Introduction

This collection of 53 stencil designs features rare and unusual birds from all around the world. Here are the kiwi of New Zealand, the penguin of Antarctica, the quetzal of Central America and the secretary bird of Africa. There are birds everyone is familiar with, like the hummingbird and peacock, and others that will be new to most people, like the pagoda starling and the wire-tailed manakin. Use these illustrations singly or combine them to form your own colorful and lively aviary.

These stencils can be cut out and used again and again. Border elements can be repeated indefinitely to form frames and borders, and all designs can be flopped to reverse the image for symmetrical repetition. The illustrations on the covers give examples of attractive color patterns.

The designs can be used for decorating walls, floors, furniture, fabrics, tin, leather and almost any other surface. All materials needed are inexpensive and easy to find in most well-stocked hardware or art-supply stores. The method is easily mastered and projects quickly completed.

LIST OF MATERIALS

boiled linseed oil
turpentine
rags
stencil knife and blades
knife sharpener or carborundum stone
large knitting needles or ice pick
cutting surface (glass, wood, etc.)
masking tape
paint
textile paint (for fabric)
stenciling brushes
newspaper
fine sandpaper
desk blotters (for fabric)
varnish (for floors, wood, tin)
#4 artists' brush

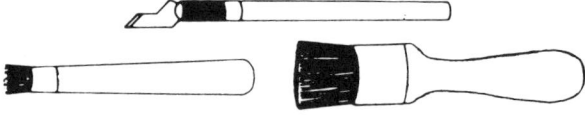

Stencil knife and two stenciling brushes of different sizes.

First, cut out an entire page (= stencil plate) from the book with a pair of scissors. When more than one design appears on a page, a dotted line serves as the cutting guideline for separating each design onto a distinct stencil plate. The margin of ¾ inch or more around the design makes the stencil sturdy and durable while in use and protects the surrounding areas from paint when stenciling.

The pages of this book are of medium-weight manila paper, which must be treated with oil to make it tough, leathery and impervious to moisture. Oiled manila will become semi-translucent, allowing light to penetrate slightly. A knife blade will cut through an oiled plate more easily. The oiling process takes place after the plate (page) is cut from the book but before the blacked-in areas of the design are cut out, so there will be no chance of bending or ripping delicate ties (bridge areas) when applying the oil.

A mixture of 50% *boiled* linseed oil and 50% turpentine is applied with a rag to both sides of the plate until it is thoroughly saturated. Using a thumbtack, the plate is then hung to dry. It will dry to the touch in about 10 minutes. Any excess can be wiped off with a dry rag or the plate can be allowed to dry for a longer period. The rag should then be immersed in water until it can be incinerated or removed by regular garbage disposal service. Spontaneous combustion can occur if the rag is stored for later use.

The stencil knife is used for cutting out the small pieces through which the paint will reach the surface to be decorated. Only the solid black areas of each design are cut out. Suitable cutting surfaces for this task are hard wood, a piece of plate glass with the edges taped, or a stack of old newspapers. The oiled stencil plate is placed on the cutting surface and allowed to move freely. Grasp the stencil knife as you would a pencil. Apply even pressure for the entire length of a curve or line. Frequent lifting of the knife causes jagged, uneven edges. The small details of the stencil design are cut out first and larger areas last to prevent weakening the plate before cutting is completed. Sharpen the blade frequently on a carborundum stone or knife sharpener.

Cutting requires careful and accurate work. A jagged line or ragged corner will stencil exactly that way in every impression of the stencil plate.

The narrow bridges of paper between the cut-out areas in the design are known as ties. If you accidentally cut through a tie, apply tape to both sides of the tear and replace the tape when needed. Circles and small dots are difficult to cut with a knife. Various large needles can be used to punch out the circles. Ice picks and different-size knitting needles work well. Carefully use the knife or a small piece of fine sandpaper to trim and smooth the edges.

Paints used for stenciling can be water-base or turpentine-base. Any paint used must be mixed to a fairly thick consistency. Acrylic paint is an excellent water-base paint because it is fast-drying and easy to clean up. Acrylics are sold in tubes or jars and come in the right consistency for stenciling. Japan paints come in small 8-ounce cans and must be thinned slightly with turpentine. Turpentine-base paints must be allowed to dry for 24 hours. Both acrylic and japan paint dry to a flat finish. As soon as stenciling is completed, brushes are cleaned, using water for water-base paints and turpentine for oil- or turpentine-base paints.

Stenciling on fabrics requires textile paints or inks made especially for decorating on fabric. Textile paints and inks come either water- or turpentine-soluble and are mixed thinner than regular paints. The fabric must be prewashed or drycleaned to remove any sizing and allow for shrinkage. Blotters must be used underneath the fabric to absorb excess moisture and paint. After the stenciled fabric has dried, ironing will set the textile paint or ink and make the colors permanent and washable. All these coloring mediums can be purchased at an art-supply store.

Brushes used for stenciling are cylindrical. The bristles are cut all the same length, forming a circular flat surface of bristle ends. Stencil brushes come in various sizes. A good selection of sizes would be ¼ inch in diameter, ½ inch in diameter, and 1 inch in diameter. A clean brush is used each time a new color is introduced.

Stenciling begins by securing the stencil plate on two sides with masking tape to the object being stenciled. If the plate is not secure, the action of the stencil brush will cause the design to smear. The brush is grasped like a pencil but held perpendicular to the work surface. Dip only the flat bottom of the bristles into the paint. Do not overload the brush with paint, or it will run under the plate and ruin the design. Have several sheets of newspaper nearby for pouncing out the freshly loaded brush. Pouncing is a hammerlike movement that disperses the paint throughout the bristles. When an even speckling of paint is evident on the newspaper, the brush is ready for use. Stippling is the proper term for the rapid up-and-down motion of the brush over the stencil plate. Stippling continues until the openings in the plate are completely filled in with color.

Masking tape is used to keep different colors clean and separate if you desire to use more than one color for a single stencil plate. The varying parts of the design are masked with tape as each color is transferred. Changing the masking tape is done without removing the plate from the project being stenciled.

As soon as stenciling with any plate is finished, the plate is wiped gently with a rag or sponge dampened with water or turpentine depending on the paint in use. This increases the life expectancy of the stencil plate by helping prevent the accumulation of paint around the edges of the design.

Colors can be lightened by the addition of white and grayed and neutralized by the addition of a small amount of the complementary color. Red and green are complements as are blue and orange, yellow and purple. The grayer the color the more faded and aged the final result. Metallic bronzing powders added to paint give the appearance of iridescence. Darker colors mixed to a thinner consistency with varnish or acrylic polymer over a light ground give the effect of translucency. Sanding the stenciled design with fine sandpaper will make it appear worn. Stencilwork on floors, woodwork and tin should be protected with several coats of a good varnish.

A more detailed and specific account of the art of stenciling is contained in *The Complete Book of Stencilcraft* (Dover, 0-486-25372-4), by JoAnne C. Day.

1 Wood hoopoe

2 Nicobar pigeon

3 Yellow robin

4 Fairy wren

5 Eurasian curlew

6 Macaws

7 Lovebirds

8 Cockatoo

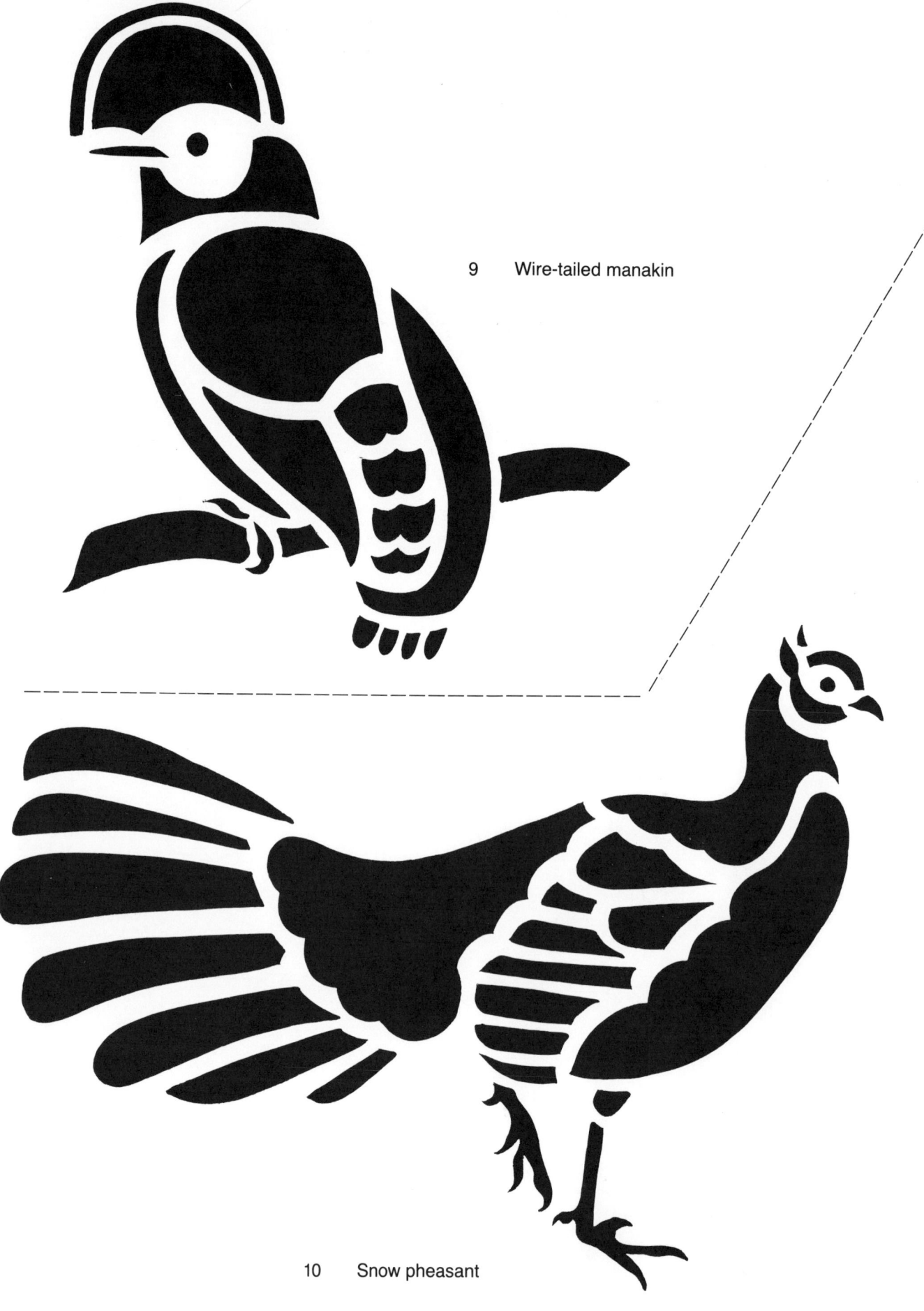

9 Wire-tailed manakin

10 Snow pheasant

11 Swallow-tailed bee eater

12 Superb fruit dove

13 Penguins

14 Pin-tailed whydah

15 Penguins

16 Racket-tailed kingfishers

17 Parakeets

18 Fairy bluebird

19 Peacock

20 Pagoda starling

21 Green jay

22 Wattled curassow

23 Green-tailed sylph

24   Willie wagtail

25   Secretary bird

26 African darter

27   Flamingos

28   Roadrunner

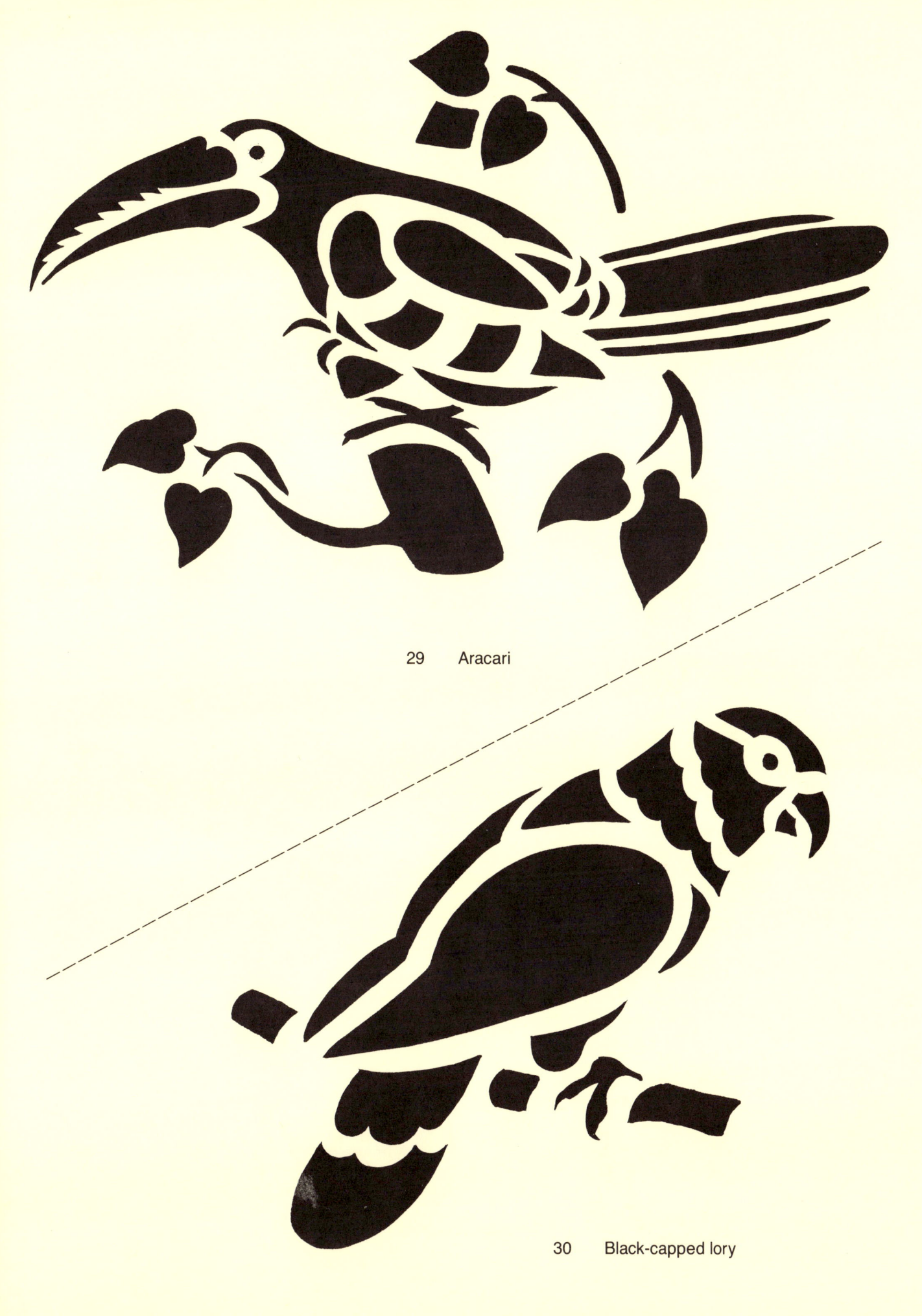

29 Aracari

30 Black-capped lory

31   Rainbow lorikeets

32 Ostriches

33   Cranes

34　Lilac-breasted roller

35　Puffin

36 Hummingbird

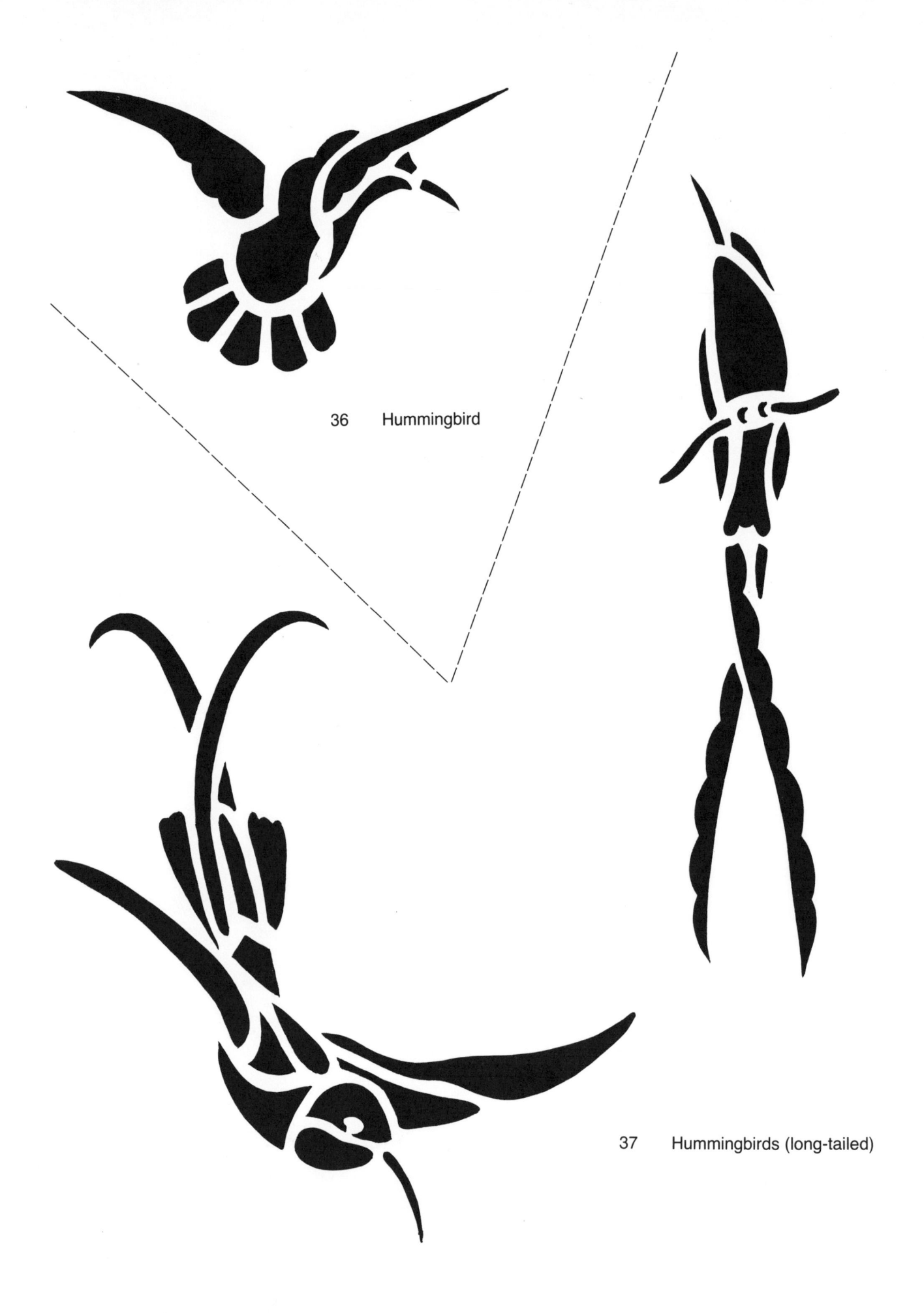

37 Hummingbirds (long-tailed)

38 Crowned crane

39 Crowned pigeon

40 Red-billed hornbill

41 Crimson sunbird

42 Egret

43　Racket-tailed hummingbirds

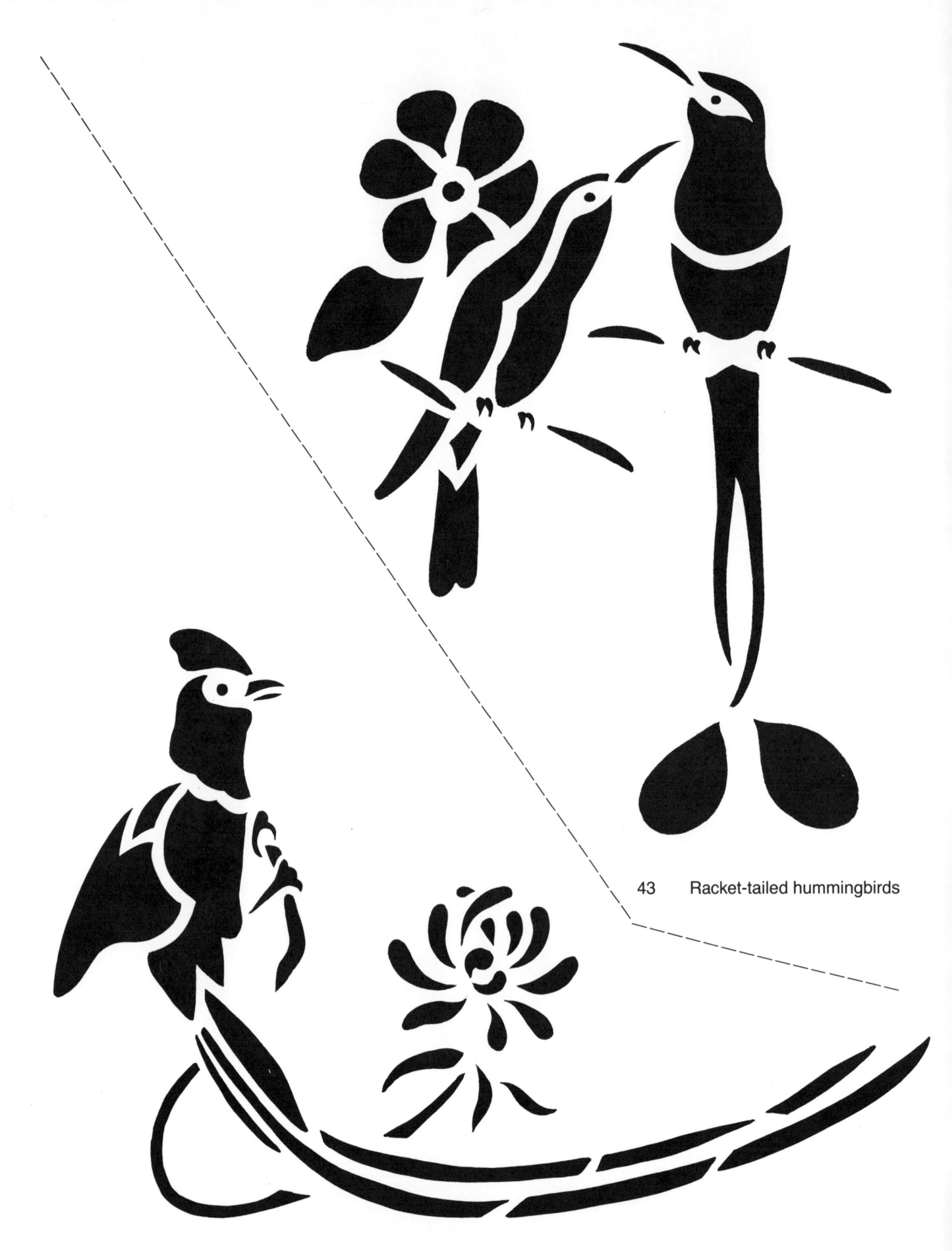

44　Bird of paradise

45   Little egret

46   Sulfur-breasted toucan

47 Peacock

48 Blacksmith plover

49　Quetzal

50　Kiwi

51 Pied kingfisher

52 Frogmouths

53   Lyrebird

GLOBAL STYLE
·JEWELRY·

Inspiration and Instruction for
25 EXOTIC BEADED JEWELRY PROJECTS

Anne Potter

INTERWEAVE
interweave.com

Global Style Jewelry Copyright © 2016 by Anne Potter. Manufactured in China. All rights reserved. No part of this book may be reproduced in any form or by any electronic or mechanical means including information storage and retrieval systems without permission in writing from the publisher, except by a reviewer who may quote brief passages in a review. Published by Interweave Books, an imprint of F+W Media, Inc., 10151 Carver Road, Suite 200, Blue Ash, Ohio 45242. (800) 289-0963. First Edition.
www.fwcommunity.com

fw
a content + ecommerce company

21 20 19 18 17 16   5 4 3 2 1

Distributed in Canada by Fraser Direct
100 Armstrong Avenue
Georgetown, ON, Canada L7G 5S4
Tel: (905) 877-4411

Distributed in the U.K. and Europe by
F&W MEDIA INTERNATIONAL
Brunel House, Newton Abbot,
Devon, TQ12 4PU, England
Tel: (+44) 1626 323200
Fax: (+44) 1626 323319
E-mail: enquiries@fwmedia.com

SRN: 16JM05
ISBN-13: 978-1-63250-391-6

Editor: Michelle Bredeson
Technical Editor: Bonnie Brooks
Cover Designer: Frank Rivera
Interior Designer: Nicola DosSantos
Beauty Photography: Jack Deutsch (except where noted)
Step Photography: Ann Sabin Swanson
Stylist: Jodi Andriella

We make every effort to ensure the accuracy of our instructions, but mistakes occasionally occur. Errata can be found at jewelrymakingdaily.com/errata.

CONTENTS

Introduction...................5
Tools and Supplies 6

Europe
Ireland: Celtic Knot Bracelet...............12
Poland: Polish Pottery Earrings 18
Spain: Gaudí Tile Bracelet 24
Norway: Sølje Chain Maille Necklace 28
Ukraine: Vyshyvka Bracelet.................34

Asia
Thailand: Bangkok Street Necklace..........40
Japan: Raked Pebble Bracelet 44
Turkey: Iznik Tile Earrings 48
Cambodia: Apsara Cuff Bracelet 52
Persia: Kilim Cross Earrings 56

India
Goa: Azulejo Tile Necklace 62
Gujarat: Mehndi Hand Bracelet 68
Udaipur: Inlaid Pearl Earrings...............72
Mumbai: Sari Gold Necklace 76
Bagru: Print Block Earrings 80

Africa
Uganda: Paper Bead Necklace..............86
Kenya: Maasai Cuff Bracelet 90
Egypt: Modern Pharaoh's Collar 94
Morocco: Tea Glass Earrings................98
Senegal: Recycled Tin Necklace............104

Latin America
Mexico: Frida Kahlo Earrings...............112
Western Amazonia: Shipibo Wrap Bracelet..116
Guatemala: Mayan Weaving Necklace 120
Oaxaca: Retablo Charm Bracelet 124
Peru: Incan Quipu Necklace 128

Helpful Techniques............. 132
Resources...................... 138
Suppliers....................... 140
About the Author................ 142
Acknowledgments 142
Dedication 142
Index.......................... 143

PASSPORT
Trondheim
Dovrefjell
Glittertind 2470
Bergen
Oslo
Göteborg
Kattegat
Moray Firth
Aberdeen
BİRLEŞİK
KRALLIK
Glasgow
Dundee
Edinburgh
Belfast
İRLANDA
Dublin
Cork
Liverpool
Manchester
Leeds
Sheffield
Newcastle upon Tyne
Middlesbrough
Kingston upon Hull
Nottingham
KUZEY
DENİZİ
Esbjerg
Frizya adaları
Amsterdam
HOLLANDA
Den Haag
Rotterdam
Cardiff
Bristol
Hamburg
Bremen
Hannover
Kiel
Lübeck
Rostock
Berlin
BALTIK
Liepaja
Riga
Klaipeda
Daugavpils
LİTUANYA
Kaunas
Vilnius
Kaliningrad
Gdańsk
Szczecin
Toruń
POLONYA
Poznań
Varşova
Białystok
Minsk
Baranoviçi
Brest
Pripet
Pripet Bataklıkları
Essen
Antwerp
Düsseldorf
Köln
BELÇİKA
Lille
Brüksel
Bonn
ALMANYA
Magdeburg
Leipzig
Dresden
Wrocław
Łódź
Lublin
Frankfurt
Mainz
Prag
Katowice
Krakov
Lvov
Reims
LÜK
Lüksemburg
Nancy
Strasbourg
Karlsruhe
Nürnberg
Regensburg
Stuttgart
Münih
Plzeň
Brno
ÇEK CUM
Ostrava
Gerlachovka 2663
Przemyśl
Ternopol
Jitomir
Brest
Cherbourg
Le Havre
Rouen
Orléans
Nantes
Tours
La Rochelle
FRANSA
Bordeaux
Dijon
Lyon
Basel
Zürih
Berne
LİHT
Lausanne
Cenevre
İSVİÇRE
Mt Blanc 4807
Milano
Torino
Cenova
La Spezia
Bologna
Salzburg
Linz
Viyana
Bratislava
SLOVAK CUM.
Miskolc
AVUSTURYA
Gr.Glockner
Graz
Budapeşte
Debrecen
Oradea
Cluj
MACARİSTAN
Maribor
Ljubljana
Pécs
Szeged
Trieste
Venedik
Zagreb
HIRVATİSTAN
Novi Sad
Belgrad
BOSNA HERSEK
Saraybosna
SAN MARINO
Floransa
Ancona
Zadar
Split
Dubrovnik
SIRBİSTAN
Toulouse
Nîmes
Bilbao
Andorra
Barselona
Tarragona
Tortosa
Madrid
Valencia
Cartagena
Ibiza
Bari
Brindisi
Korfu
Tiran
Üsküp
MAKEDONYA
ARNAVUTLUK
Lárisa
YUNANİSTAN
Atina
Korint
Kalámai
Bükreş
Ploieşti
Braşov
Ruscuk
Balkan dağl.
Burgas
Plovdiv
BULGARİSTAN
Edirne
İstanbul
Marmara Denizi
Çanakkale boğ.
Midilli
Girit
Rodos
200
100
EURO
50
EURO

INTRODUCTION
An Artist's Travelogue

Fascinated by other cultures, I have always loved to travel. For the last twenty years, however, I have been on a layover to raise my five children. This wonderful season has been worth every minute, and in the end, I'm still the girl who loves the people and places of far-off lands. Most other adventurers I know are on layover, too. Demanding jobs, raising small children, paying for college, caring for aging parents: there are a lot of things that keep us from traveling the world. But no matter our situations, there's no quelling the creative soul! So if you're an artist with wanderlust like me, I hope you'll enjoy this book.

Global Style Jewelry features twenty-five designs inspired by different design traditions from around the world: global design. Arranged like a world tour, the book is divided into five sections: Europe, Asia, Latin America, Africa, and India. Thanks to such a varied fount of inspiration, the projects are diverse, exploring different facets of jewelry design, from chain maille, to beadweaving, to macramé. Some pieces are more laborious than others, but all are approachable for the intermediate beginner and a great introduction to new techniques. On this level, *Global Style Jewelry* will be a great addition to your crafting library. And because we artists respond to the setting, the context, and the story of a piece, I set these projects into a narrative. A romantic tale that lovingly pays homage to the cultures and artisans that make the beautiful designs that inspire us. As a teenager I enjoyed reading *The Travels of Marco Polo* and the J. Peterman catalog. Both inspire my own writing and read similarly—just as in those works, the people and stories featured in this book are fictionalized, but the narrator is real.

Enjoy and bon voyage!

© GettyImages.com/seb_ra

The stringing materials you use can be purely functional or a major design element.

TOOLS AND SUPPLIES

Each project in this book includes a complete list of tools and materials needed.
Here is some background on the supplies I like to use.

Stringing Materials

The right stringing material is a crucial part of your design, so make sure you choose a material that is strong enough to support your design but lends the right flexibility for your piece, as well. And design matters, too! While some projects call for the "strong and silent" type of stringing material, other pieces employ it as a feature, as in macramé and knotted pieces.

Silk Beading Thread: I turn to silk thread time and again for my stringing projects. Silk thread is perfect for seed bead work because it's fine, strong, and smooth. Then when you're done, it knots perfectly. Nylon options also do the deed.

Waxed Linen: This slightly stiff thread provides the necessary structural base for macramé projects, while its waxed finish makes knots "stay." I find this casual stringing material is well-suited for bohemian-style jewelry.

Memory Wire: With its great "memory," this wire returns back to its original shape every time. Be sure to use memory-wire cutters when cutting, though, because the tempered steel of the wire will dent the blades of your everyday wire cutters.

Wire: Wire is a workhorse (and a chameleon) in my designs: I use it for everything from stately earring forms to sloppy wraps on beaded dangles. Besides good sterling silver and gold-filled wire, my favorite wire is by Vintaj because the rich, warm patina enhances every design. Wire is classified by hardness and gauge. Hardness—hard (H), half-hard (HH), dead soft (DS)—indicates the wire's rigidity and malleability. And for gauge: the higher the gauge, the skinnier the wire. So while 18-gauge hard (H) wire is perfect for making something structural with wire, 26-gauge half-hard (HH) wire is just right for wrapping.

Flexible Beading Wire: Look to the "break" listed on the package when choosing strong wire for heavier projects. A "10-pound break" means that the wire can hold 10 pounds before breaking. While we don't usually make 10-pound necklaces, this measure of strength also accounts for 10 pounds of tension (like catching your necklace on a cabinet pull while making dinner!).

Findings

Though findings can seem to be insignificant to a piece's overall look, I've found that head pins, clasps, and chains with great patina or good form can make all the difference. I like to use vintage or handmade findings in my designs because they lend another layer of interest, and I avoid cheap findings with a garish finish, as they always detract from the finished piece.

Clasps: Depending on the design, I choose clasps according to how prominent I want them to be. Sometimes the clasp has a place in the design, either as a resting spot for the eye, or to give a necessary metallic element to the palette. For these jobs, I love to use decorative S-hooks or toggles for their architectural interest. And for busier pieces, I happily choose a small lobster clasp that recedes design-wise. No matter which clasp you choose, make sure it can manage the weight of the design and not come unclasped too easily.

Chain: My favorite source for cool chain at a great price is vintage costume jewelry. Ignore ugly pendants and look for chain with interesting links and a quality (or beautifully worn) finish. And even better: finished jewelry comes with a matching clasp and findings.

Ball-End Head Pins: I use ball-end head pins for most of my beaded dangles because the tiny little ball lends a visual balance to these components.

Eye Pins: One eye pin, and you're halfway to a beaded link! Make a beaded link by adding your beads and bead caps to the eye pin, and finish with a simple loop. I like to match my loop to the loop of the eye pin, keeping the loop size and direction the same. Fussy, yes, but I always like the finished product this way.

Crimp Beads: There is nothing more stressful in beading than crimping the last crimp on your stringing project because if you get it wrong, it's back to square one. So get some good light and practice, practice, practice to save yourself tears and heartache.

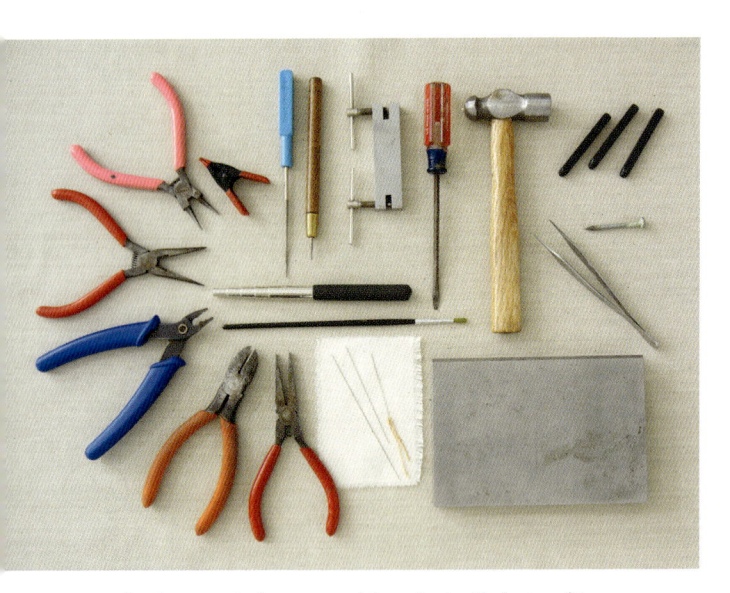

Purchase new tools as you need them, buying the best quality you can afford. Your jewelry will thank you!

Crimp Covers: These little guys go far to finish a piece. Match the metal to your design, and they will lend a polished, professional, and unassuming finish to unsightly (or poorly done!) crimps. I use 4mm crimp covers as a basic, but larger 6mm crimp covers can cover even beastly knots of beading thread.

Neck Wires: These rigid neck rings are a great necklace foundation, giving designs the structure they need. While they may look like chokers, they size more as a flattering short necklace length. To add beads, just unscrew the ball end, then when your design is complete, screw the ball end back on and gently curve the wire to lie gracefully.

Stamping Tags: These shaped metal charms are such a fun building block, and there are so many interesting shapes to try! Certainly stamp them, but don't stop there: they can be painted, patinaed, and wire wrapped, too. Then use your metal hole punch to turn them into links and more.

Jump Rings: I have a massive collection of jump rings, because when it comes to jump rings for projects, one size does not fit all (literally). Besides the myriad of metal finishes, you'll need fine 4mm jump rings for linking pendants to fine chain, up to heavy-gauge 14mm jump rings for supporting the weight of a chunkier piece—and everything in between.

Tools

If you're serious about beading, invest in a good basic set of tools. The better the tools, the easier your beading and the better the finished piece will be.

Pliers: You'll use two pairs of pliers to manipulate wire, open jump rings, finish head pins, and wrangle chain links. Flat-nose or chain-nose pliers are most common, but use whatever works for you; I actually use a flat-nose pliers and a crimping pliers for its narrow, flat nose. Get comfortable with this technique of using two pliers at once, because you'll be using it a lot!

Round-nose Pliers: Necessary for making simple loops and wrapped loops—you'll grab these pliers over and over again. Consistent loops take practice as you train your eye and your hands to learn the motion and tension of this basic step, so use a whole spool of wire to practice if you want—wire's cheap.

Wire Cutters: I recommend investing in wire cutters before all other tools. Choose a quality pair with precise blades and a fine nose so your wire cuts are perfect, and perfectly placed.

Beading Needles: Don't try beadweaving without beading needles. Don't even bother. These super-skinny needles can pass through seed bead holes that other needles can't, saving you the frustration of getting "stuck" in a bead! My favorites come with a very large collapsible eye that's easy to thread but still holds the thread securely.

Cup Bur: This tool's a one-trick pony, but you'll need it if you plan to make your own ear wires. After cutting your wire, use the cup bur to smooth the edges ("burs") off the end of your wire so your ear wires are rounded and comfortable to wear.

Metal Hole Punch: Available at your craft store, this simple tool can turn coins, stampings, and found metal into links and pendants. It also gives you the freedom to make holes where you need them for your design.

Metal Stamping Supplies: Invest in a basic hammer and bench block for easy metal stamping. In addition to an alphabet/number set in a plain, sans serif font, I'll use anything I can find to make interesting stamps: screws, tiny screwdrivers (+ and -), square nails. There are a ton of cute metal stamps on the market, but I prefer simple stamps repeated to make a design, like you'd find on old tinwork.

Bead Clamps: Simply, these little clamps secure the end of your stringing material to keep beads from sliding off. I also use them in the middle of a project when it's time to try a piece on. Dropping all the beads off a tedious project just one time taught me to take three seconds and add clamps. A folded piece of clear tape also works well on flexible beading wire and thread.

Tweezers: Necessary for precision work, such as placing tiny beads in epoxy clay—look for fine-point tweezers at the craft store and leave your everyday tweezers in the bathroom, where they belong.

Mandrel: While my beading style is pretty laid-back, there are times when I need a perfect (or perfectly sized) loop. Mandrels come in all sizes: skinny ones to make little 4mm loops, up to larger ones that make precise and perfect bracelets and rings.

Paintbrush: I keep a small old paintbrush around for applying patina and paint. Nothing fancy, but choose a natural-bristle brush for the best application.

Beads

Very simply, beads are why I love beading. My favorite beads are like little works of art: beautifully wrought from interesting materials, with colors and textures that delight. And thanks to all the beautiful beads out there, the excitement of jewelry design will never get old. How cool is that?

Cornerless Cubes: With their pretty facets that catch the light, these beads are stand-alone beautiful, but also the pack mule of my designs. Strung together, they lend a beautifully textured element, but they do also work well as spacers, fillers, stabilizers for large-hole beads, and crimp covers.

Turkish Glass: I love these beads because each one is different and noticeably handmade. These beads come from a collective of Mediterranean artisans who make them from odd lots of

Often underappreciated, findings can make or break a design.

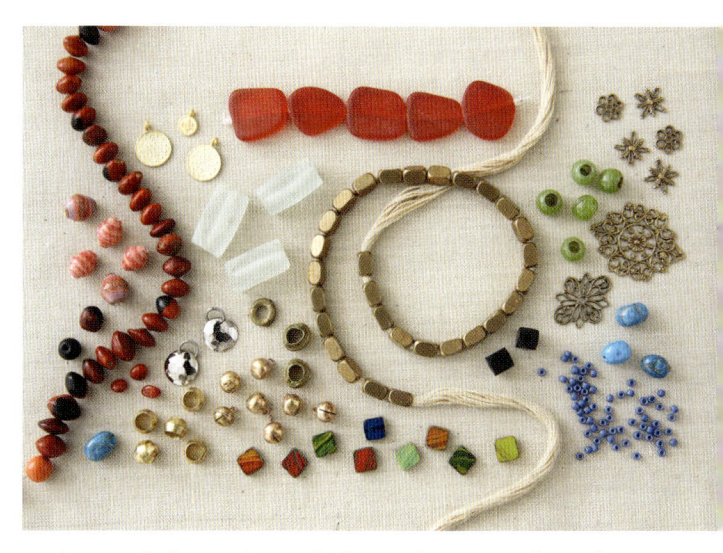

Beads are usually the stars of my jewelry designs. Choose ones you love and don't be afraid to substitute!

recycled glass in small kilns outside their homes. Dyelots will vary as much as each individual bead, so be flexible.

Paper Beads: One of my all-time favorite beads. Rolled from recycled paper and finished with a shiny lacquer, these beautiful beads are intrepidly colored, and each is unique. And because they are most often made by women in developing countries as a means of income, they're more than just a pretty bead: they're supporting a family!

Natural Beads: Each different, nut and seed beads give an organic warmth to designs. These beads often come with very small holes, so choose stringing materials accordingly: flexible beading wire or silk thread usually works best.

Recycled Glass Beads: I think the matte finish of recycled glass is hauntingly beautiful, and that's why I turn to these beads so often. Their translucency plays well with other finishes, so these beads work well in lots of designs, always lending a dose of unexpected texture.

Indian Brass: Another design workhorse. The mellow gleam of Indian brass beads is bright enough to serve as a metallic element, but not so bright as to steal the show.

Seed Beads: While seed beads from Japan are perfectly uniform and ideal for exact beadweaving, I usually choose seed beads from the Czech Republic. Czech seed beads are just imperfect enough to lend a little character, but still keep a reliable size that's easy to work with.

Filigree: These pretties bring a lot of romance to your designs and can really lighten things up. Their lacy pattern gives a nice counterpoint to bolder beads and heavier metals.

TOOLS AND SUPPLIES ~ 9

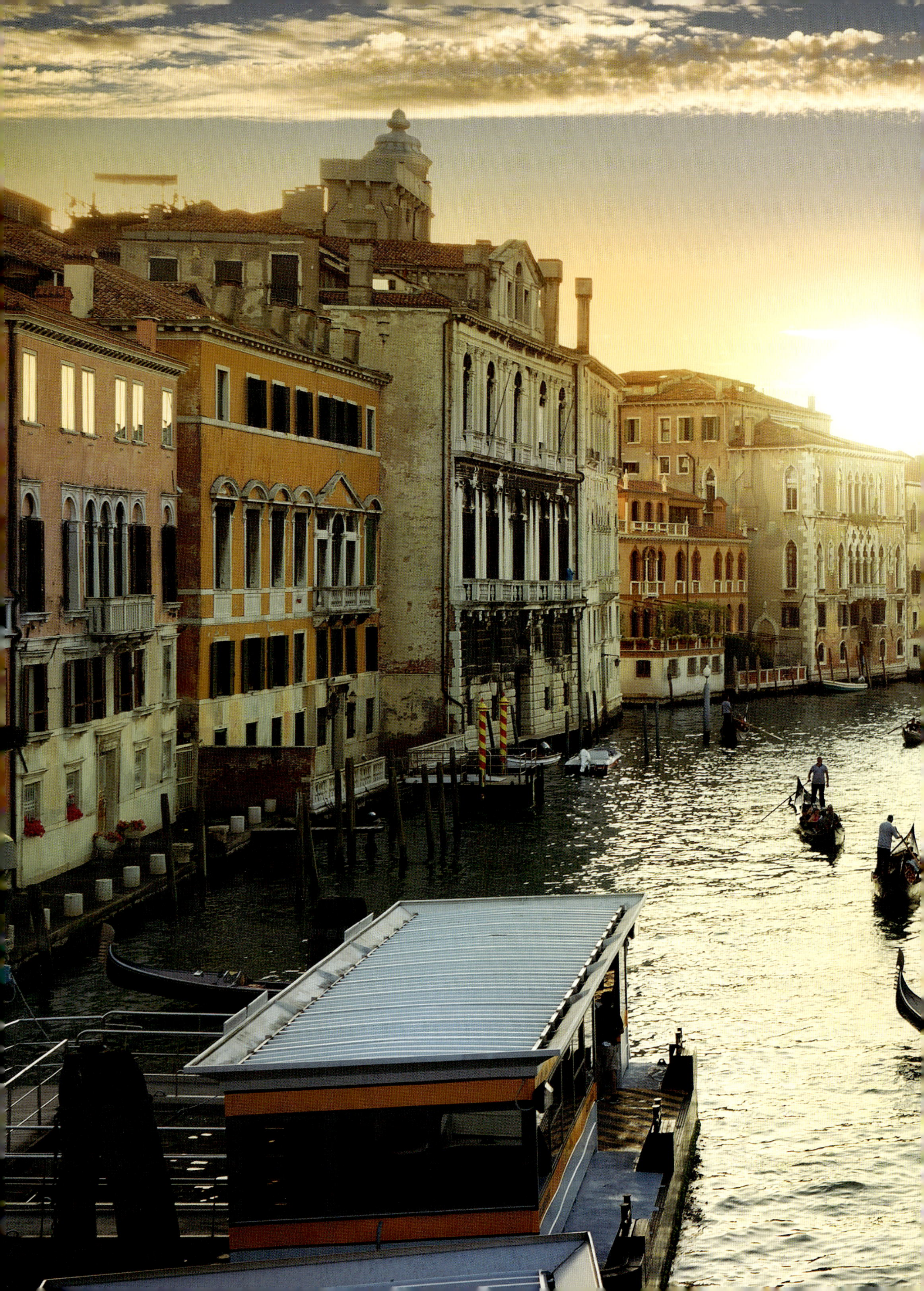

Chapter One

EUROPE

Travel through Europe and you'll find a mash-up of thoroughly modern cultures. Scandinavia is ideologically progressive, Germany technologically advanced, Spain achingly hip, and France forever fashion's gold standard. Europe is a rousing place to experience What's New, What's Next, but alongside this modernity, Europe bears its bedrock Old World heritage, too.

I'm enthralled with the cathedrals, the cobblestones, the bridges, the fountains of Old World Europe, and I especially love how these landmarks seem to live and breathe within the bustle of modern life. Tour the sites of any major European city, and you will take them in with low-key locals living life. Maybe you'll travel 3,000 miles to see some Gothic cathedral, but it's part of someone else's everyday scenery. Europe is the place to take in precious, historic sites with the people who continually renew their culture to make it new and modern and hip.

© GettyImages.com/Givaga

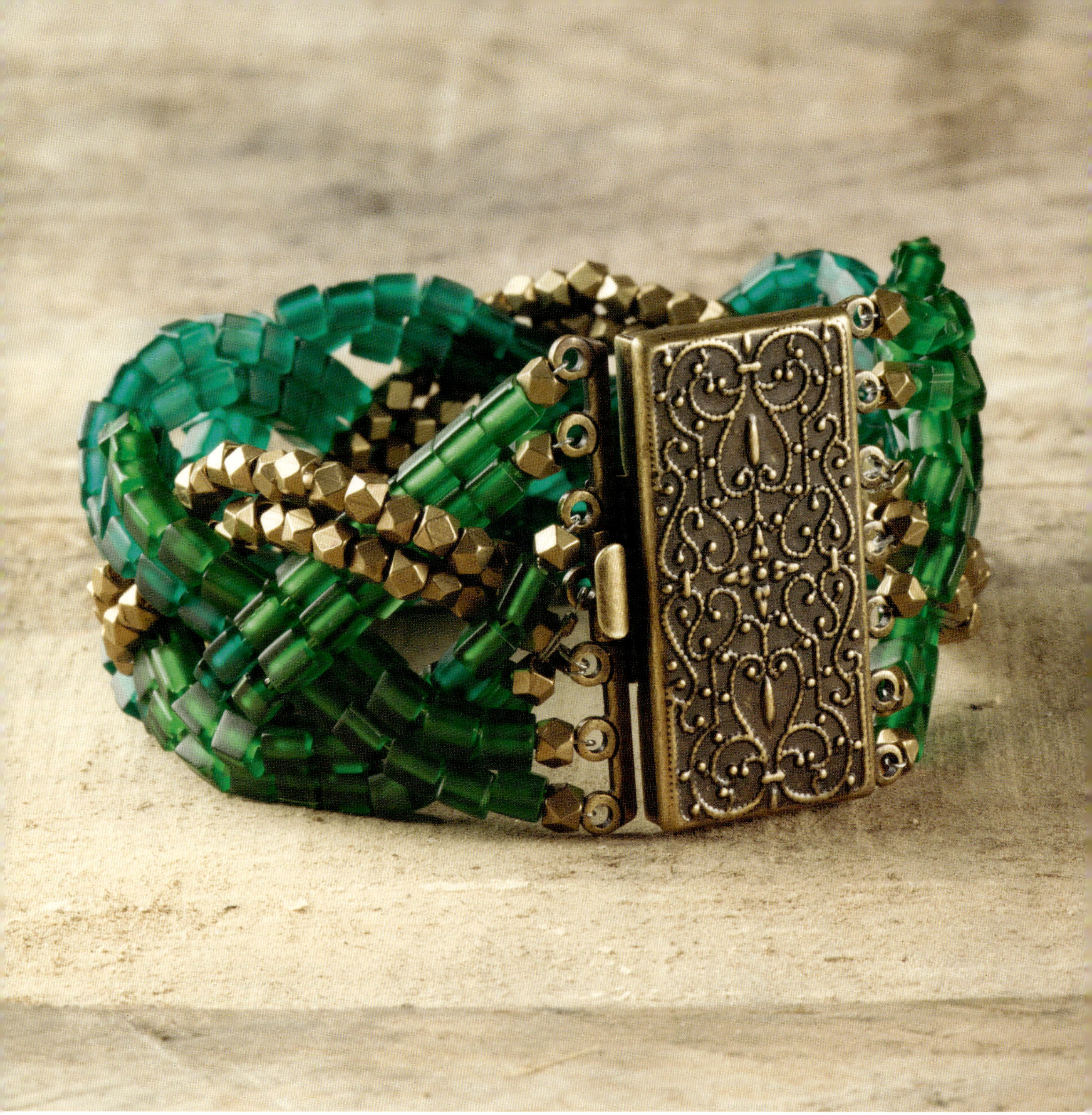
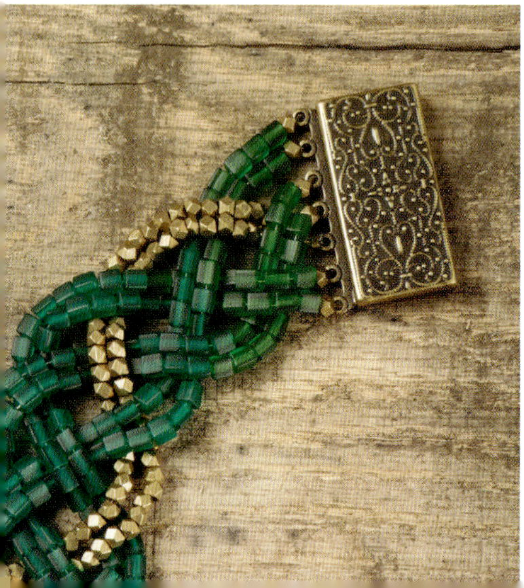
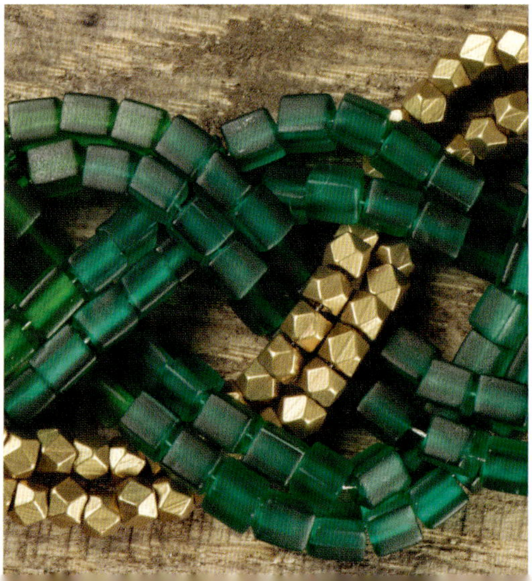
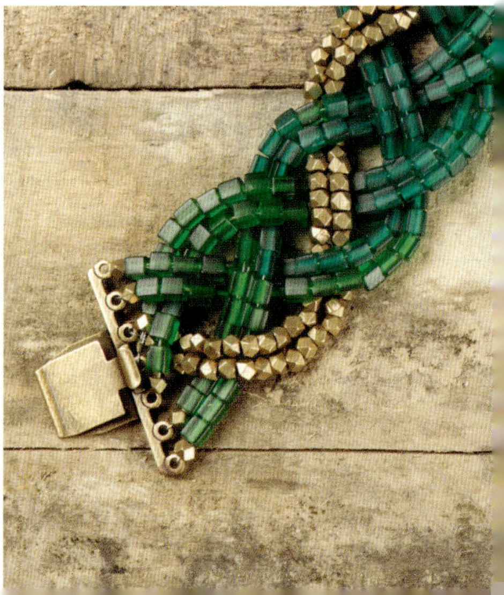

IRELAND
Celtic Knot Bracelet

Forgoing a James Joyce tour, I decide to spend my last day in Dublin taking in the city, just enjoying "a day in the life." Strolling around Dublin, I feel the years of history that made this place. Cobblestone streets and soaring cathedrals, unchanged over years, set an Old World scene. Slim alleys, like rabbit holes, lead to pubs and hipster shops. But for all its antiquity, the city buzzes with all things modern: take-out counters, traffic, and smokers leaning against buildings.

I notice Celtic knots throughout the city, on everything from tombstones to tattoos. With their roots in Roman design, Celtic knots evolved into their recognizably Irish style. The complex and continuous braids mesmerize: a mix of straight-grid lines and sweeping curves, all primly contained in their geometric confines. This ancient design somehow looks brilliantly modern. The Book of Kells features knotwork drawn 1,200 years ago by monks who lavishly embellished the illuminated text of the Gospels. Never called "artists," these scribes used colored ink on paper-thin sheets of leather. Yellows and reds glow with a warm brightness, while indigo inks cast a plum-purple tint. And surrounding each lavish design there is a ghostly halo of rust from the iron in the gall ink, giving the entire piece a haunting beauty.

The Celtic Knot Bracelet featured here is an interpretation of modern Celtic knots, rather than those from the Book of Kells. The knot design is simpler, with just four "cords" plaited together, because it was more appropriate for the medium of beads strung on flexible beading wire. I chose green for the palette as a nod to modern Ireland and its national identity, graduating the green, from teal to emerald and back to teal, for added interest and dimension. A decorative antiqued brass box clasp finishes the piece, emulating both an intricate Celtic knot and Dublin's Old World beauty.

While working this piece I often took breaks, taping the whole braided piece to my work surface. While the braiding itself is simple to do, it takes patience to make the strands even and equally spaced. And crimping the crimp beads on the second end of the clasp is tricky, with very little room to maneuver. Break your work into smaller steps to help ensure that your quality does not diminish in these last steps, or that you don't throw the whole bracelet across the room (especially when you're almost done and it's going to be so pretty!).

MATERIALS

1 antiqued brass 7-hole box clasp

150 antiqued brass 3.3mm cornerless cubes

124 matte emerald 4mm glass cubes

175 matte teal green 4mm glass cubes

14 antiqued brass 2mm crimp beads

16' (4.88 m) flexible beading wire

TOOLS

Tape

Wire cutters

Crimping pliers

FINISHED SIZE

7 ½" long × 1" wide (19 × 2.5 cm).

1. With wire cutters, cut flexible beading wire into eight 24" (61 cm) lengths.

2. Open clasp. Tape one end of clasp to work surface and set second end aside to use in Step 10.

3. The holes in the clasp are numbered 1–7 from left to right. Pass length of one flexible beading wire through crimp bead, through first hole of clasp, and back through crimp bead. Crimp (**Figure 1**). Repeat for Holes 2, 3, 4, 6, and 7. (Hole 5 will be treated differently on this clasp end.)

4. Onto first wire, string 1 antiqued brass cornerless cube, 7 emerald cubes, 35 teal cubes, and 9 emerald cubes (**Figure 2**). Fold a small piece of tape at end of flexible beading wire to keep beads secure and rather taut on flexible beading wire. Set aside.

5. Repeat for wires 2, 3, 4, 6, and 7, according to the following sequences (**Figure 3**):

   Wire 2: 1 antiqued brass cornerless cube, 9 emerald cubes, 30 teal cubes, and 12 emerald cubes

   Wire 3: 1 antiqued brass cornerless cube, 12 emerald cubes, 26 teal cubes, and 14 emerald cubes

   Wire 4: 1 antiqued brass cornerless cube, 10 emerald cubes, 29 teal cubes, and 10 emerald cubes

   Wire 6: 1 antique brass cornerless cube, 12 emerald cubes, 24 teal cubes, and 12 emerald cubes

   Wire 7: 1 antiqued brass cornerless cube, 7 emerald cubes, 31 teal cubes, and 10 emerald cubes.

6. Pass length of one flexible beading wire through crimp bead, through Hole 5 of clasp, and back through crimp bead. Crimp. Repeat again to make two crimped lengths of flexible beading wire in Hole 5.

7. Onto the first wire attached to Hole 5, string 69 antiqued brass cornerless cubes. Fold a small piece of tape at end of flexible beading wire to keep beads secure and rather taut on flexible beading wire. Set aside. Repeat for second wire attached to Hole 5, but first pass beading wire through first cornerless cubes from first wire (**Figures 4–6**). Proceed to string 68 antiqued brass cornerless cubes.

Fig. 1

Fig. 2

Fig. 3

Fig. 4

Fig. 5

Fig. 6

IRELAND: CELTIC KNOT BRACELET ~ 15

8. Lay all eight beaded strands out flat, with #1 and #2 positioned together on the far left, #3 and #4 in the center left, brass strands in the center right, and #6 and #7 on the far right (**Figure 7**).

9. Braid in a four-strand plait pattern, starting with brass strands going under strands #3 and #4 (**Figures 8–12**).

10. Once plaiting is complete, carefully even out the strands so they "finish" at the same time. The plait should be flat, with each strand running with its twin as "railroad rails." Plait should measure about 7" (18 cm) long. (According to the number given as their starting position [see Step 8], beaded lengths should end in the following order from left to right: 1, 2, brass, 3, 4, 6, 7.)

11. String 1 antiqued brass cornerless cube onto #1 and pass its flexible beading wire through crimp bead, through Hole 1 of second clasp end, and back through crimp bead. Crimp. Repeat for remaining beaded strands, passing strands in order through Holes 2, 4, 5, 6, and 7. (Hole 3 will be treated differently on this clasp end.)

12. String 1 antiqued brass cornerless cube onto left-most brass strand and pass its flexible beading wire through crimp bead, through Hole 3 of second clasp end, and back through crimp bead. Crimp. Pass flexible beading wire of right-most brass strand through the last cornerless cube of left brass strand. Pass through crimp bead, through Hole 3, and back through crimp bead. Crimp. This will be a little tricky.

Fig. 7

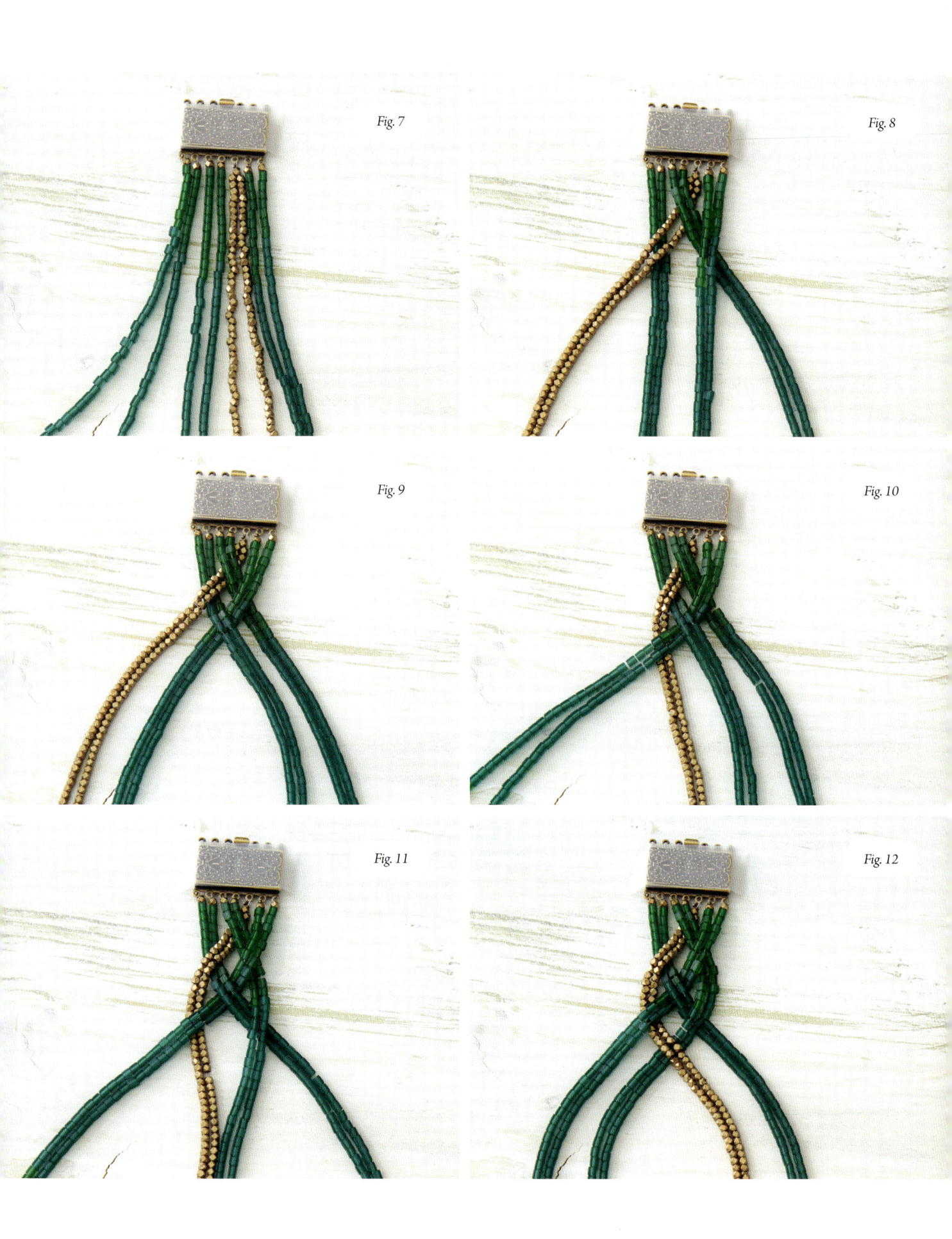

Fig. 8

Fig. 9

Fig. 10

Fig. 11

Fig. 12

IRELAND: CELTIC KNOT BRACELET ~ 17

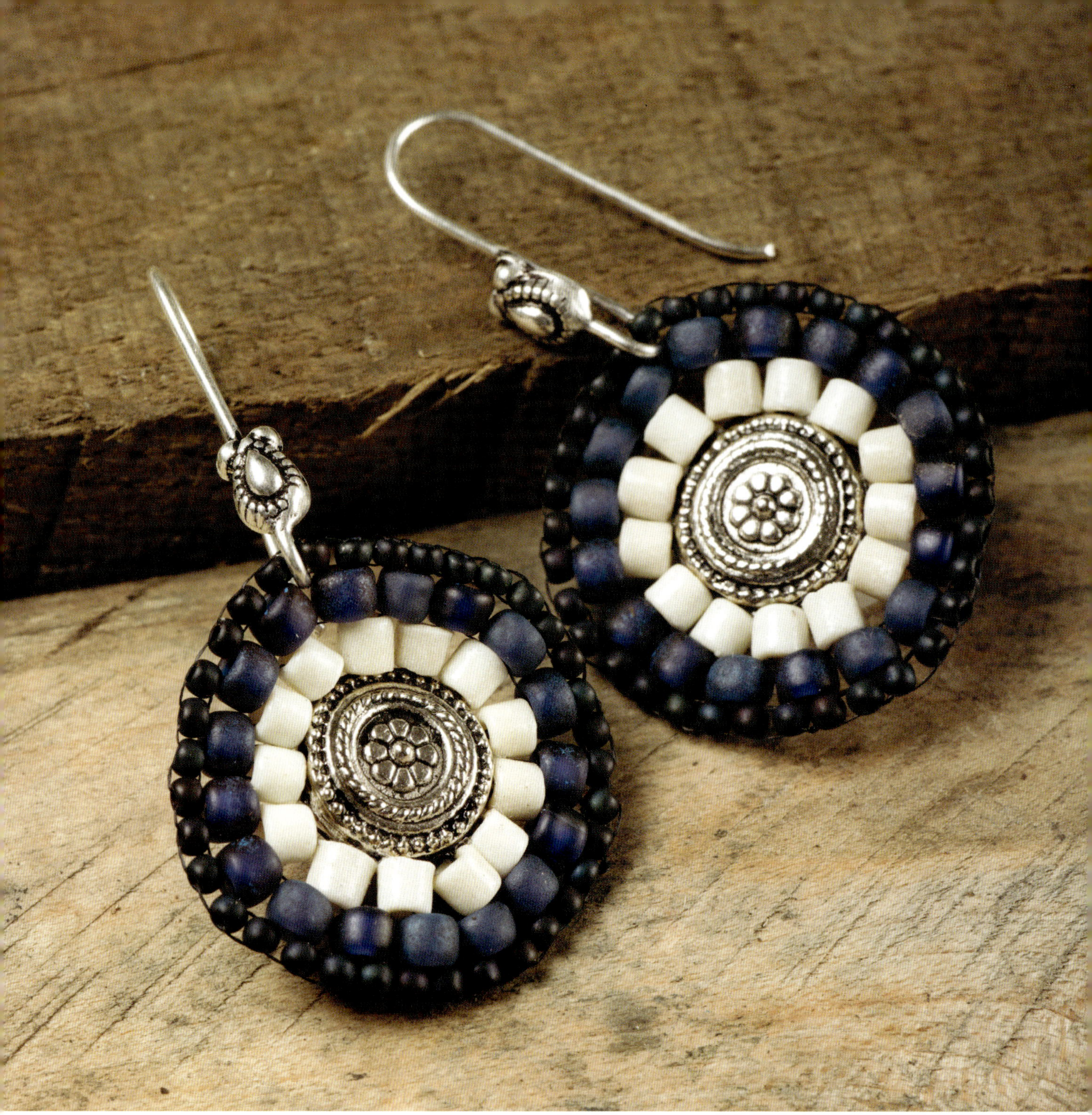
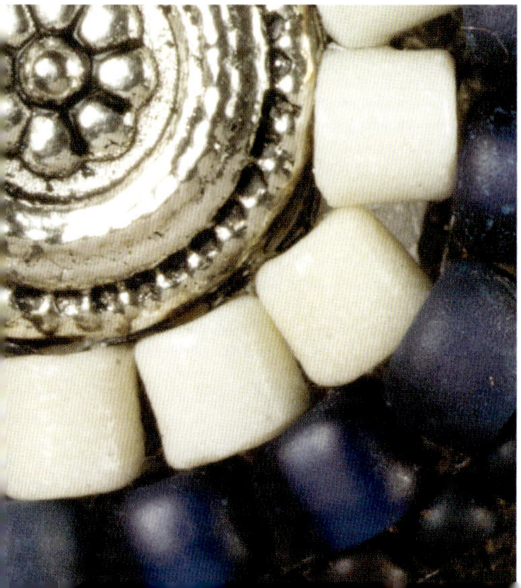
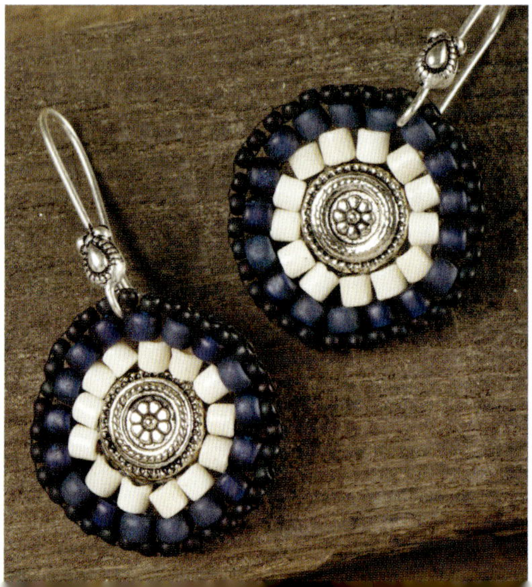
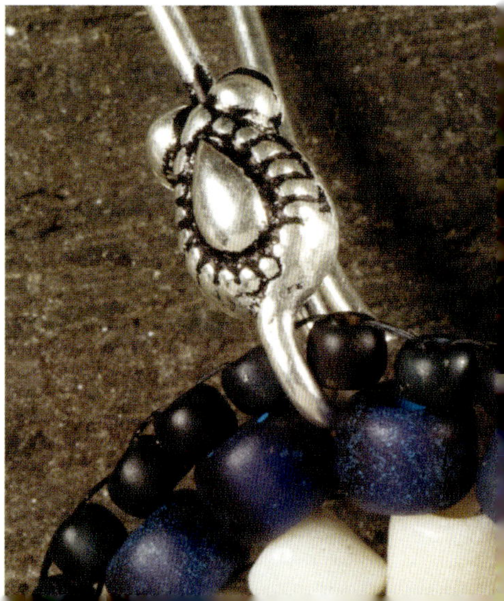

POLAND
Polish Pottery Earrings

The deep ruts of the lane lead us along a golden rye field and away from the trucks and traffic of town. Marek is driving me to his aunt's house because he thinks I will like her collection of pottery. As we bounce along in this Soviet-era jalopy, I am struck by how pure the farmland looks: yellow fields rippling under a clear blue sky, with dark green trees specking the landscape here and there.

The farmhouse has a heavy thatched roof and whitewashed walls; two horses eavesdrop by a small barn. Alicja is a small old woman with a round, smiling face. *"Wejdź, wejdź,"* she says, and ushers us inside. Alicja pours us tea while Marek shows me the plates and saucers and teacups, all patterned with cobalt blue and creamy white circles and dots. He picks up a plate and explains, "See, the clay comes from right here in Silesia and it is very good clay. See, it is very beautiful." "Oh, it's *so* beautiful!" I agree.

"What is her favorite piece?" I ask. *"Która jest jej ulubionym?"* he asks Alicja. She fetches a lone plate from a shelf by the sink and places it carefully in front of me. It's rimmed with rows of blue circles with googly rust brown rings in each one. She is telling Marek a story, her face smiling, but tears start to run down her cheeks. When she is done, Marek translates for me: "Her favorite aunt left for America when Alicja was seven years old. She was very beautiful and Alicja loved her very much. These plates were a gift and she packed them to bring with her. The night before her aunt left, Alicja took one plate out of the suitcase. She thought that when her aunt got to America and found that a plate was missing, she would have to come home to get it!" Alicja smiles and shrugs sheepishly at the failed plan. I smile and nod, sniffing back tears. I tell Marek, "Please tell her that I think it was a great plan."

For these pottery-inspired earrings, I chose tiny ivory bone heishi for their rustic, creamy color, but if you prefer uniform beads, then I would recommend 6º matte opaque bone Japanese seed beads. The beaded circle is built around a mandala-like silver coin bead. Though this is not a Polish-looking element per se, I think the concentric circles and dot details really evoke the Polish pottery look I was going for. Humble components all, but they combine for an elegant design.

MATERIALS

1 pair decorative sterling silver ear wires

2 silver-plated 12mm patterned coin beads

26 bone 3mm heishi beads

34 matte navy 6º seed beads

70 matte metallic nebula midnight blue 11º seed beads

6' (1.8 m) beading thread

G-S Hypo Cement adhesive

TOOLS

Beading needle

Scissors

Two pairs of pliers (for opening and closing ear wires)

FINISHED SIZE

1¾" long × 1" wide (4.5 × 2.5 cm), including ear wire.

1. Leaving a 6" (15 cm) tail, pass needle through coin bead once, and again, and again in the same direction, making two floats of thread. Position these two threads along one edge of coin bead. They should run 180 degrees along one half of the rim of the bead. These will be your beading "base threads" (**Figure 1**).

2. String 2 heishis on needle and position them so they are both sitting square on rim of coin bead. (The first bead will be sitting as it was strung, and the second bead will be sitting upside down from how it was strung. The thread should be connecting the 2 beads on the outside ends [**Figures 2 and 3**].) Holding heishis here, pass needle under base threads, from back to front. Now pass needle up through second heishi, starting at end sitting on rim of coin bead. Pull snugly, but keep your base threads running around rim of bead (**Figure 4**). (You will need to keep base threads snug, but running around rim of bead, at all times during this first round.)

3. String a third heishi onto needle and position bead right next to second bead (**Figure 5**). (This bead and every subsequent bead will be sitting upside down from how it was strung.) Holding heishi here, pass needle under base threads, from back to front. Now pass needle up through the heishi, starting at end sitting on rim of coin bead. Repeat this step four more times until 6 or 7 heishi are strung around roughly one half of coin bead (**Figure 6**).

Fig. 1   *Fig. 2*

Fig. 3   *Fig. 4*

Fig. 5   *Fig. 6*

POLAND: POLISH POTTERY EARRINGS ~ 21

4. Pass needle through coin bead once, and again, and again in the same direction, making two new floats of thread. Position these two threads along other edge of coin bead. They should run 180 degrees along other half of rim of bead. These will be your "base threads" for the second half. You should be back at the start.

5. Pass needle through first bead from rim end to outside end.

6. Turning your work if necessary, repeat Step 3 for remaining 6 or 7 heishis, ending with your thread coming out the very first heishi (**Figure 7**).

7. To begin second ring, string 2 matte navy 6º beads on needle (**Figure 8**) and position them so they are both sitting square on the first row of heishi beads. Holding matte navy beads here, pass needle under base threads, from back to front, then pass needle through second matte navy bead starting. Continue in this manner, stringing 17 matte navy seed beads around, passing thread through connecting threads from previous ring (**Figures 9 and 10**).

8. For third ring, repeat Step 7 using 35 matte midnight blue 11º beads.

9. With beading needle, secure thread by tying half-hitch knots (see page 137) over next 5 beads. Pass thread through bead and trim end close with scissors.

10. Repeat Steps 1–9 for second earring.

11. Using two flat-nose pliers, open loop on ear wire and slip on one beaded disk at a point reinforced with half-hitch knots (**Figure 11**). With pliers, close loop. Repeat for second earring.

12. On a flat surface, run a line of adhesive around center disc bead and position heishi row so it is flush to edge of coin (**Figure 12**). Repeat for second disc bead and let dry.

Fig. 7

Fig. 8

Fig. 9

Fig. 10

Fig. 11

Fig. 12

POLAND: POLISH POTTERY EARRINGS ~ 23

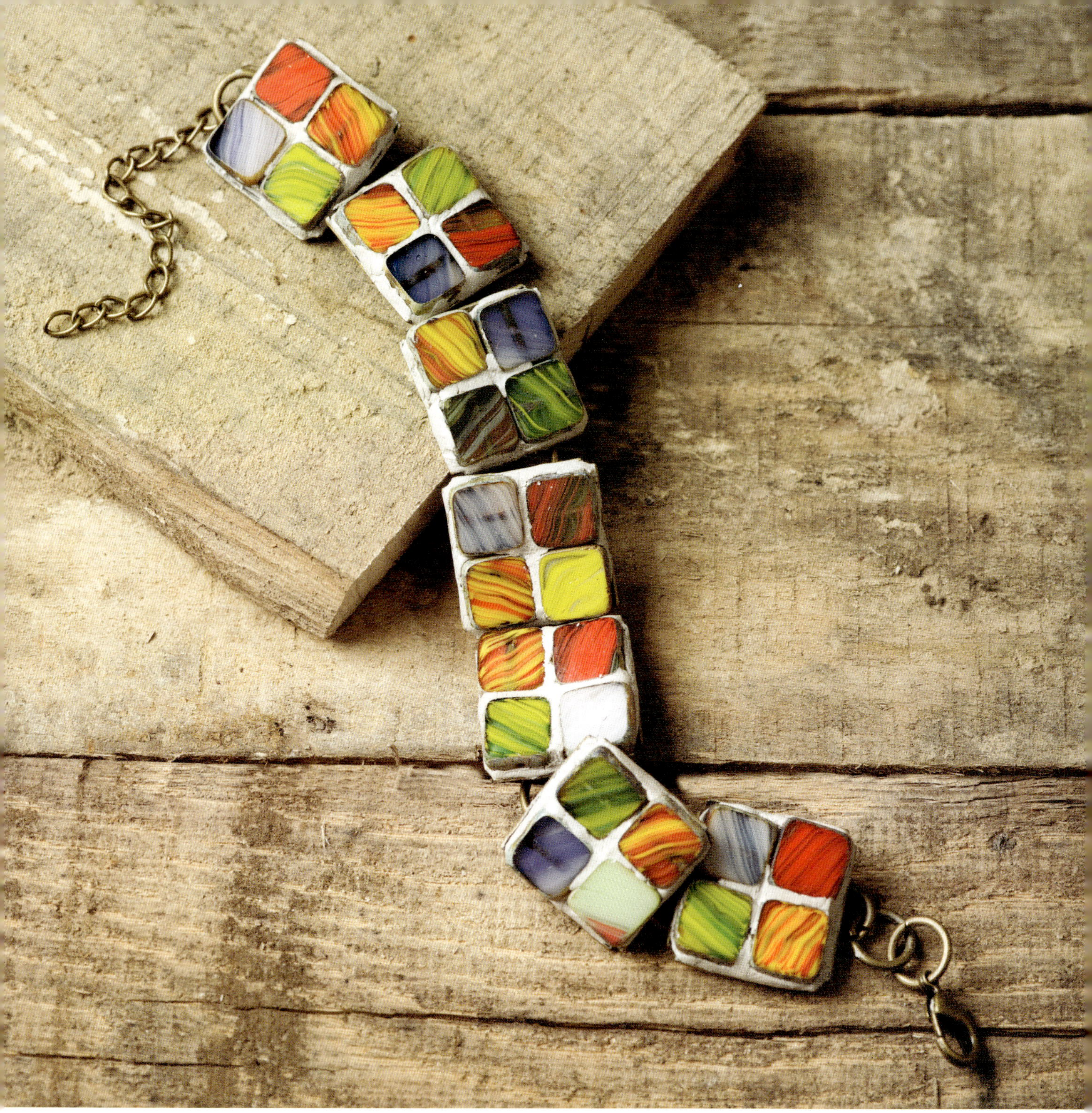
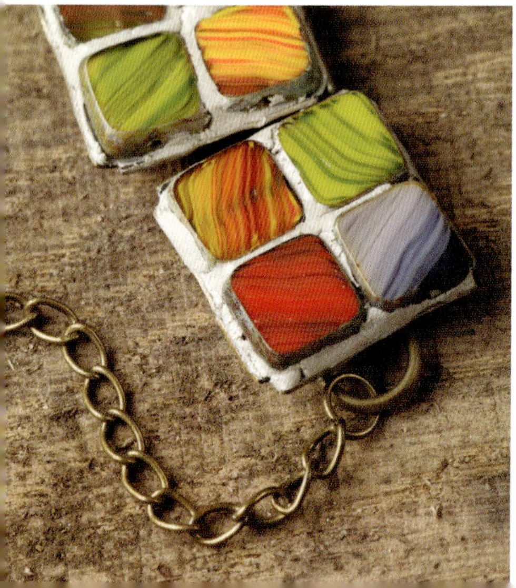
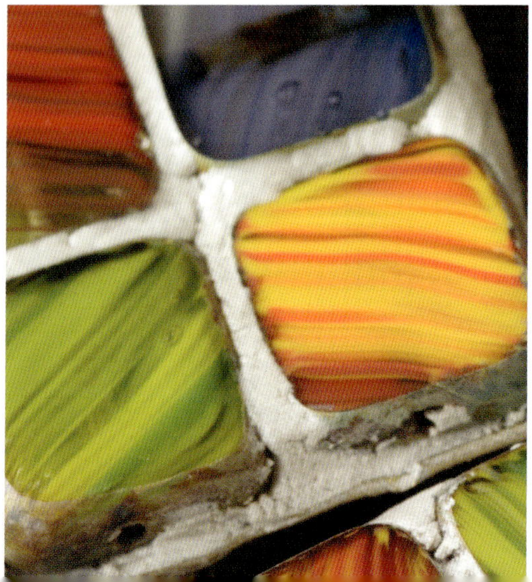
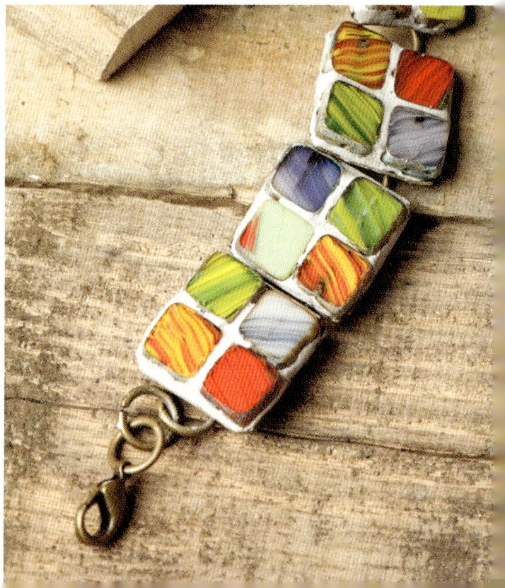

SPAIN
Gaudí Tile Bracelet

At a table just off a narrow brick street we sit around plates of tapas drinking *jarras* of beer. Miguel and Pilar have lived in Barcelona their whole lives and we're talking about Park Güell.

"What do you love about it? Why do you go there?" I ask.

"It's very Catalonian. Gaudí's work comes from *this* place, you know?" Miguel explains. "It feels very…*íntimo*…eh, 'familiar.' I think you will like it!" Miguel says with a confident smile.

Commissioned to design and build a park overlooking Barcelona as part of an urbanization movement, Antoni Gaudí completed Park Güell in 1914, and it stands today as one of the most popular and successful city parks in the world. This whimsical park flaunts Gaudí's surreal modern-baroque style and is covered with *trencadís*-style mosaics, which use reclaimed pottery such as ceramic plates instead of new tiles. The park is a multicolored wonderland.

Broken shards fit together, neatly reforming their original floral pattern, or easily melding with other pieces. It's very tidy, not messy like I was expecting. A light gray cement grouts the tiles—a counterpoint to the boisterous colors of the glazed ceramic pieces. A proper tea rose china plate cozies up to a crimson Spanish baroque shard. Surprisingly, the effect is a harmonious patchwork. As the setting sun casts a golden wash over the city, encroaching shadows paint the park. What was white a few minutes ago is now an energetic, electric blue. Patches of red and green and yellow pop with saturation now, as if switched on from underneath. Miguel and Pilar take a self-portrait together with gingerbread gatehouses and beautiful Barcelona in the background. Leaning together, they are wearing sunglasses and smiling big, laughing smiles. I wonder if Gaudí knew that his park would feel like this? What a playground, what a happy place to be!

It's easy to evoke the beauty of Gaudí's trencadís mosaic work with Czech glass beads. One short strand of tile beads will give you plenty of design options, because each bead is unique. For the base of this bracelet, I went with a craft store bezel-link bracelet because they're readily available and (almost) perfect for this project. These bezels were actually too small to fit the four 8mm square tiles that I chose, so I had to improvise. With flat-nose pliers, I opened up the bezels to make a wider base setting. I thought it was worth the trouble, but choose smaller tile beads and you won't have to worry about this step at all.

MATERIALS

Twenty-eight 8mm table-cut square Czech glass beads for tiles

5 grams silver two-part epoxy clay

1 square bezel link bracelet, each bezel link 18mm × 18mm

TOOLS

Plastic knife

Paper towel

Flat-nose pliers (to open up bezels)

FINISHED SIZE

7–9" long × ¾" wide (18–23 × 2 cm).

1. Optional: If your beads don't lie flat in the base of the bezels, with flat-nose pliers, open up bezel links to make a large setting base (**Figure 1**). Start at corners and gently pull bezel walls out.

2. Plan out your bead placement and arrange tile beads as you like (**Figure 2**).

3. Cut two equally sized, small pieces of the resin and hardener, about the size of a nickel each (**Figure 3**). According to manufacturer's directions, mix two parts of epoxy clay together until completely blended.

4. Pinch off a piece of the mixed epoxy clay about the size of a pencil eraser. With finger, press epoxy clay into bezel base, covering completely (**Figure 4**).

5. Press 4 tile beads into epoxy clay (**Figure 5**). With finger, press epoxy clay up sides of beads to hide hole.

6. Pinch off a tiny piece of clay and roll into a 1" (2.5 cm) long "snake." Use this snake of clay as "grout" and fill in the cross formed between the 4 tiles (**Figure 6**).

7. Repeat Steps 4–6 for remaining 6 bezel bases.

8. With very little water, dampen paper towel. Polish each four-tile link to remove excess clay from tile surface, and smooth any fingerprints or impressions left on clay (**Figure 7**).

9. Place in safe place to cure for at least 24 hours.

10. Wash hands.

Fig. 1

Fig. 2

Fig. 3

Fig. 4

Fig. 5

Fig. 6

Fig. 7

Spain: Gaudí Tile Bracelet ~ 27

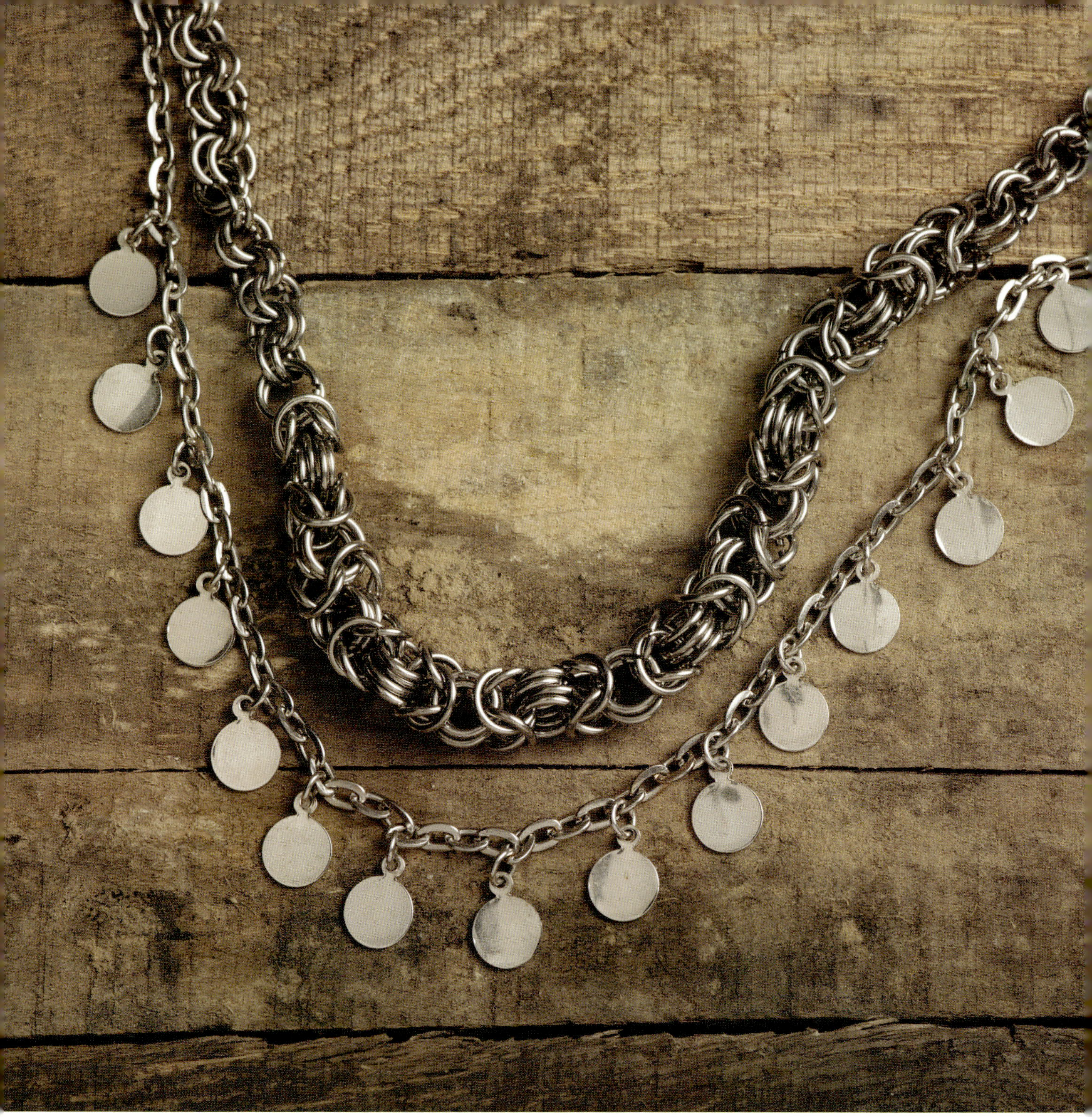
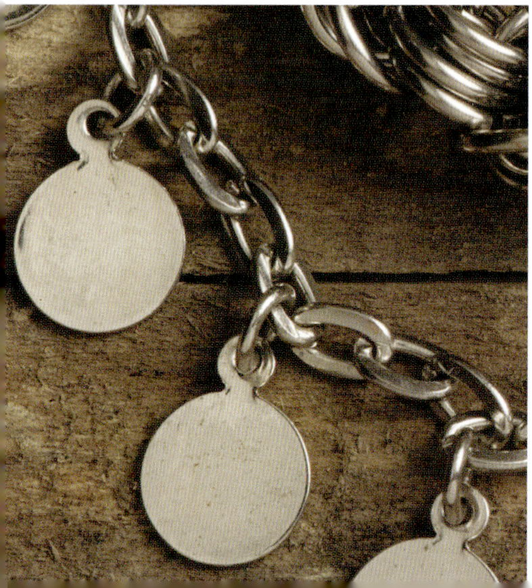
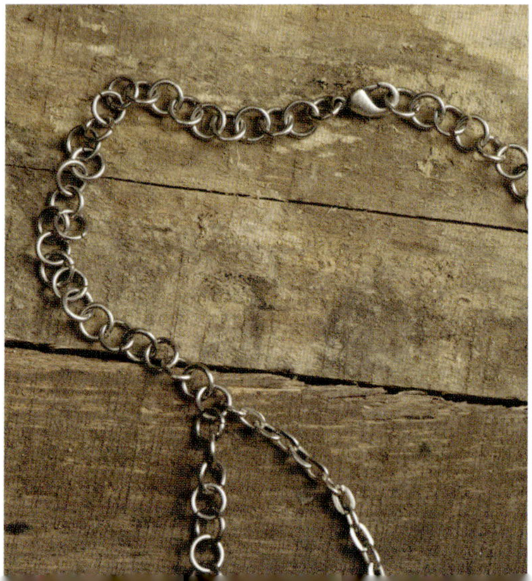
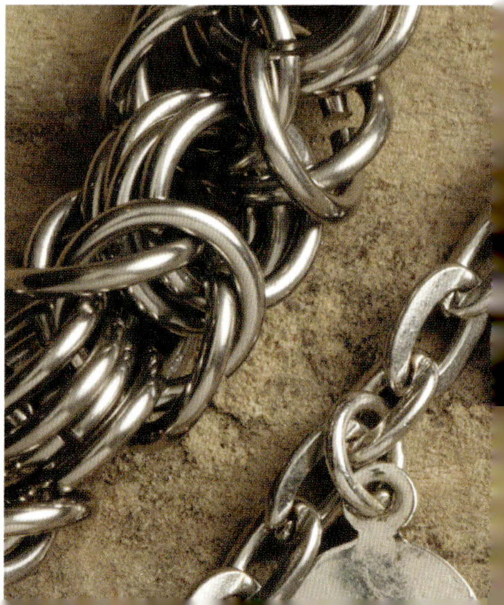

NORWAY
Sølje Chain Maille Necklace

Under the watch of a midnight sun we dive into the still chill of the bottomless fjord. The sky above is awash with purple and peach, and the sun is twilight bright. Hoary mountains surround us, ancient and uncommon. This landscape, this place, is mystical. It's said that *nisse*—those gnomes that make mischief for farmers—turn into mountains when they fall asleep and die. This is magical Norway. A mystical place, where mountains are old souls, and I can swim at midnight with a sun that doesn't set.

Earlier today, after a mountain train ride and an uphill hike, we reached my cousin Effi's house. Effi is my favorite cousin. She is small and industrious and hosts us with easy grace, all while running a farm solo. She spread out a table of flatbread, farmer cheese, and blueberries, and as we ate our lunch she excused herself to—no joke—milk the cow. Effi's a Viking. Such cool, hardy stock! Such pulled-together competence.

Catching up over knitting, I admired her brooch. "Oh! A *sølje*!" I said, recognizing the pretty silver pin. When I was baptized as a baby my grandmother gave me a little sølje pin just like Effi's. Søljes are a classic, if esoteric, piece of Norwegian jewelry. They have an open circle frame that represents the sun. Filigree dangles hang symmetrically around the pin like numbers on a clock, and from each dangle hangs a bright silver spangle, or "spoon," that quivers like an aspen leaf.

"I have one just like this, Effi! It's the sun, right?" I asked her.

"Oh, I suppose," she replied, "but it is really for the *huldrefolk*."

"The what?" I asked.

"The huldrefolk," she repeated, snorting at my ignorance. "They are the demons that roam the countryside and steal children. We wear søljes to protect us from the huldrefolk."

"Of course we do," I said.

While wrought entirely in a stainless steel palette, this double-strand necklace boasts craftsmanship and style. The shortest layer is chain maille, made in a simple adaptation of the basic Byzantine pattern. It's a little hard to get started, but once you grasp the concept after a few repeats, it works up more quickly. Don't hesitate to find a friend who does chain maille or a video, as chain maille is easier to learn "live-action." The longer layer of the necklace will come together much more easily! It is not as complicated, but its sølje-like spangles make a sprightly counterpoint to the chain maille.

MATERIALS

148 stainless steel 5/32" (4mm) 18-gauge jump rings

122 stainless steel 13/64" (5mm) 16-gauge jump rings

1 stainless steel lobster 12mm clasp

17" (43 cm) stainless steel 5×4mm oval chain

17 nickel-plated 8mm round tag drops

17 stainless steel 4mm open jump rings

TOOLS

Twist tie

Two pairs of pliers (for opening and closing jump rings)

FINISHED SIZE

27" (68.5 cm) long.

1. With two pairs of pliers, open all 5/32" (4mm) stainless steel jump rings.

2. To make modified Byzantine chain maille section, link 2 jump rings to 2 jump rings. Close rings. This will make a 2-2 starter chain. Thread a twist tie through first 2 links to mark beginning of chain maille and make it easier to handle (**Figures 1 and 2**).

3. Flip second set of 2 jump rings back toward twist tie so they form a V alongside first set of rings (**Figure 3**). Now, working into non-twist-tie end of first set of rings, link 4 jump rings to first 2 jump rings (**Figures 4 and 5**). Close rings.

4. Into 4 rings, link 2 rings. Close rings (**Figure 6**).

Fig. 1

Fig. 2

Fig. 3

Fig. 4

Fig. 5

Fig. 6

Norway: Sølje Chain Maille Necklace ~ 31

5. Into these 2 rings, link 2 rings. Close rings (**Figure 7**).

6. Flip second set of 2 jump rings back toward twist tie so they form a V alongside first set of rings off of the 4 jump rings (**Figure 8**). Now, working into this set of 2 rings, link 4 jump rings to the first 2 jump rings (**Figures 9 and 10**). Close rings.

7. Repeat Steps 3–6 thirteen more times.

8. Flip second set of 2 jump rings back toward twist tie so they form a V alongside first set of rings, and link 4 jump rings to first two jump rings. Close rings.

9. Returning to twist-tie end, remove twist tie. Link 4 jump rings to very first set of 2 rings. Close rings.

10. With two pairs of pliers, open all $^{13}/_{64}$" (5mm) stainless steel jump rings.

11. Link 2 smaller rings to 4 larger rings of one end of modified Byzantine chain maille section. Close rings.

12. Link 2 smaller rings to 2 smaller rings, beginning a 2-2 chain pattern. Close rings. Repeat this step fifteen more times.

13. Onto other end of modified Byzantine chain maille section, repeat Steps 11 and 12.

14. Link 1 smaller ring to 2 rings on the end of one of the 2-2 sections, beginning a 1-1 chain pattern. Close ring. Repeat this step thirty-seven more times.

15. Link one smaller ring to the end of the other 2-2 section, beginning a 1-1 chain pattern. Close rings. Repeat this step thirty-seven more times (**Figure 11**).

16. Add lobster clasp to one end of 1-1 chain. Close ring.

17. With two pliers, open all 4mm stainless steel jump rings.

18. Beginning in the center of stainless steel oval chain, add 1 stainless steel drop to link of chain with one 4mm jump ring. Close ring.

19. Continue adding stainless steel drops every four links in this manner, working on both sides of center link.

20. Lay chain maille section out flat, being careful not to twist. Lay chain section with stainless steel drops out flat, being careful not to twist (**Figure 12**).

21. With pliers, open up twelfth link of 1-1 chain of chain maille section, counting from end attached to 2-2 chain section. Attach one end of stainless steel drop chain. Close ring. Repeat for other end of stainless steel section and twelfth link of other side of chain maille section.

Fig. 7

Fig. 8

Fig. 9

Fig. 10

Fig. 11

Fig. 12

Norway: Sølje Chain Maille Necklace ~ 33

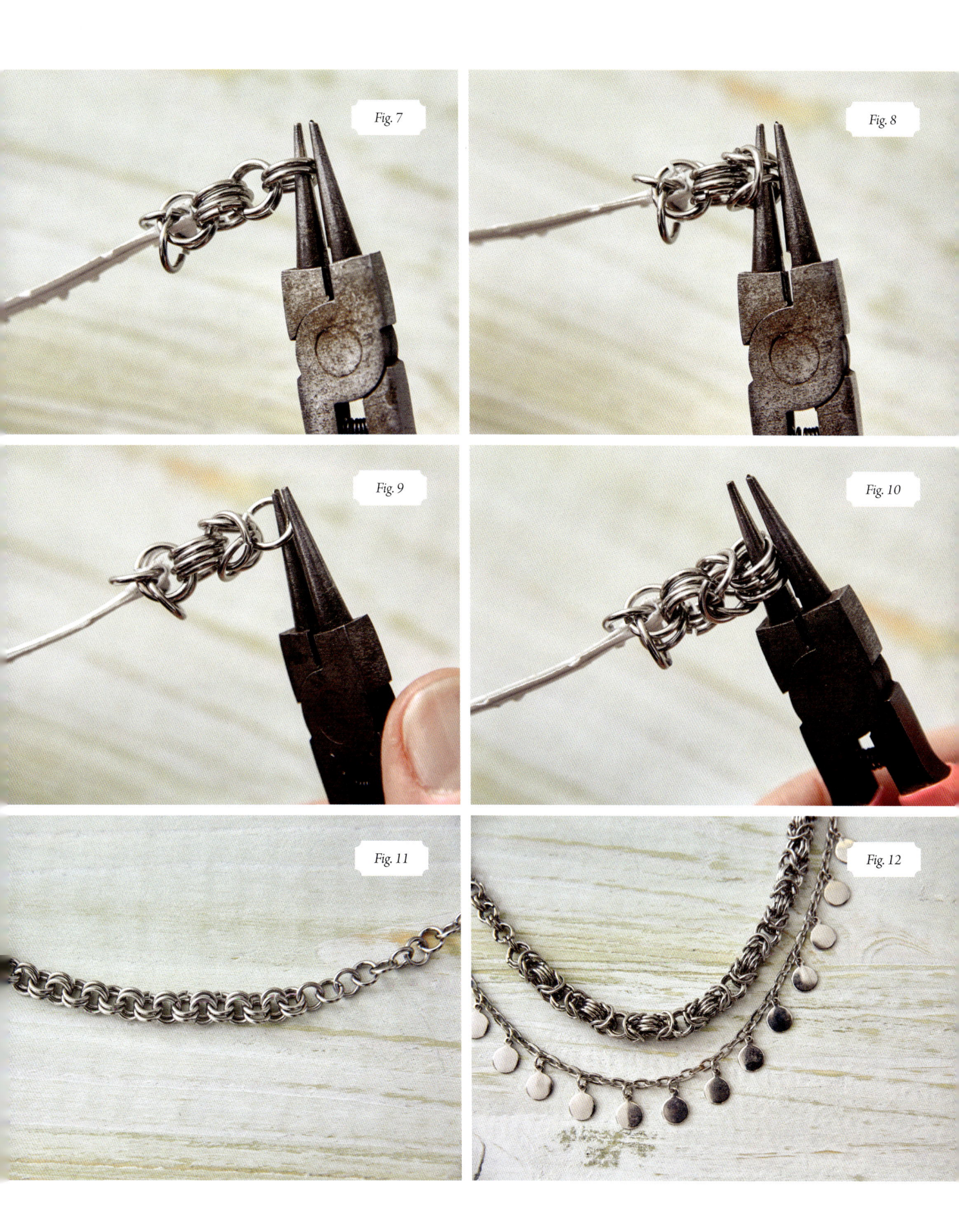

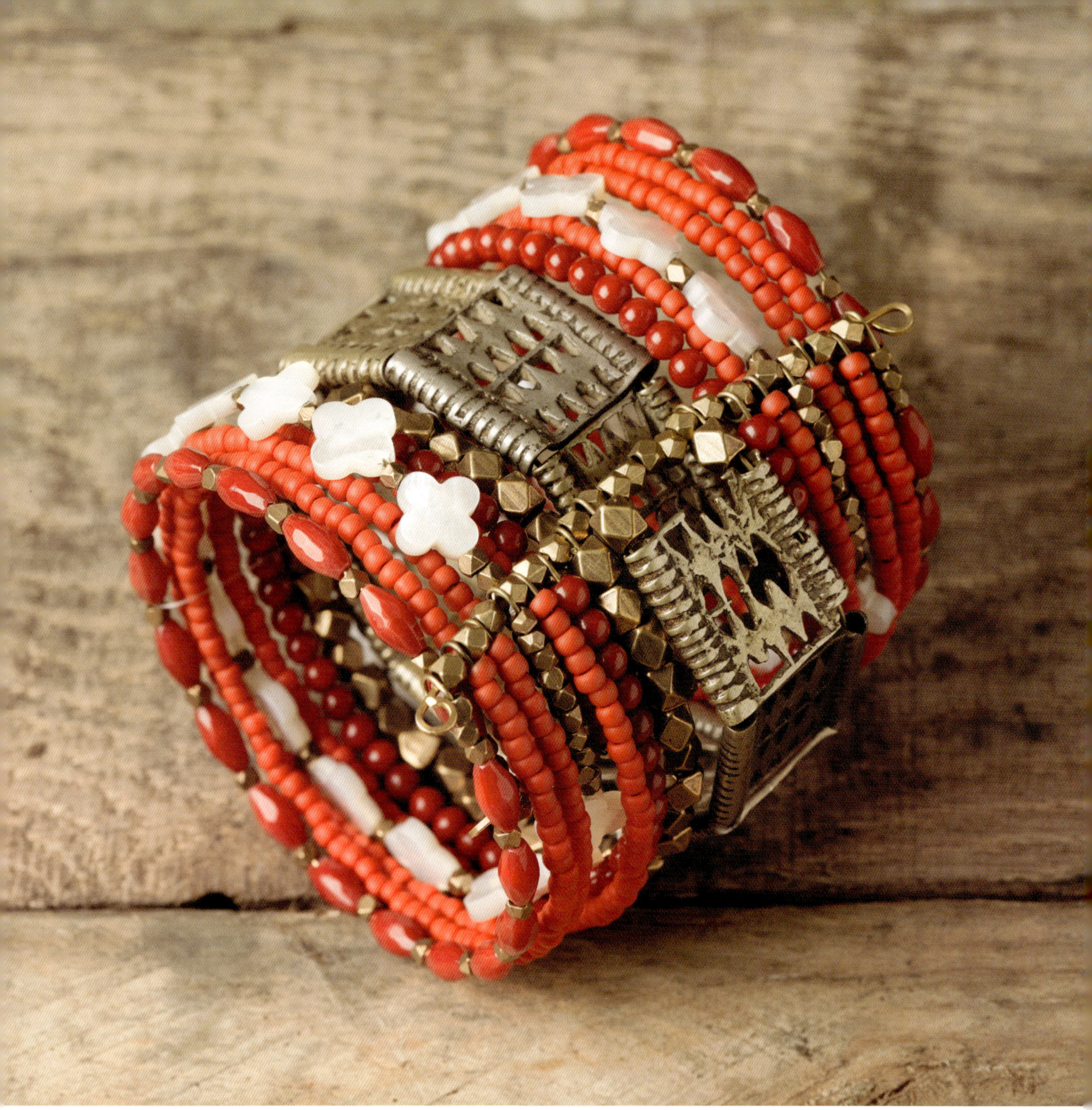
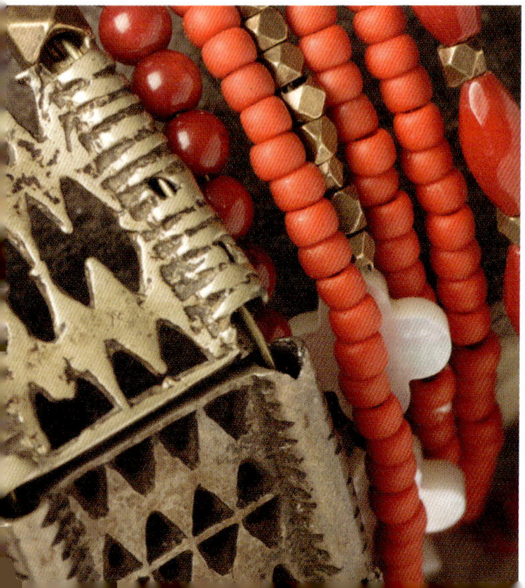
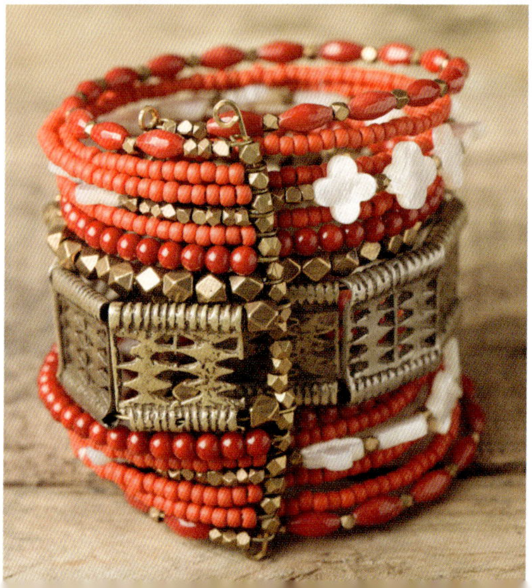
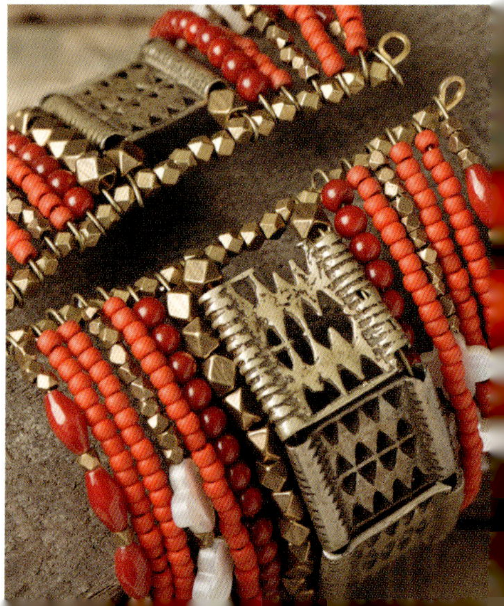

UKRAINE
Vyshyvka Bracelet

Twenty minutes into the old woman's lecture seems a little late to say, "I don't speak Ukrainian," but I don't think it matters. This isn't some chat over tea; this is a sermon. A sermon on *vyshyvka*—Ukrainian embroidery—and I'm a rapt audience. She holds the embroidered blouse and passionately preaches to me, explaining, exhorting (I think). Wide-eyed, I nod in submissive accord as she points to an element and then expounds on . . . something (I don't know what).

Looking at this masterpiece, it is easy to appreciate this classically Ukrainian needlework, even if I can't understand her homily. It is geometric and exact, symmetrical and grid-like, yet combines for a lacy, floral effect. Elaborate motifs, linked together, make up the four-inch-wide band that decorates the hem of the blouse. The red and black threads pop on the stark white linen. She points to a large diamond motif that repeats down the center of the band and expounds. In the center of each diamond is a cross, each arm formed by two angled wedges, like a snowflake motif on a Norwegian sweater. The snowflake cross is surrounded by bent barbs that jut from the inside walls of the diamond, while the outside of the diamond is embellished with a small dentil border, softening the hard edges. Other diamonds, smaller versions of the first, boast tiny plus-sign crosses and little dentil trim around the edge, like pickets on a tiny fence. Simple cross-stitches fill in between the diamonds; the thousand tiny stitches splinter like frost on a windowpane. It's divine.

When she is finished, she leans back in her chair, smiling in satisfaction at enlightening me, and a little worn out, too. I don't know what to do, so I tell her in loud English, "Ukrainian embroidery is just exquisite; this is a masterpiece!"

"так!" she exclaims.

I think we agree (I think).

Instead of making a very precise interpretation of Ukrainian embroidery—maybe a perfect replica beaded in brick stitch—I decided to instead try to capture the glorious busyness of this embroidery by collecting different bead shapes and scales. The centerpiece of this bracelet are Akha belt pieces from the hill regions of Thailand. Their diamond cutouts capture the diamond repeats of the embroidery and create a dynamic focal point. Quatrefoil mother-of-pearl beads represent the cross designs nicely, and a nice collection of red beads captures the simple, bold palette of the complex redwork.

MATERIALS

36 red coral 8×3mm faceted barrels

570 matte red 6º seed beads

26 mother-of-pearl (MOP) 10mm quatrefoils

46 antiqued brass 5mm cornerless cubes

10 antiqued brass 20×20mm Akha belt links

102 red coral 4mm rounds

112 antiqued brass 2.5mm cornerless cubes

38 antiqued brass 3.3mm cornerless cubes

12' (3.35 m) antiqued brass 55mm memory wire

8" (20.5 cm) raw brass 18-gauge square wire

TOOLS

Memory-wire cutters

Round-nose pliers

FINISHED SIZE

7" around × 2½" high (18 × 6.5 cm).

1. With wire cutters, cut memory wire into fifteen 9½" (24 cm) lengths.

2. With round-nose pliers, form a simple loop (see page 134) at one end of each length.

3. For faceted coral layers (A): onto one memory wire length, string 3 antiqued brass 2.5mm cornerless cubes, [1 faceted red coral barrel, 1 antiqued brass 2.5mm cornerless cube] seventeen times, and 3 antiqued brass 2.5mm cornerless cubes. With round-nose pliers, form a simple loop at the free end. Repeat with another length of wire.

4. For seed bead layers (B): onto one memory-wire length, string 95 matte red seed beads. With round-nose pliers, form a simple loop at the free end. Repeat with five more lengths of wire to make a total of six seed bead loops.

5. For MOP quatrefoil layers (C): onto one memory-wire length, string 11 antiqued brass 2.5mm cornerless cubes, [1 MOP quatrefoil, 1 antiqued brass 2.5mm cornerless cube] twelve times, and then 11 antiqued brass 2.5mm cornerless cubes. With round-nose pliers, form a simple loop at the free end. Repeat one more time.

6. For coral round layers (D): onto one memory-wire length, string 51 red coral 4mm rounds. With round-nose pliers, form a simple loop at the free end.

7. For brass cornerless cube layer (E): onto one memory-wire length, string 42 antiqued brass 5mm cornerless cubes. With round-nose pliers, form a simple loop at the free end.

8. For Akha link layer (F): onto one memory-wire length, string 1 antiqued brass 5mm cornerless cube, one side of 10 Akha links, and 1 antiqued brass 5mm cornerless cube. With round-nose pliers, form a simple loop at the free end. Onto one memory-wire length, string 1 antiqued brass 5mm cornerless cube, the other side of 10 Akha links, and 1 antiqued brass 5mm cornerless cube. With round-nose pliers, form a simple loop at the free end.

9. With wire cutters, cut 18-gauge wire into two 4" (10 cm) lengths.

10. With round-nose pliers, form a simple loop at one end of each length.

11. Line up openings of completed memory-wire layer in the following order: A, B, B, C, B, D, E, F, D, B, C, B, B, A. String one end loop of first layer and then 1 antiqued brass 3.3mm cornerless cube. Repeat, alternating first seven layers and 3.3mm cornerless cubes. Then string one loop of Akha layer (F), 6 antiqued brass 3.3mm cornerless cubes, then second loop of Akha layer. Continue alternating 3.3mm cornerless cubes and a layer ending with last completed loop. Repeat for second loops of completed memory-wire layers. With round-nose pliers, form a simple loop at free end of each wire close to last memory-wire loop (**Figure 1**).

Fig. 1

Ukraine: Vyshyvka Bracelet ~ 37

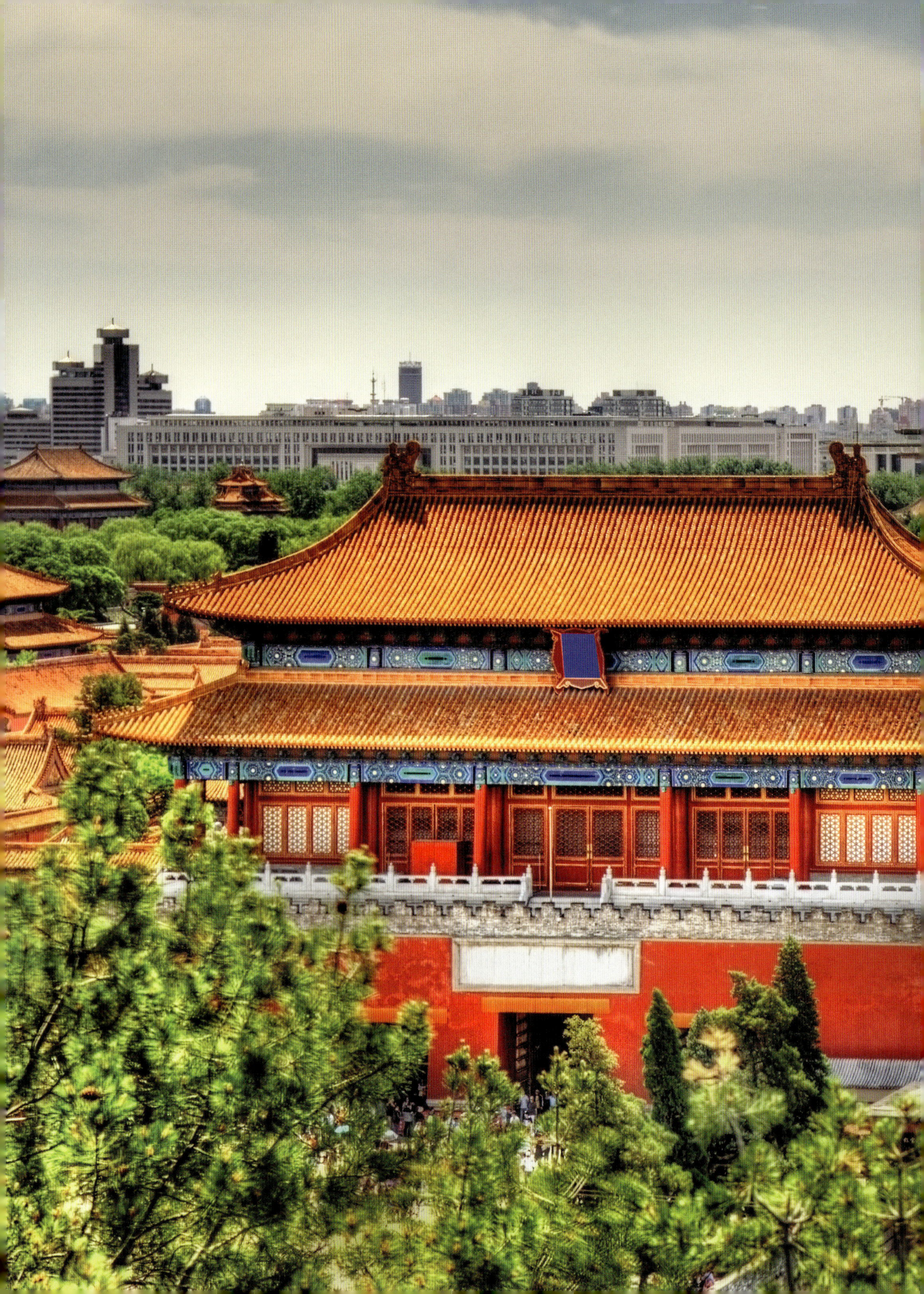

Chapter Two

ASIA

In this chapter, you will not see a cohesive "Asian" design identity, but rather just the opposite. With Asia being such a massive continent (and composed of so many subcontinents), it was difficult to choose just a few pieces from such a broad display of design inspiration. The Far East—China, Japan, and Korea—has a look very distinct from that of Southeast Asia and certainly Middle Eastern cultures. I decided to make my selections as if sampling from a seriously large Asian buffet. Pieces that at once capture Japan's meticulous attention to detail and the boisterous busyness of Bangkok's street culture. And not forgetting the millennium-old arts of nomadic people in the Hindu Kush. This chapter gives you a cool selection that just grazes on Asia's design diversity. Cohesive it is not, but neither is Asia.

© GettyImages.com/Leonid Andropov

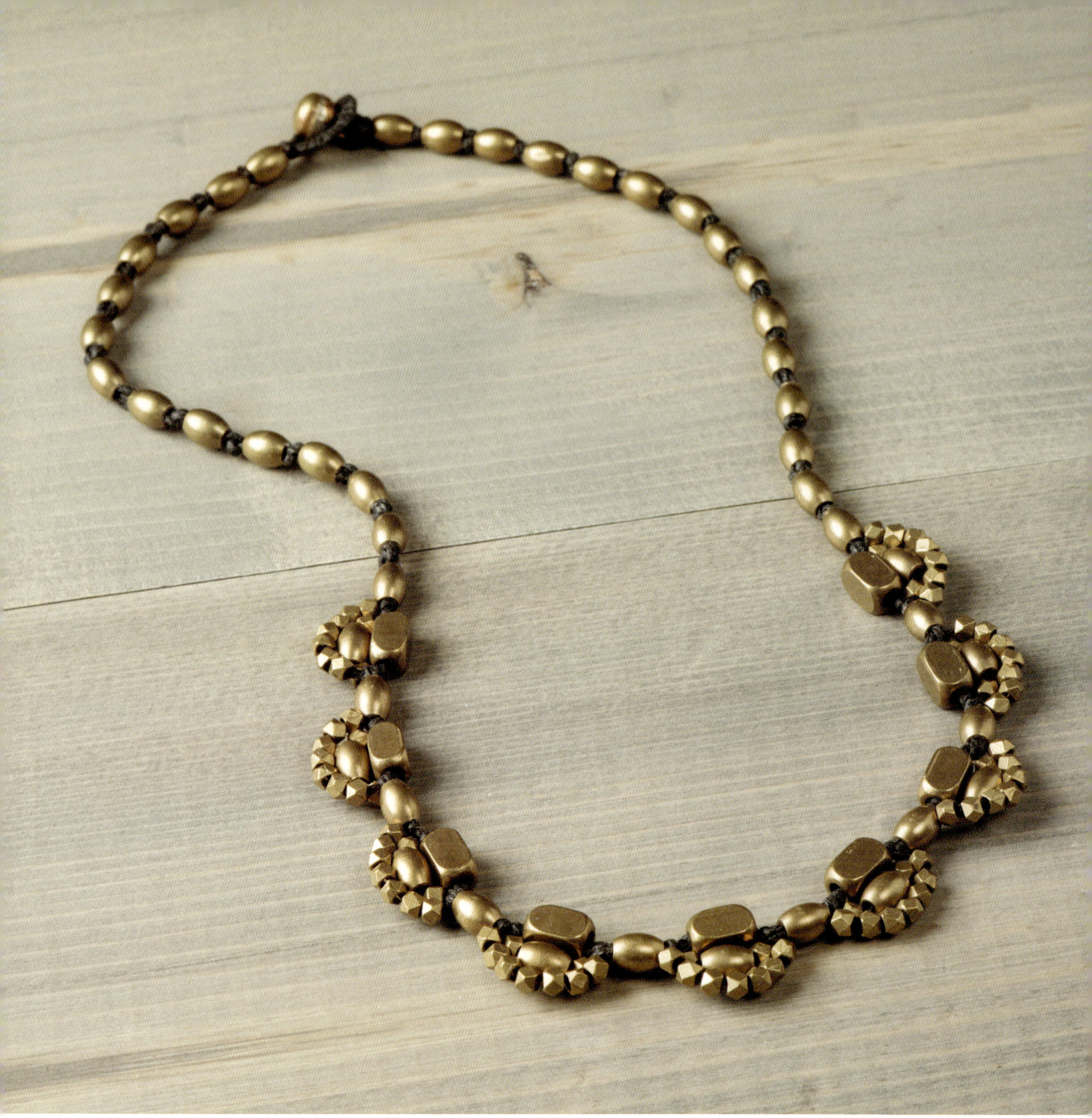
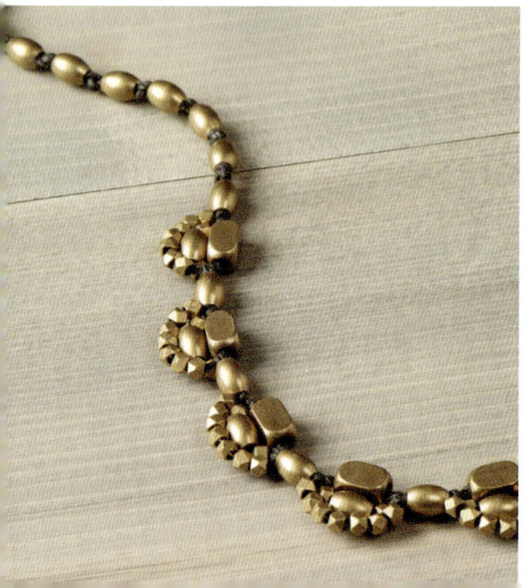
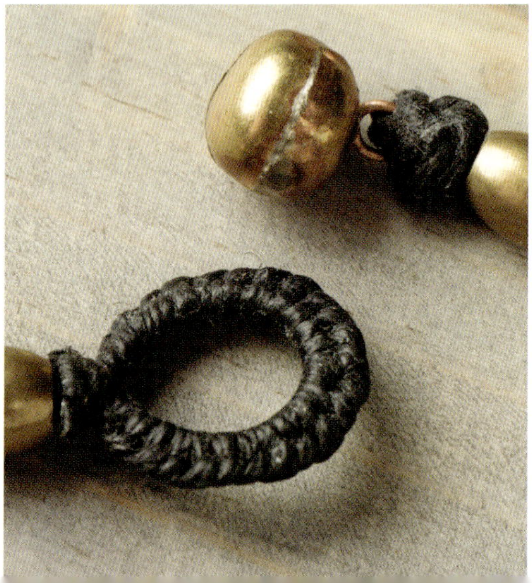
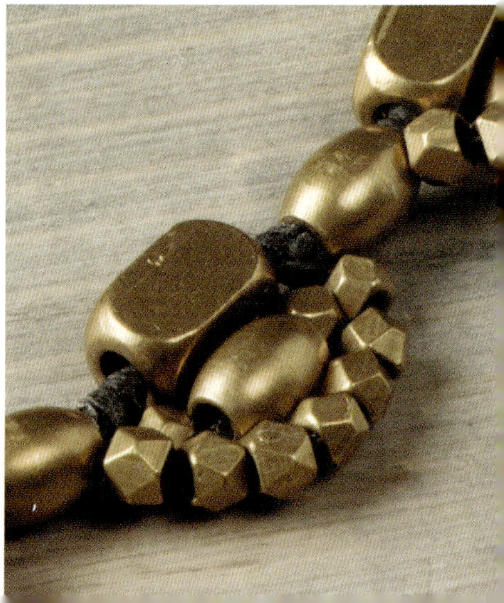

THAILAND
Bangkok Street Necklace

Walking through Bangkok's crowded streets, I can't think about anything except the heat. I wish monsoon season would come. Now. As I stagger along, fanning myself, I see an older woman across the street. Looking through the bustle of street traffic, she seems so serene, tranquilly making something with her hands. Tidy rows of *something* make an unassuming display on the small, low table in front of her. Hoping for jewelry, I cross the street, nearly getting swiped by a scooter.

It is jewelry, and her wares remind me of friendship bracelets. Little bands of neatly knotted linen threads, with twisted tail ties, in an understated palette of dark brown and black. With her head cocked a little to one side, she doesn't look up. Her fingers move quickly, throwing black thread over black thread to make half-hitch knots and square knots. Sliding a bead up sometimes, she locks it in place with another knot. The bracelet is simple, and I like it: the unfussy design and minimal materials combine for an understated elegance.

Abruptly she unclips the bracelet, ties a knot, and cuts the ends with a small scissors. I want *that* one.

"Fifty *baht?!*" I ask loudly. She doesn't answer so I dig out the bill from my pocket and hold it out to her. "Fifty baht?!" She has moved on to the next bracelet, cutting lengths of dark brown linen thread. (These are for sale, right?) "Yeahfiffybaht," she says without looking up. I lay down the money and pick up my new bracelet. I admire the perfect lines of knots, the even tension, and how the brass beads gleam next to the rustic linen. The woman, swiftly tying knots, doesn't look up. Oh, to be that cool.

This necklace is a version of the macramé jewelry sold to tourists all over the world. Using inexpensive materials, artisans can produce a high volume of low-priced jewelry to make a meager income. I call this style of jewelry "street jewelry": often artful, humbly produced jewelry made by artisans and hawked to tourists. It's easy to undervalue this type of jewelry because of the low price, but I've found it's usually very well made, and I just love the innovative creativity I see from street jewelers. There's always a lot to learn by buying a piece and studying the workmanship. For this necklace, I used simple waxed linen and inexpensive brass beads. Innovative, confident craftsmanship and humble materials combine to make a seriously eye-catching design. Be prepared to take it off and show the whole piece to admirers.

MATERIALS

12' (3.5 m) black waxed linen cord

46 antiqued brass 6×4mm rice beads

9 antiqued brass 8×4mm rectangles

81 antiqued brass 3.3mm cornerless cubes

One 10mm brass bell

TOOLS

Tape

Scissors

FINISHED SIZE

20" (51 cm) long.

Note: The three cords are named A, B, and C, in order from the base cord (A), the medium scallop cord (B), and the longer scallop cord (C).

1. With scissors, cut waxed linen cord into three 4' (122 cm) lengths. Tie all three lengths with an overhand knot (see page 136) about 8" (20.5 cm) from one end. Tape ends securely onto surface.

2. String 1 rice bead onto all three lengths. Holding cord A in right hand, tie a half-hitch knot (see page 137) with cords B and C. Repeat twelve more times (**Figure 1**).

3. Onto cord A, string 1 antiqued brass rectangle bead (**Figure 2**).

4. Onto cord B, string 1 antiqued brass 3.3mm cornerless cube, 1 antiqued brass rice bead, and 1 antiqued brass 3.3mm cornerless cube. Holding cord A in right hand, tie a half-hitch knot with cord B (**Figure 3**).

5. Onto cord C, string 7 antiqued brass 3.3mm cornerless cubes. Holding A and B in right hand, tie a half-hitch knot with cord C (**Figure 4**).

7. Repeat Steps 3–5 eight more times.

8. Repeat Step 2 to make 13 knotted rice beads total.

9. At beginning end, string bell onto all three lengths and tie several knots to secure (**Figure 5**). With scissors, cut ends close.

10. At other end, tie cord C into a half-hitch knot around cords A and B (**Figure 6**). Thread end of C through last rice bead and cut close with scissors.

11. Holding cord A in right hand, tie half-hitch knots with cord B for about 1" (2.5 cm) (**Figure 7**). Loop knotted length into a ring that barely fits over brass bell (**Figure 8**). Secure by tying cords A and B into three very tight square knots (see page 137). Cut close with scissors.

Fig. 1

Fig. 2

Fig. 3

Fig. 4

Fig. 5

Fig. 6

Fig. 7

Fig. 8

THAILAND: BANGKOK STREET NECKLACE ~ 43

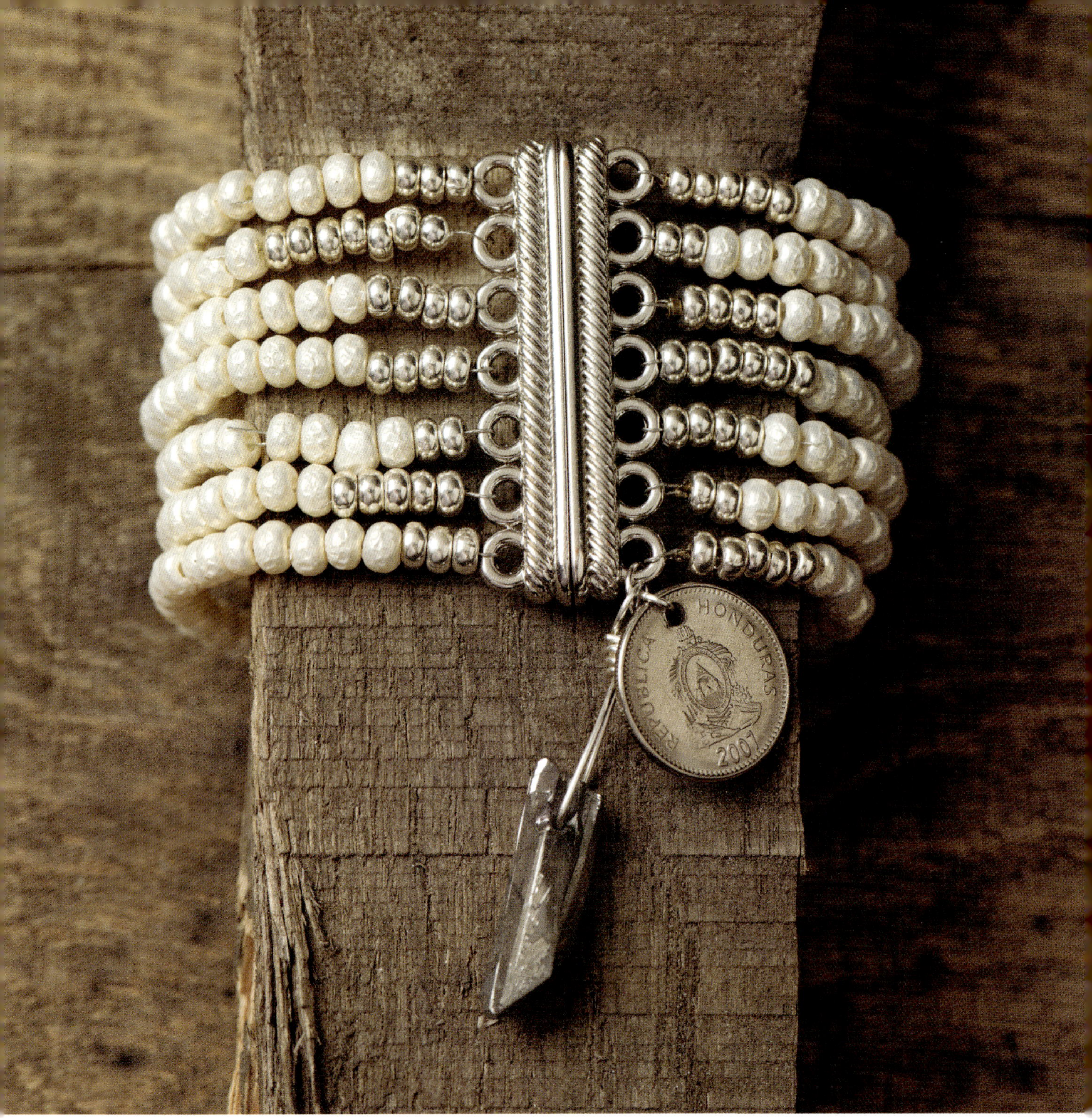
REPUBLICA HONDURAS
2007

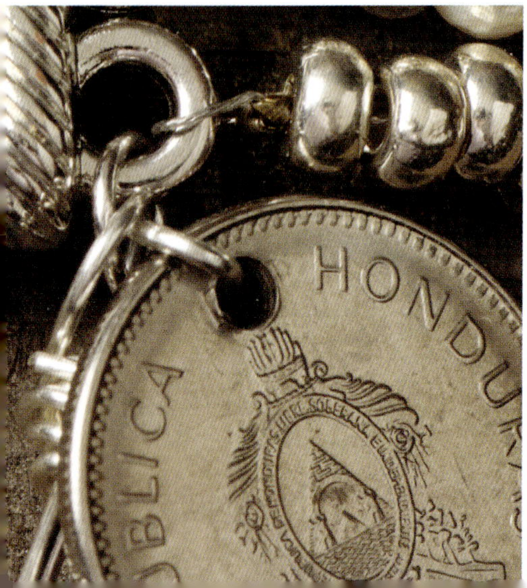
HONDURAS

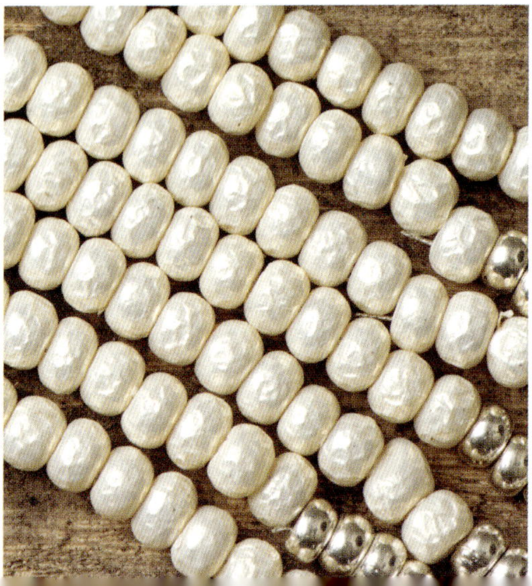

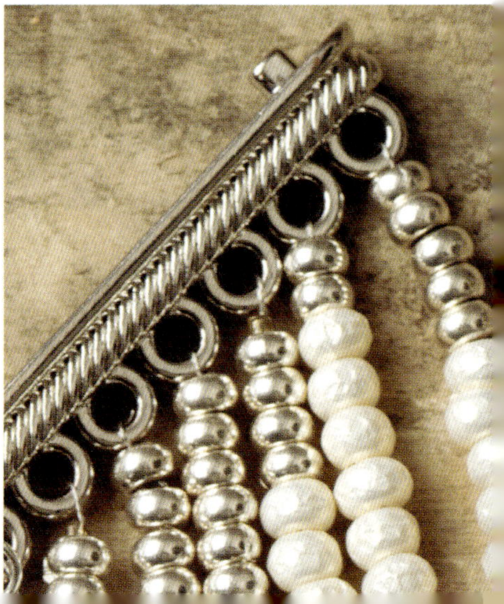

JAPAN
Raked Pebble Bracelet

Under the shelter of a red maple tree, the rock garden, still and perfect, looks like a stolen moment from a placid dream. Large, flat boulders encased in ancient velvet moss bask like turtles. The moss is a sprightly yellow—almost golden—green. With its thick, lush pile, the moss turns the boulders into tuffets, their edges soft and smooth.

In the middle of the garden are three large boulders, jagged and gray. Two tall, and one large and squat, they look like three craggy old sentries standing guard. Their harsh, rough-hewn rocky forms play against the mossy rocks beside them: cold gray on soft green. The layout of the garden seems effortless, like some gardener once just dealt with these rocks as they were. But really, the arrangement is pure art. A studied composition of color and space and form, with a wabi-sabi beauty.

Surrounding each focal rock are swaths of raked pebbles, like concentric waves rippling over a lake's surface. The pebble rings are pristine and perfect. Linking the craggy rocks and the mossy boulders, these light-bright pebbles act as a liaison, a calming sea that soothes the rocks' sore heaviness. For a thousand years, these pebbles have played the part of Lake with Rippling Waves. I trace my eyes along the raked ridges, and, like a labyrinth, they meander around rocks, then outline the square confines of the small garden. I realize this place is a sanctuary, a precious reverie, and I am inspired.

Irregular glass pearl seed beads capture the raked pebbles of a Japanese garden in this bracelet. Their color is bright and pure, while their blistered texture captures the perfectly imperfect, organic beauty of the pebbles. I didn't want to detract from the uncluttered beauty of strands of pearls, so I kept a light hand with other elements. A graphite-colored quartz point represents a craggy garden boulder, while a silver coin gives a nod to Japan's storied empire.

MATERIALS

32 grams glass pearl 6º seed beads

56 silver-plated 4×2mm rondelles

1 magnetic 44×18mm silver 7-hole clasp

84" (2 m) flexible beading wire

14 silver crimp beads

1 silver 20×7mm quartz point

One 18mm non-magnetic coin

2 silver 6mm open jump rings

6" (15 cm) sterling silver round 20-gauge wire

TOOLS

Wire cutters

Round-nose pliers

Flat-nose pliers

Crimping pliers

Two pairs of pliers (for opening and closing jump rings)

Metal hole punch

FINISHED SIZE

6" × long × 1½" wide (15 × 3.8 cm).

---

1. With wire cutters, cut flexible beading wire into seven 12" (30.5 cm) long lengths.

2. With metal hole punch, punch hole at top center of coin (**Figure 1**).

3. To make quartz dangle, string quartz point onto sterling silver wire. With round-nose pliers and flat-nose pliers, form elongated wrapped bail that measures about 1½" (3.8 cm) long. Make wrapped loop (see page 135) in center of sterling silver wire. String quartz point onto wire, leaving about ½" (1.3 cm) between quartz point and wrapped loop. Wrap tail of wire around wrapped loop several times and cut wire. (**Figure 2**).

4. Pass one length of flexible beading wire through crimp bead, through first loop of one side of magnetic clasp, and back through crimp bead. Place crimp bead close to loop. With crimping pliers, crimp the crimp bead (**Figure 3**).

5. Onto this length of flexible wire, string 5 silver rondelles, 44 glass pearls, and 3 silver rondelles.

6. Pass end of flexible beading wire through crimp bead, through first loop of second side of magnetic clasp, and back through crimp bead. Place crimp bead close to loop. With crimping pliers, crimp the crimp bead (**Figure 4**). Run beginning tail through 6–8 beads and trim (**Figure 5**).

7. Repeat Steps 4–6 for next six strands, stringing beads in the following sequence:

    Strand 2: 2 silver rondelles, 44 glass pearls, and 6 silver rondelles

    Strand 3: 4 silver rondelles, 44 glass pearls, and 4 silver rondelles

    Strand 4: 6 silver rondelles, 44 glass pearls, and 2 silver rondelles

    Strand 5: 4 silver rondelles, 44 glass pearls, and 4 silver rondelles

    Strand 6: 2 silver rondelles, 44 glass pearls, and 6 silver rondelles

    Strand 7: 5 silver rondelles, 44 glass pearls, and 3 silver rondelles

8. Attach quartz dangle to coin with 1 jump ring. With two pairs of pliers, close jump ring (**Figure 6**). Attach coin and dangle to last loop of clasp with 1 jump ring (**Figure 7**).

Fig. 1

Fig. 2

Fig. 3

Fig. 4

Fig. 5

Fig. 6

Fig. 7

Japan: Raked Pebble Bracelet ~ 47

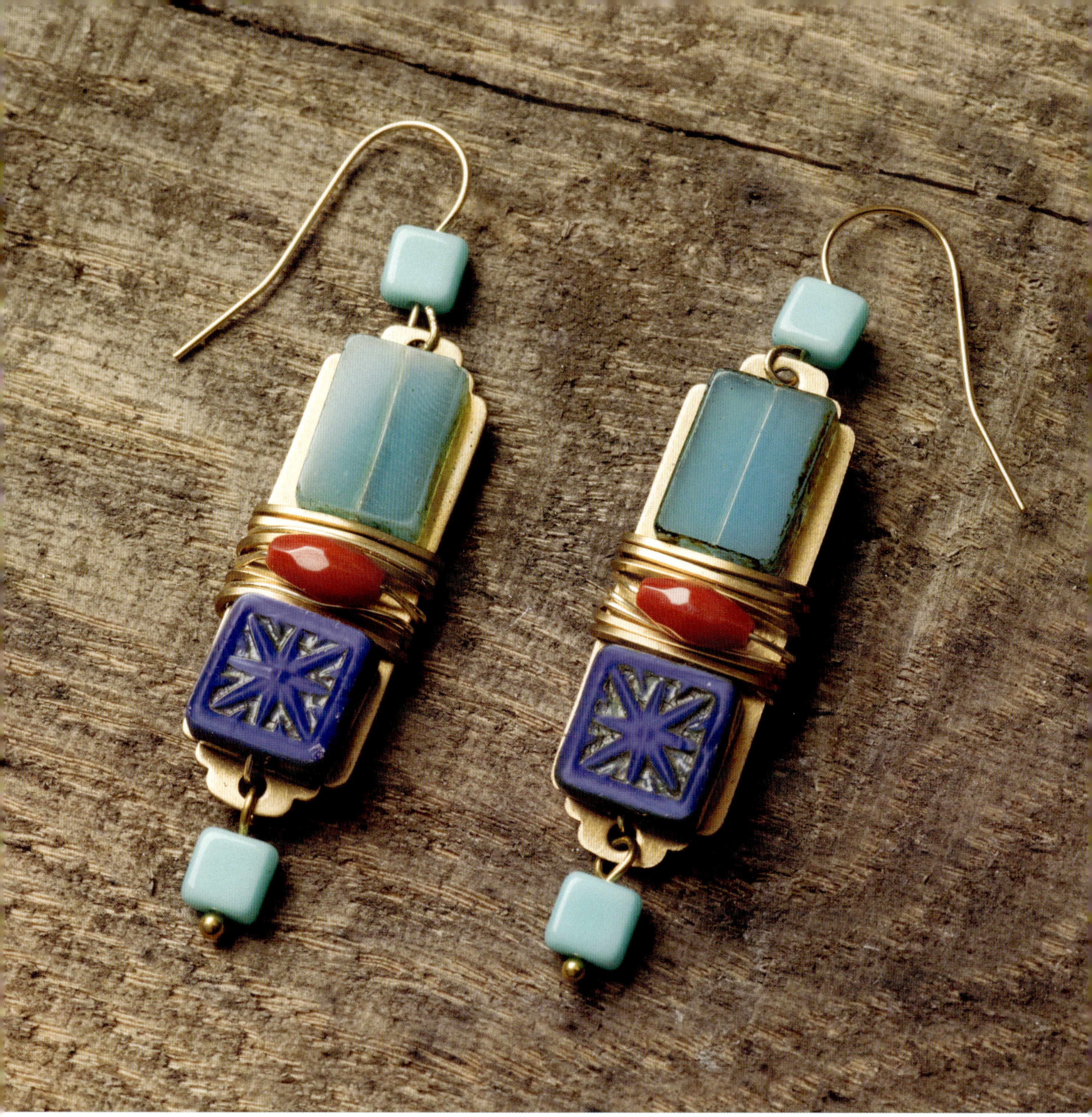
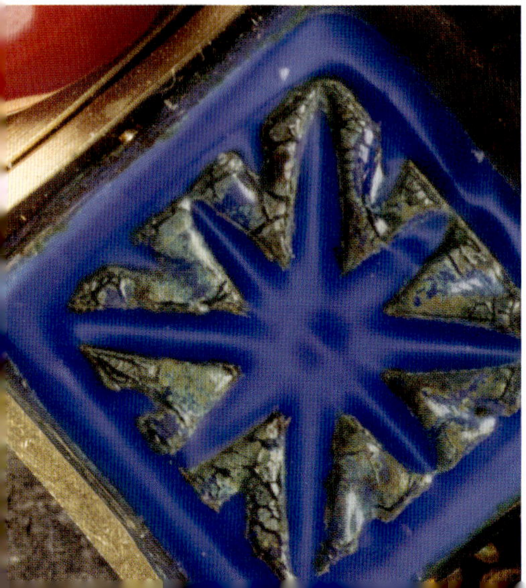
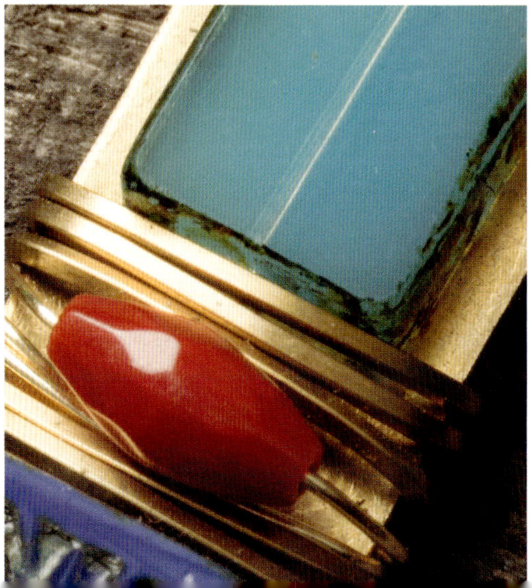
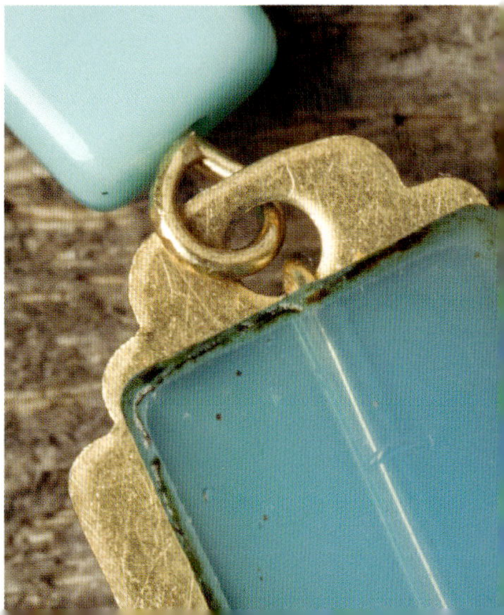

TURKEY
Iznik Tile Earrings

Yesterday, I toured the Topkapi Palace to take in its rich tilework and left with a headache. Almost every surface is decorated with an expanse of tile: decadent and pulsating, purring with Turkish blue designs. The walls sizzle with a myriad of flourishes and flora. Domed ceilings soared above my head with fully loaded patterns—explosive, exquisite, a sky full of flowers. Alcoves disclose kaleidoscopic secret gardens. This palace is impossibly ornate, and I was sated.

Tilework seems to cover all of Istanbul, from palace walls to public drinking fountains, and I find I'm most taken with the Iznik tiles. These graceful, traditionally Turkish tiles combine to form ornate, allover patterns of arabesques, flowers, and flourishes. I expected more geometric patterns, but mainly I see iterations of blooming carnations, tulips, and pomegranates with feathery, paisley-shaped leaves. And the color palette is consistent nearly everywhere the tiles appear: aqua blue and cobalt blue with tiny touches of red and green on a plain white background. The tilework is everywhere, seemingly growing wild, coloring humble walls and ceilings with a ubiquitous aqua-turquoise hue.

"Turquoise" is French for Turkish, after all.

I chose to focus on the colors of Iznik tile for these earrings, and not the exuberant pattern, so these earrings are about a Turkish (*"turquoise"*) color palette, not Turkish decoration. A simple selection of turquoise, cobalt, and red nicely interprets the classic harmony of Iznik tiles' color palette. To further the theme, I opted for shapes that copy Ottoman elements of design. Most obviously, the beads are squares and rectangles, like tiles. But the brass base has ogee corners, like an alcove at the Palace. I opted for brass elements because brass evokes the luxe gilding found throughout Topkapi Palace, a well-loved feature in Turkish decoration. Lastly, I went with ear wires that gave me a little bit more design room. These ear wires come with a long, straight shaft that you can cut to suit your design: add up to 40 mm of beads to the uncut shaft (I added just one 6mm square bead) or forget beads altogether and cut the wire for a simple loop. Either way, these ear wires give you lots of flexibility, which I like.

MATERIALS

2 table-cut aqua 12×10mm glass rectangles

2 cobalt sunburst 12mm Czech-glass squares

2 red faceted 10×5mm coral barrels

4 aqua 6mm opaque glass squares

2 raw brass 10×36mm 2-hole ID tags

2 gold-plated ear wires with 35mm shanks

2 gold-plated 2" (5 cm) ball-end head pins

12" (30.5 cm) gold-plated 22-gauge wire

20" (51 cm) raw brass 18-gauge square wire

TOOLS

Wire cutters

Flat-nose pliers

Round-nose pliers

FINISHED SIZE

2½" (6.5 cm) long.

1. With wire cutters, cut 22-gauge gold-plated wire into two 6" (15 cm) lengths. With middle of wire at the center of the back of 1 ID tag, thread each end of wire through one hole (**Figure 1**). Pull so wire is flat against back of ID tag. On wire end emerging from top hole, string 1 aqua rectangle. On wire end emerging from bottom hole, string 1 cobalt square (**Figure 2**). Pulling tightly, twist wire ends once in between the 2 beads (**Figure 3**). Repeat for second wire and second ID tag.

2. Wrap one wire end around ID tag once. String coral barrel onto wire and place in between the 2 beads wired to front of tag (**Figure 4**). Continue wrapping this wire, hiding end beneath other wraps of wire. Coral barrel should be situated horizontally, while blue glass beads should be situated vertically. Wrap second wire end in opposite direction around ID, not covering coral barrel. Repeat for second coral barrel and second ID tag.

3. With wire cutters, cut 18-gauge square wire into two 10" (25.5 cm) lengths. Wrap one length of wire over wraps that secured coral barrel on 1 ID tag. With wire cutters, cut ends and hide with flat-nose pliers if necessary. Repeat for second length of square wire and second ID tag.

4. Onto one ball-end head pin, string one 6mm aqua square. With wire cutters, cut head pin about ½" (1.3 cm) from bead. With pliers, form simple loop (see page 134; **Figure 5**). Repeat for ball-end head pin and second aqua square.

5. With flat-nose pliers, open simple loop of aqua square dangle and attach to bottom hole of ID tag. With pliers, close loop. Repeat for second dangle and second ID tag.

6. Onto shank of ear wire, string one 6mm aqua square (**Figure 6**). With wire cutters, cut head pin about ½" (1.3 cm) from bead. With pliers, form simple loop very close to bead so bead cannot move. Repeat for second ear wire and second aqua square.

7. With flat-nose pliers, open simple loop of ear wire and attach to top hole of ID tag. With pliers, close loop. Repeat for second dangle and second ID tag.

Fig. 1

Fig. 2

Fig. 3

Fig. 4

Fig. 5

Fig. 6

TURKEY: IZNIK TILE EARRINGS ~ 51

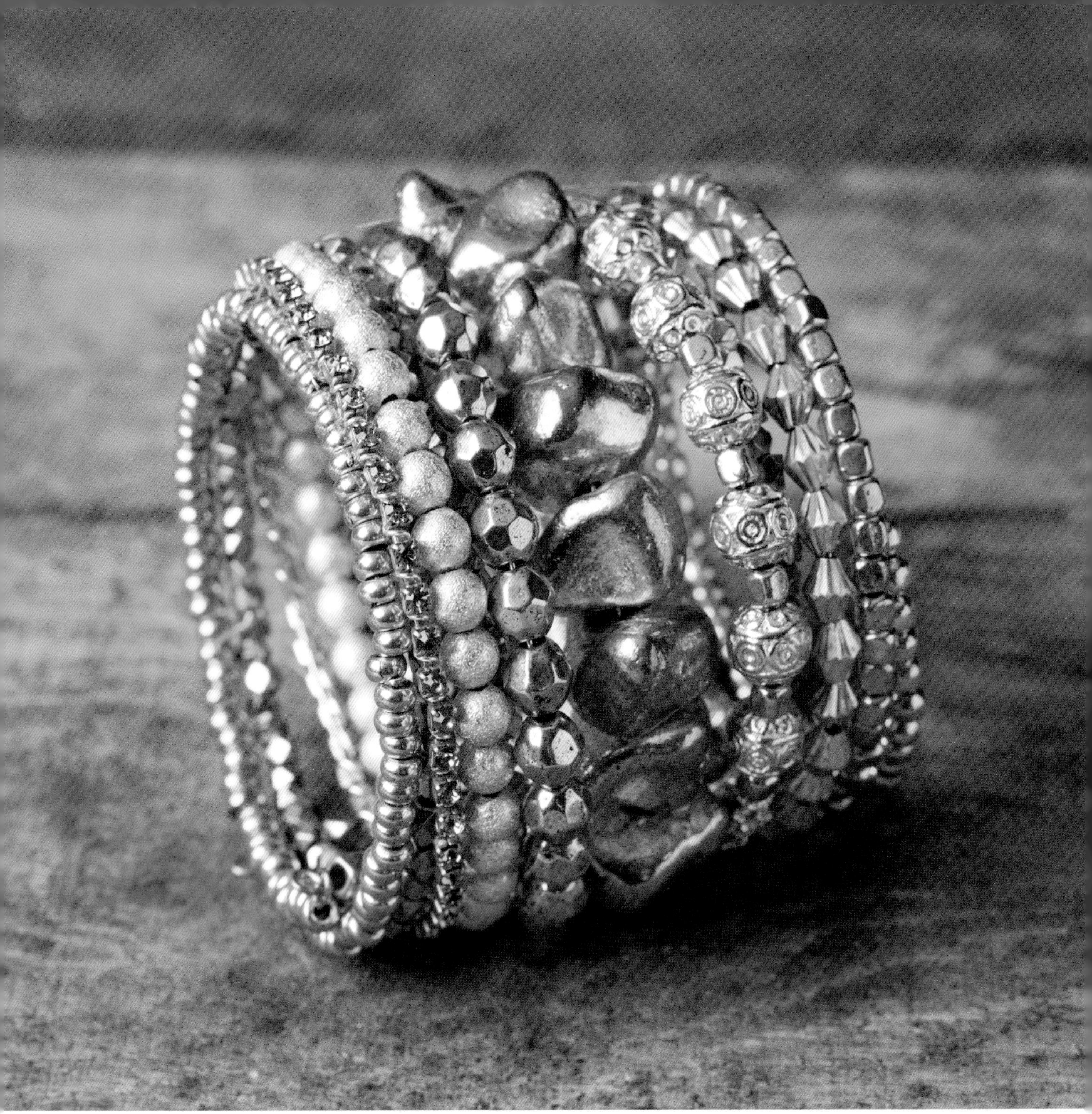
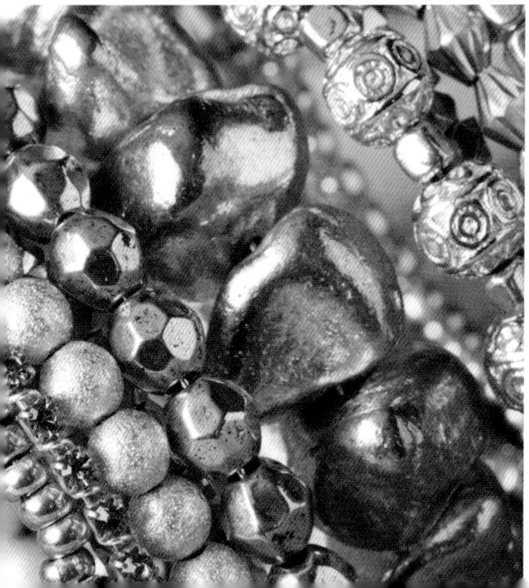
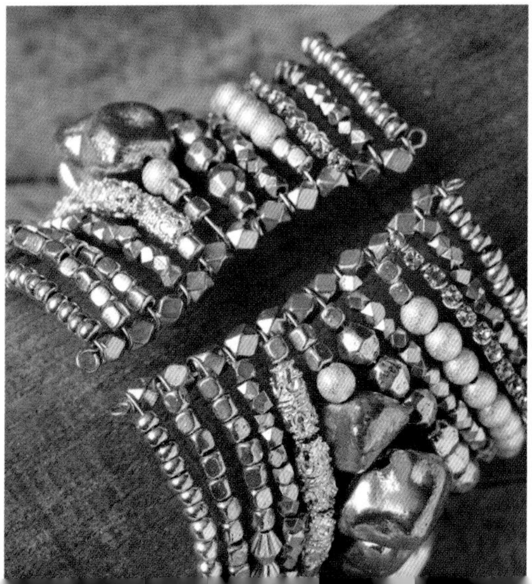
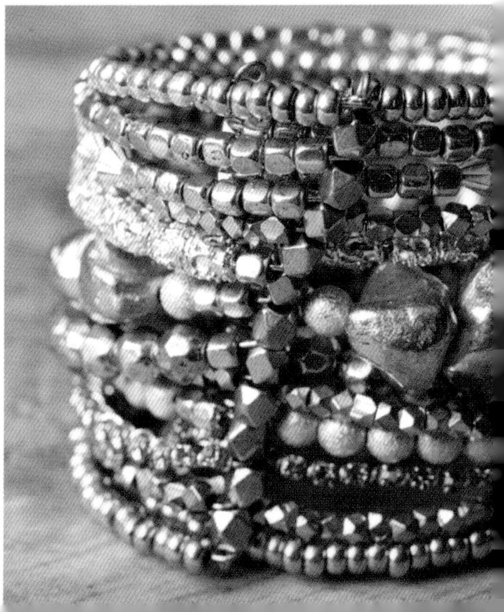

CAMBODIA
Apsara Cuff Bracelet

As intricate carvings stretch along ancient temple walls, the jungle encroaches. Thick tree roots ooze over the mossy-green walls like squid tentacles, slowly devouring the Ta Prohm temple and stretching forth. Twilight settles and the open temple courtyard takes on a mystical quality. Looking at the ornate carvings, I cannot decode the grand story they tell; I can only admire the beauty of such a rich work: epic scenes of deities and creation and mythological metaphors. And dancing girls. Lots of 'em.

I am visiting the great Angkor Wat temple complex in Cambodia, where hundreds and hundreds of *apsara*—celestial dancing girls—cover the walls, entertaining and seducing gods and men. They captivate, with impossibly curvy figures and flexible movements meant to enchant. Ancient sex symbols. I'm enchanted by their adornment. Bracelets stack high on their arms; thick anklets sit low on their ankles like shackles. Their dresses are festooned with richly ornamented collars and wide encrusted hip belts. And on their heads are elaborate, showstopping headdresses. These headdresses are unlike anything I've ever seen. Arresting. Built like a cathedral façade, with ornate pointed spires rising high above wheel-like ornaments that resemble gothic windows. And so richly decorated! They're completely encrusted in warm vermeil goldwork.

The apsaras' headdresses are over-the-top opulent. And I'm completely enchanted with them.

This cuff bracelet is a concession: opulent and spectacular, but much more wearable than an apsara headdress. To mimic the encrusted texture of apsara crowns, I pulled together lots of different gold-tone beads that combine for a high-drama look. Stardust beads, huge golden nuggets, smooth faceted cubes, cut-work bicones, and even rhinestone chain. The beads have different pedigrees and different gold tones even, but they work together because the goal is a dynamic collection. Feel free to follow my source list, or make your own collection of golden beads. And this bracelet will translate well in different metals and more. If gold isn't your favorite, try making this cuff in bright silver, antiqued brass, or even wooden beads or blue glass! It's a simple "statement" design, so go ahead and make the statement you like.

MATERIALS

101 gold-plated 5×3mm rondelles (A)

40 gold-plated 5mm rounds (B)

91 gold-plated 4mm cornerless cubes (C)

24 gold-plated 7×5mm cut bicones (D)

210 gold-plated 3.3mm cornerless cubes (E)

6 gold-plated 12×6mm textured barrels (F)

10 gold-plated 8mm textured rounds (G)

15 gold-plated 18×15mm nuggets (H)

28 raw brass 8mm faceted rounds (I)

35 gold-plated 6mm stardust rounds (J)

10" (25.5 cm) gold-plated 2mm topaz rhinestone cup chain

22 gold-plated 5mm cornerless cubes

16" (40.5 cm) gold-plated 22-gauge round wire

8" (20.5 cm) gold-plated 18-gauge round wire

12' (3.35m) antiqued brass 60mm bracelet memory wire

TOOLS

Memory-wire cutters

Round-nose pliers

Crimping pliers

FINISHED SIZE

9" around × 2½" high (23 × 6.5 cm).

1. With wire cutters, cut memory wire into twelve 9½" (24 cm) lengths.
2. With round-nose pliers, form a simple loop (see page 134) at one end of each length.
3. Onto one memory wire length, string 10 rondelles (A), 40 rounds (B), and 10 rondelles (A). With round-nose pliers, form a simple loop at the free end. (Do this after stringing each memory wire length in the steps that follow).
4. Onto one memory wire length, string 56 cornerless cubes (C).
5. Onto one memory-wire length, string 7 cornerless cubes (C), 24 bicones (D), and 7 cornerless cubes (C).
6. Onto one memory-wire length, string 72 cornerless cubes.
7. Onto one memory-wire length, string 1 cornerless cube (C), 3 textured barrels (F), 1 cornerless cube (C), 10 textured rounds (G), 1 cornerless cube (C), 3 textured barrels, and 1 cornerless cube (C).
8. Onto one memory-wire length, string 2 cornerless cubes (C), 1 stardust round (J), 15 nuggets (H), 1 stardust round (J), and 2 cornerless cubes (C).
9. Onto one memory-wire length, string 1 cornerless cube (C), 28 faceted rounds (I), and 1 cornerless cube (C).
10. Onto one memory-wire length, string 72 cornerless cubes (E).
11. Onto one memory wire length, string 2 cornerless cubes (C), 33 stardust rounds (J), and 2 cornerless cubes (C).
12. With round-nose pliers, form a simple loop at the free end of one memory-wire length (**Figure 1**). Leaving a 4" (10 cm) tail on a length of 22-gauge wire, secure one end of rhinestone cup chain to the memory-wire length with length of 22-gauge wire near a simple loop end. (**Figure 2**). Continue wrapping the rhinestone chain around the memory wire, making sure the wire falls in between the rhinestones (**Figure 3**). When ½" (1.3 cm) from end of memory wire, cut any excess rhinestone chain off and secure with a few more wraps of wire. Cut wire with wire cutters and tighten the end with crimping pliers.
13. Onto one memory-wire length, string 72 cornerless cubes (E).
14. Onto one memory-wire length, string 81 rondelles (A).
15. With wire cutters, cut 18-gauge wire into two 4" (10 cm) lengths.
16. With round-nose pliers, form a simple loop at one end of each length (**Figure 4**).
17. Line up openings of completed memory-wire loops in the order made. On one length of 18-gauge wire, string one loop of first completed loop, and then one 5mm cornerless cube. Repeat, alternating completed loop and 5mm cornerless cube, ending with last completed loop. With round-nose pliers, form a simple loop at free end of wire close to last memory-wire loop. Repeat for second loops of completed memory-wire loops. With round-nose pliers, form a simple loop at free end of wire close to last memory-wire loop (**Figure 5**).

Fig. 1

Fig. 2

Fig. 3

Fig. 4

Fig. 5

CAMBODIA: APSARA CUFF BRACELET ~ 55

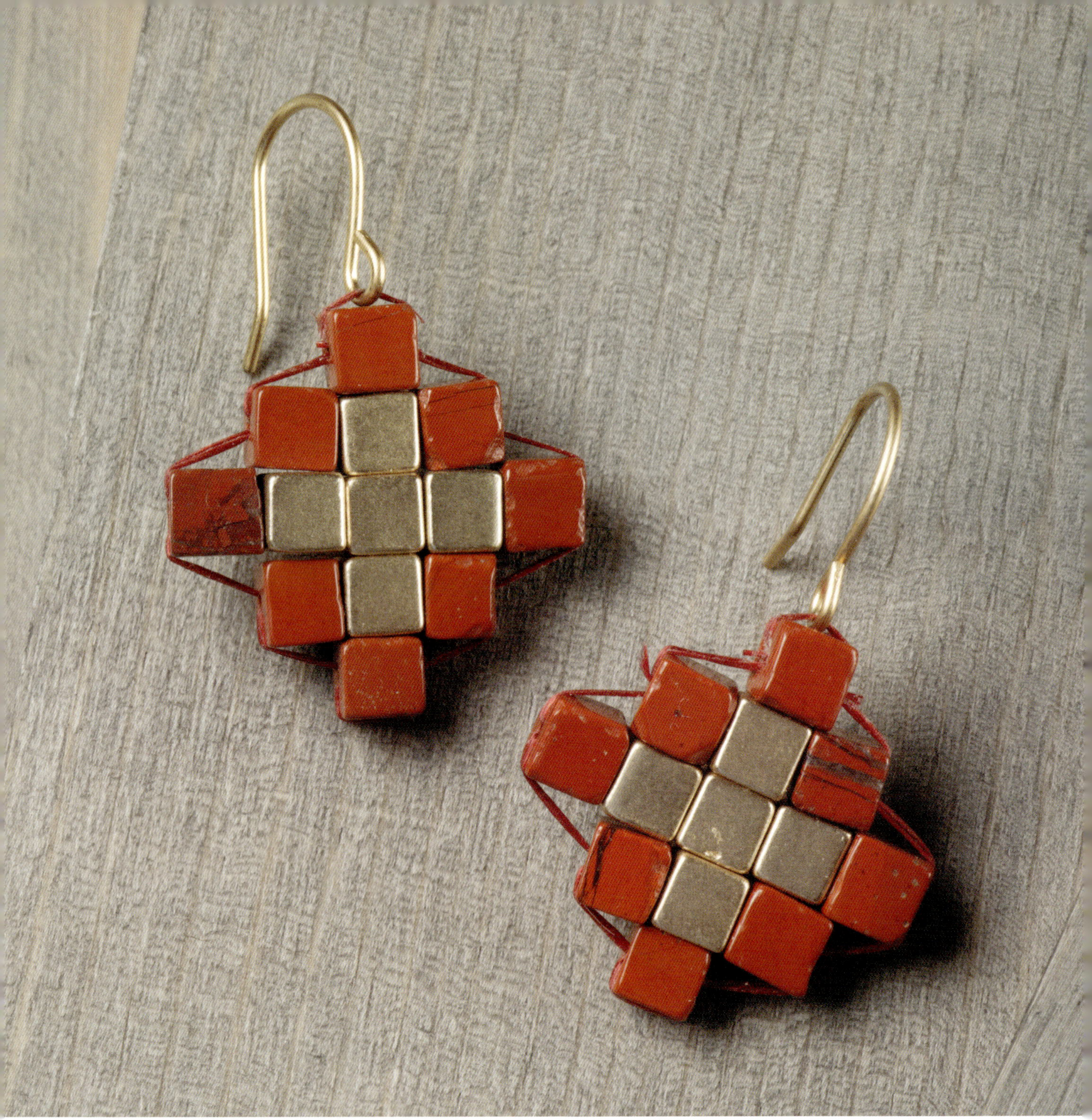

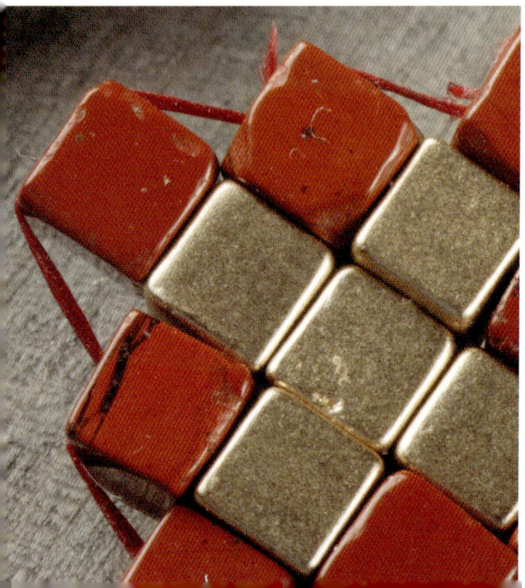

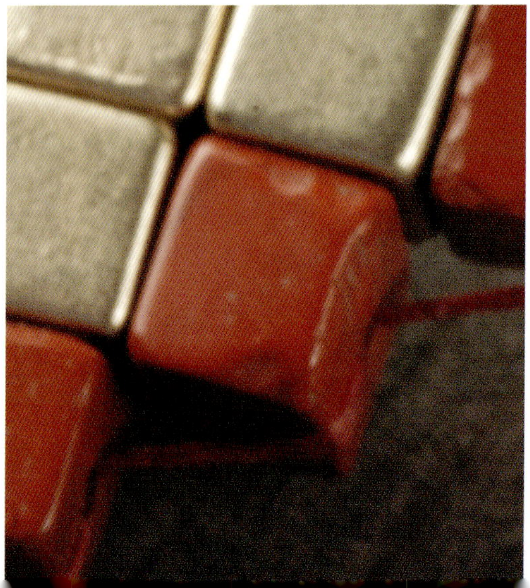

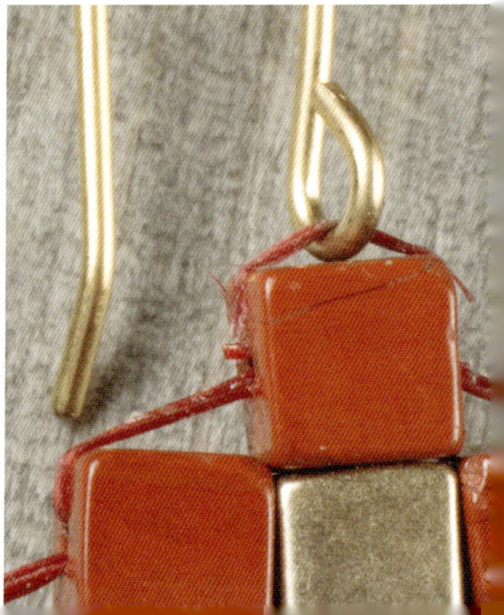

PERSIA
Kilim Cross Earrings

The Zagros Mountains of Iran crinkle and fold around this highland pasture, white snow capping their gray stone tops. Nestled in these peaks, the nomadic Lur people have summered here for a millennium. They are a pastoral tribe, speaking an ancient language, keeping customs that draw from a deep and independent cultural well. And for just as long they have been master rug weavers.

On a broad, grassy pasture outside a goat-hair tent, the woman weaves a kilim rug, while her children play around her, and her husband tends their goats. The loom is a humble setup of wooden stakes and rods. Sitting on the rug, she bends over the piece, working the red-brown stair steps of a blocky diamond. She nimbly picks up the cotton warp thread before passing the yarn through the short pass. Then she picks up threads for the pitch back, and draws the yarn back, and with a quick-slow tug the yarn nestles into place. She works quickly and carefully, shuttling yarn back and forth and picking up the tamper every few seconds, *tap tap tap,* then tossing it back down.

The Lurs weave kilim rugs, known by their geometric, symmetrical designs with repeated symbols of diamonds, crosses, and combs. Hundreds of years ago the rugs' dense weave simply kept the ground under the Lur tents dry. But over generations of craftsmanship, the rugs came to carry a great design tradition. Today, the ancient, dense weave of Lur rugs shows off the geometric patterns' sharp edges and timeless, confident designs so prized by collectors.

Using a simple combination of russet red poppy jasper and light gold cubes, these earrings employ the earthy palette of kilim rugs. Other traditional color options are brown, Persian blue, and burnt orange. But to break from tradition, you could also try alternative color combinations that would rock this ancient design: aqua and orange or white and gold. To make these earrings, you will "weave" the cubes together. Work to make your tension as tight as possible. Your first two passes will be a little looser, but your last pass should tighten everything up. And keep the design flat on your work surface and weave it flat—this will prevent tangling and knots. On your last pass, make sure you can slide an ear wire under the passes at the top of the design, as the ear wires will simply slip under the thread, and then you're good to go.

MATERIALS

16 red 4mm poppy jasper cubes

10 matte gold 4mm cubes

2 matte gold 16mm ear wires

6' (1.8 m) red silk beading thread

G-S Hypo Cement adhesive

TOOLS

Two beading needles

Scissors

Two pairs of pliers (for opening and closing ear wires)

FINISHED SIZE

1¼" long × ¾" wide (3.2 × 2 cm).

Note: The earrings in the styled photos are made with red poppy jasper and gold cubes. The ones in the instructional photos are made with blue and tan glass cubes. Choose any colors you like for these versatile earrings!

1. With scissors, cut silk beading thread into two 36" (91.5 cm) lengths. Set one length aside.

2. Thread each end of one length of thread with beading needle (**Figure 1**).

3. Lay your beads out as shown in **Figure 2**.

4. Starting at the bottom cube, pass one needle through jasper cube (**Figure 2**), around bottom of cube, and through cube again so that cube is "locked" in the middle of thread.

5. Pass right-hand needle through 1 jasper cube, 1 matte gold cube, and 1 jasper cube of second row so that needle ends up on the left. Repeat for left-hand needle so needle ends up on the right (**Figure 3**).

6. Pass right-hand needle through 1 jasper cube, 3 matte gold cubes, and 1 jasper cube of third row so that needle ends up on the left. Repeat for left-hand needle so needle ends up on the right.

7. Pass right-hand needle through 1 jasper cube, 1 matte gold cube, and 1 jasper cube of fourth row so that needle ends up on the left. Repeat for left-hand needle so needle ends up on the right.

8. Pass each needle through jasper cube of fifth row, around top of cube, and through cube again (**Figure 4**).

9. Repeat Steps 4–8 in reverse order, ending up at bottom cube. We are reinforcing the thread path here, not adding any beads.

10. Repeat Steps 4–8, without adding beads, ending up at top cube (**Figure 5**).

11. With pliers, open loop of ear wire. Slide ear wire under threads. With pliers, close loop.

12. Tie two knots and position in hole of top cube. Add a drop of adhesive and let dry (**Figure 6**). With scissors, clip ends close.

13. Repeat Steps 2–13 for second earring.

Fig. 1

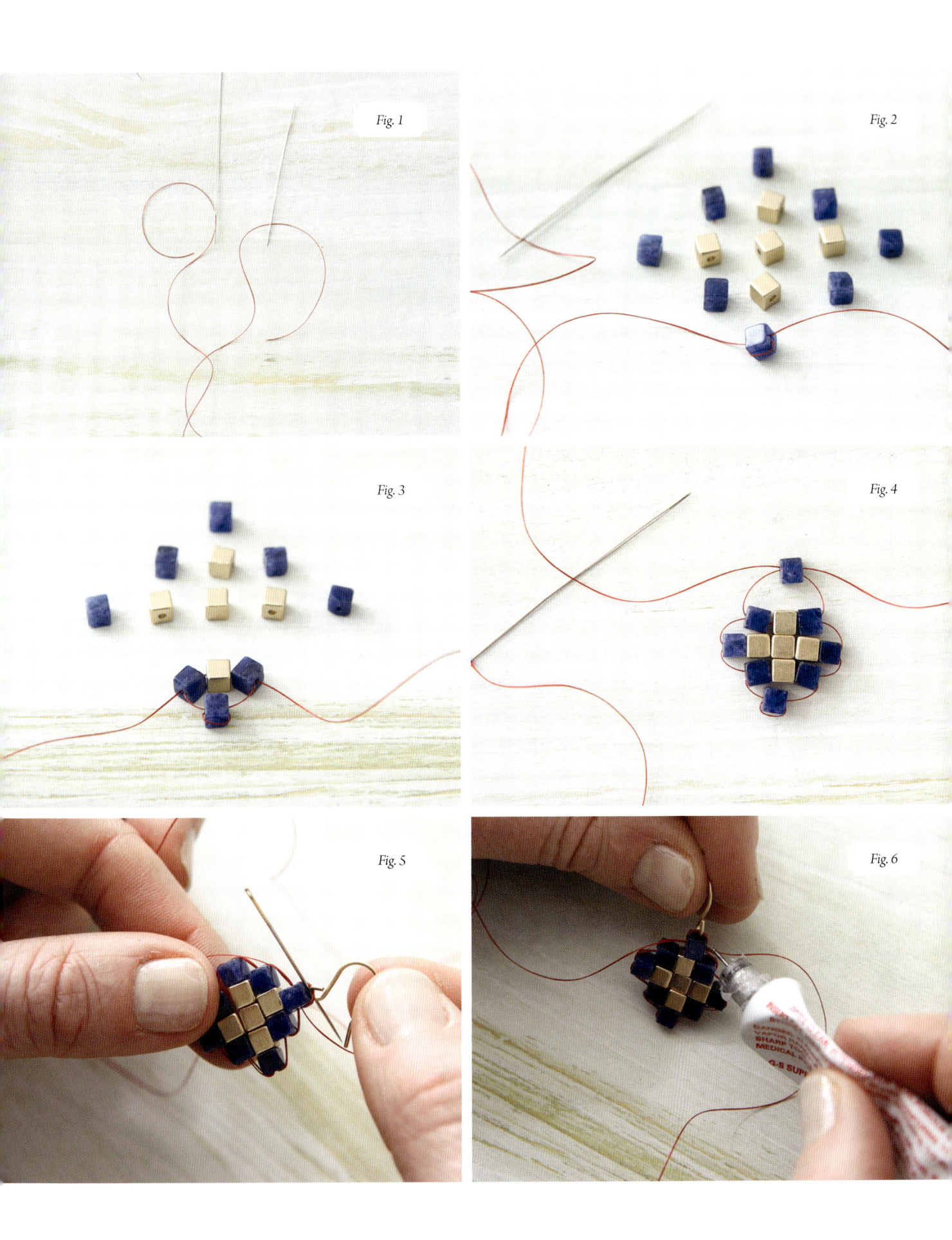

Fig. 2

Fig. 3

Fig. 4

Fig. 5

Fig. 6

Persia: Kilim Cross Earrings ~ 59

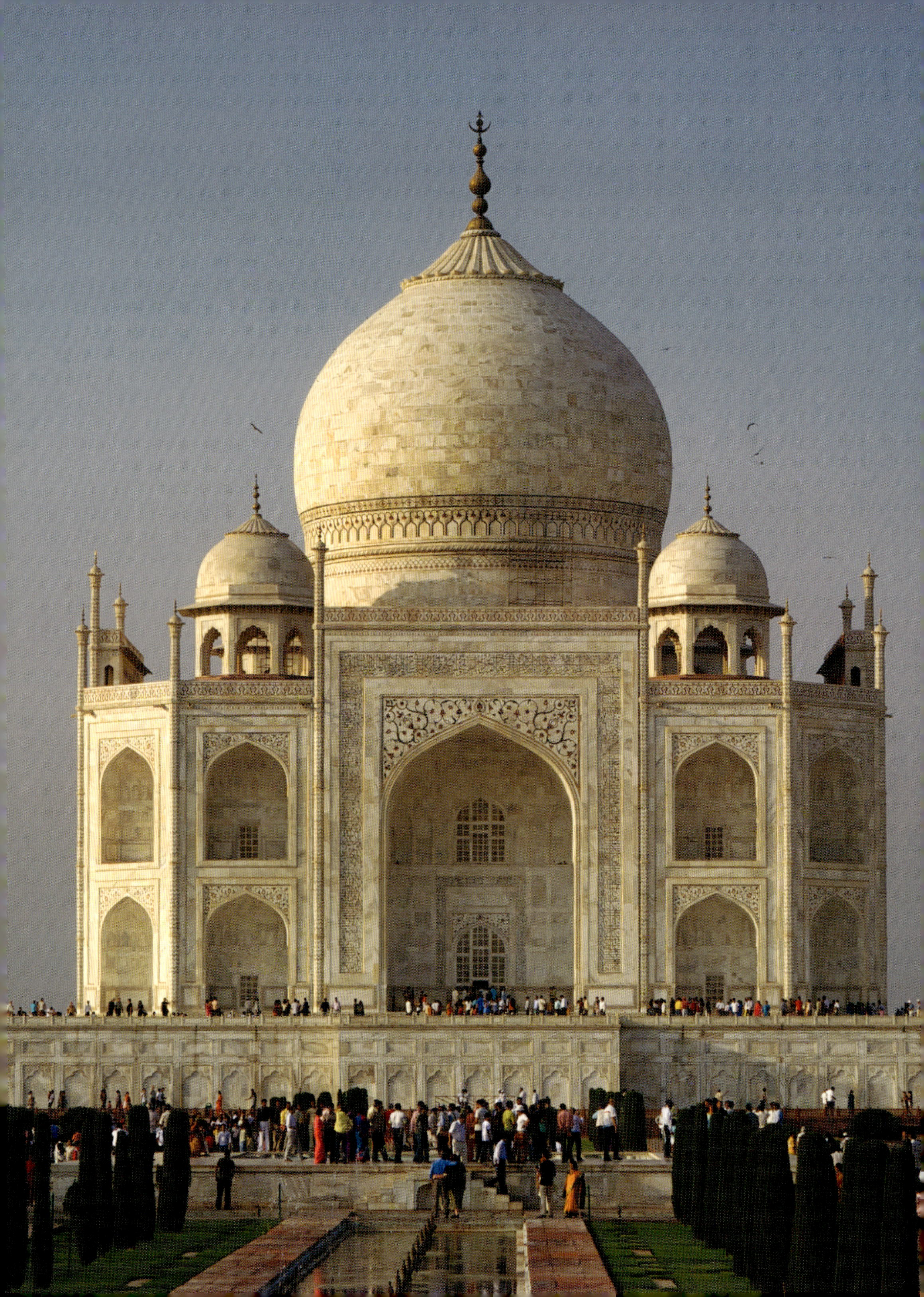

Chapter Three

INDIA

Unlike the other chapters in this book, which look at design from whole continents, this chapter is fully dedicated to the design traditions of India. The best reason for this, I suppose, is that India's varied style has always had my heart. Since I was a young girl shopping Chicago's Indian district, I've craved the riotously colored but effortlessly elegant style of all things India. Saris, paisley prints, jeweled bindis, effusive gold embroidery, over-the-top jewelry—such a design wonderland! Indian design pulls me out of any design rut I've ever had. Indian design is happily cavalier with color and layers and embellishment—if ten colors are good, why not twenty? And fringe, too? And sequins? I love this. Combine this laid-back approach to design with the rich design traditions that date back for millennia and there is enough inspiration in India to last a lifetime, I think.

© GettyImages.com/Sandra Printz

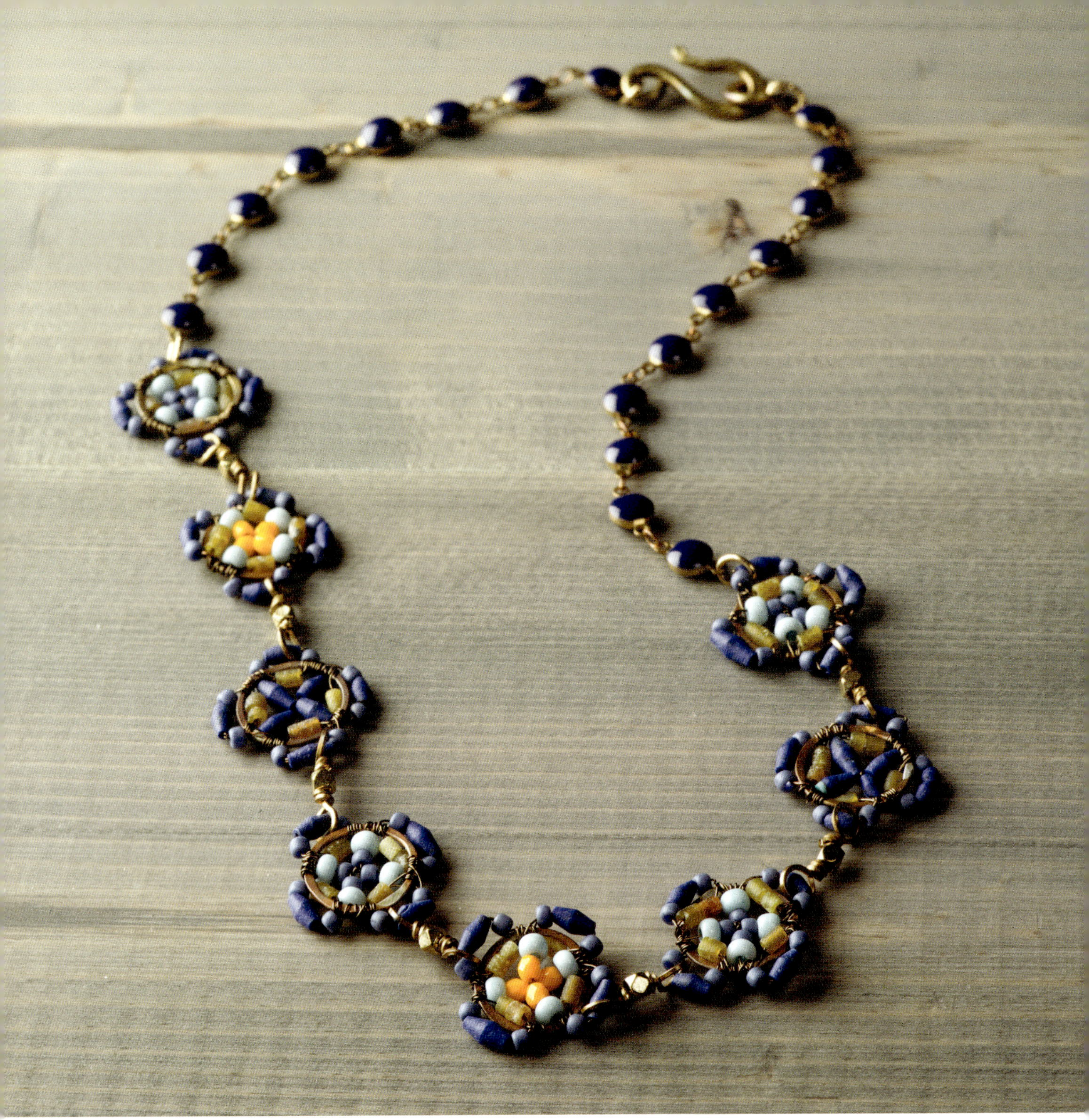

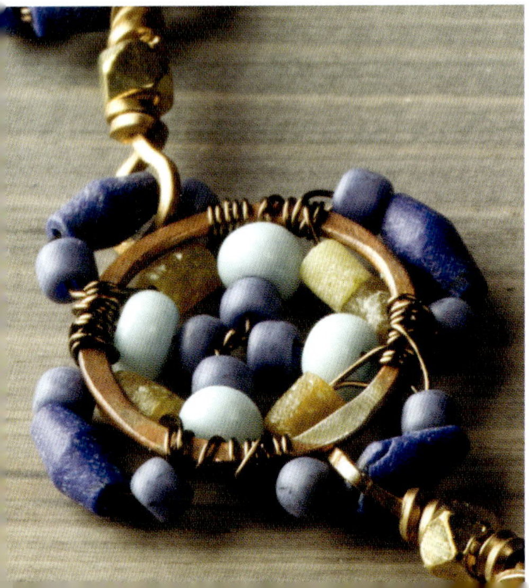

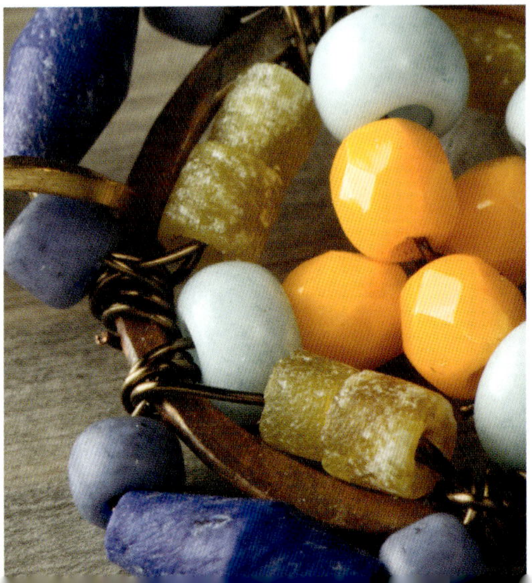

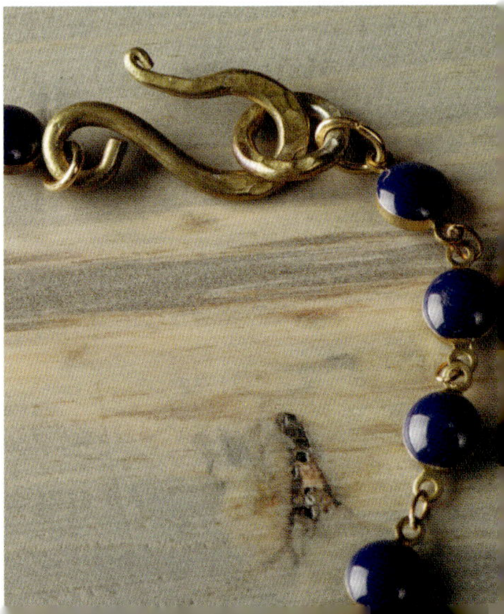

GOA
Azulejo Tile Necklace

Guiding my rented scooter around tight curves, I make my way up the hilly jungle road, dodging cows that just won't budge and dogs here and there. The sun is bright overhead, but groves of rubber trees cast dappled shade on the road before me. The drowsy, dense heat of the jungle is a sanctuary, pulling me in, away from the commotion of Panaji.

The city of Panaji is an odd mix of India and colonial Portugal. The whole state of Goa is an odd mix, really. Settled by the Portuguese centuries ago and only recently given back to India, Goa is an outpost of Portugal's Old European tradition. The look and feel of Panaji is Portuguese, but the people are Indian. Groups of women walk together wearing tropically bright saris of saffron, magenta, parrot green, and tangerine. In the market, vendor stalls are loaded with heady heaps of curry and nutmeg and chilis.

From the main road, I turn onto a dirt lane that is cloistered by pepper trees. The studio up ahead looks like an oasis from the heat: shutters prop open to let in a mountain breeze, while a dog lazes across a worn threshold. The blue and white tile placard tells me I'm at the right place: Estúdio Telha de Goa—the Goa Tile Studio—where the Portuguese tradition of painted *azulejo* tiles carries on. Inside, two women in everyday saris paint white bisque tiles with light blue, medium blue, and cadmium yellow paint. Their brushstrokes are quick and confident. And the designs are positively Portuguese. Individual tiles, each with a blooming blue flower in one corner surrounded by light blue arching flourishes, will piece together to make the tessellating pattern of corner-joined bouquets. Each tile is a one-of-a-kind work of art; pieced together, they form an Old World masterpiece. After the tiles are fired, a liquid-shiny glaze will amplify the bright colors of the designs, making them pop with a tropical punch.

Before coming to Goa, I couldn't imagine what a fusion of Portuguese-Indian cultures would look like. Now I see: it's beautiful.

This necklace employs the concept of beautiful individual tiles that marry together to make a masterpiece. Don't worry if your wire wrapping isn't perfect, but be sure to address each loose end so it can't snag clothing or come undone. You will link the tiles together by beaded links. Make sure the links' loops are large enough to let the tiles hang gracefully.

MATERIALS

8 fire-scale flat soldered 18mm copper rings

40 lapis lazuli 7×3mm hand-cut bicones

48 olive green 3mm jade heishi

80 medium blue matte 8º seed beads

8 sunflower yellow 3mm faceted rounds

7 gold 3.3mm cornerless cube beads

21" (53.5 cm) square brass 21-gauge wire

16' (4.8 m) antiqued brass 28-gauge wire

10" (25.5 cm) vintage blue enamel/brass link chain

1 hammered raw brass 27mm hook-and-eye clasp

4 gold-plated 7×5mm oval jump rings

TOOLS

Wire cutters

Crimping pliers

Round-nose pliers

Flat-nose pliers

Two pairs of pliers (for opening and closing jump rings)

FINISHED SIZE

22" (56 cm) around. Tiles measure about ⅞" (2.2 cm) square each.

1. For Tile A, cut two 4" (10 cm) lengths of 28-gauge antiqued wire with wire cutters. Make a cross form by twisting the two wires together in the center of each wire, and arrange the wires so the "arms" are at right angles (**Figures 1 and 2**).

2. Onto one arm, string 1 sunflower yellow faceted round and 1 light blue seed bead and repeat for the opposite arm of the cross (**Figure 3**). Centering the beads in the middle of 1 copper ring, wrap the wire from one arm around the ring two times (**Figure 4**). Repeat for the second beaded arm. Repeat this step for the two remaining arms. There should be a four-way cross of beads in the middle of the ring (**Figure 5**).

3. Onto one loose wire, string 1 or 2 jade heishi, depending on size. Placing heishi in ring middle, between two of the beaded arms, wrap wire two times (**Figure 6**). Repeat for remaining three wires (**Figure 7**). Center of ring should be full now. With wire cutters, cut loose wire and tighten with crimping pliers if necessary.

4. Cut two 8" (20.5 cm) lengths of 28-gauge antiqued wire with wire cutters. Holding the two wires together, secure wires to outside of ring between 2 jade heishi by wrapping round two times, leaving a 2" (5 cm) tail.

Fig. 1

Fig. 2

Fig. 3

Fig. 4

Fig. 5

Fig. 6

Fig. 7

GOA: AZULEJO TILE NECKLACE ~ 65

5. Thread onto wires 1 medium blue seed bead, 1 lapis bicone, and 1 medium blue seed bead. Place beads in an arc around outside of ring, directly outside of jade heishi. Wrap wires two times to secure in between 2 jade heishi. Repeat this step three more times, making four outside beaded arcs (**Figures 8 and 9**). With wire cutters, cut loose wire and tighten with crimping pliers if necessary.

6. Repeat Steps 1–5 three more times to make four total Tile As.

7. For Tile B, repeat Steps 1–5, but replace the blue beads from Step 2 with 1 yellow faceted round and 1 light blue seed bead. Repeat this step one more time to make two total Tile Bs.

8. For Tile C, repeat Steps 1–5, but replace the blue beads from Step 2 with 1 lapis bicone. Repeat this step one more time to make two total Tile Cs. Arrange tiles in order that you like.

9. To make beaded links: cut square brass wire into seven 3" (7.5 cm) long pieces. With flat-nose pliers and round-nose pliers, make the first part of a wrapped loop (see page 135) on one end, but do not wrap. Loop should be large enough to easily fit over outside beaded arcs of beaded tiles. String 1 cornerless cube onto wire. With flat-nose pliers and round-nose pliers, make the first part of a wrapped loop on one end, but do not wrap. Repeat this step six more times to make seven beaded links.

10. Starting at one end of arrangement of beaded tiles, slip one beaded arc of first tile onto one loop of beaded link (**Figures 10 and 11**). With round-nose and flat-nose pliers, complete wrapped loop, making sure the arc of the tile can move around freely (**Figure 12**). Slip beaded arc of second tile onto second loop of beaded link. With round-nose and flat-nose pliers, complete wrapped loop, making sure arc of tile can move around freely. Repeat this step, connecting all eight beaded tiles by link tiles together on directly opposite (not adjacent) beaded arcs.

11. With wire cutters, cut vintage enamel chain into two 5" (12.5 cm) sections.

12. With two pairs of pliers, open up 4 oval jump rings. Attach free end of first beaded tile to one end of enamel chain with jump ring. Close jump ring. Repeat for last beaded tile and second length of enamel chain (**Figure 13**).

13. Attach one free end of enamel chain to loop of hook clasp with jump ring. Close ring. Attach second free end of enamel chain to open ring of clasp. Close ring.

Fig. 8

Fig. 9

Fig. 10

Fig. 11

Fig. 12

Fig. 13

GOA: AZULEJO TILE NECKLACE ∽ 67

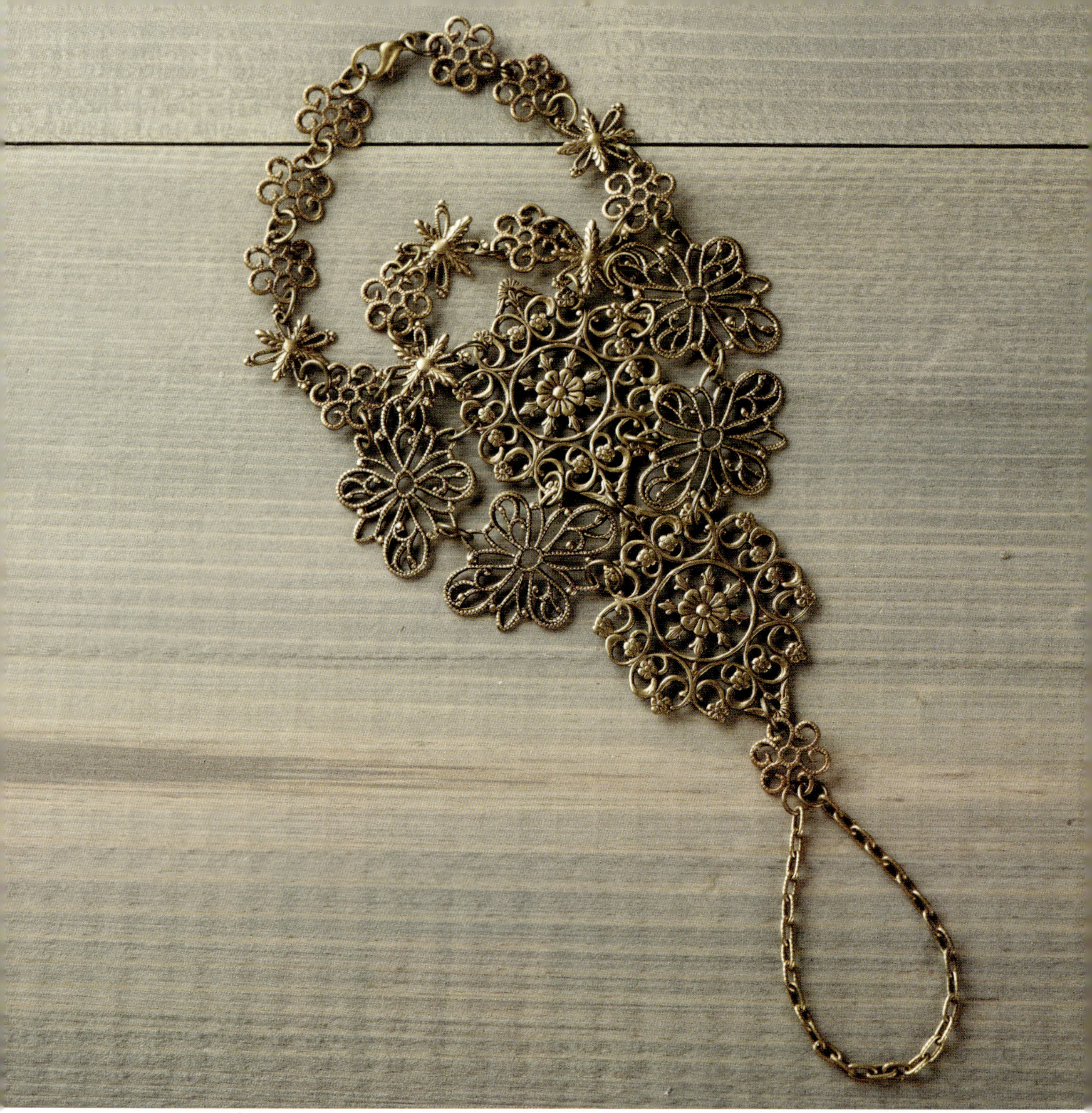
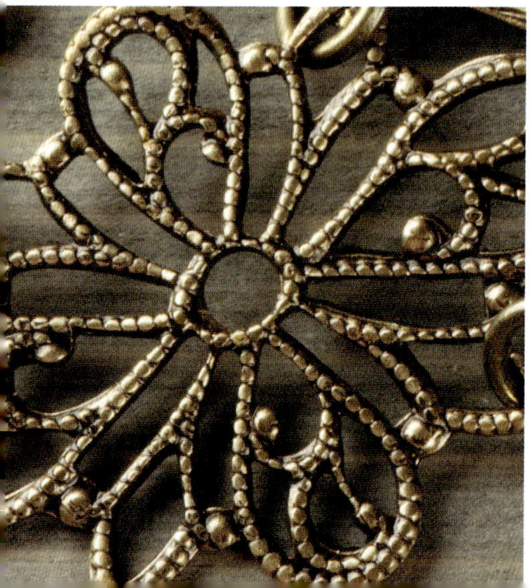

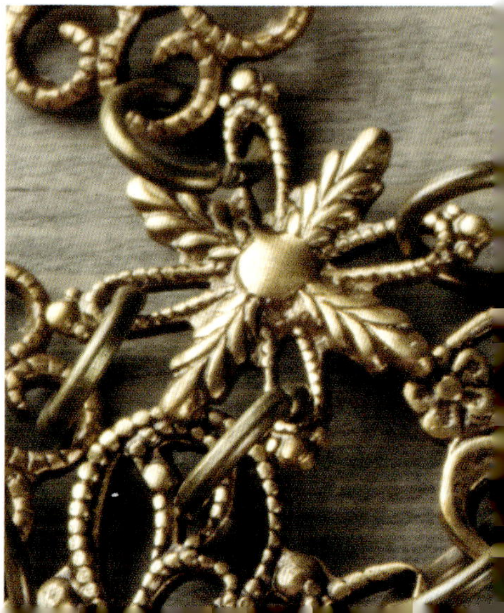

GUJARAT
Mehndi Hand Bracelet

The scene is like something out of a Bollywood movie. On huge tufted cushions, covered by colorfully festooned canopies, groups of women sit, whispering, teasing, laughing, talking. To one side, older women cluck together about the arrangement, nodding agreement and beaming with joy. A cushion of young women gossip together, fidgeting with their sari scarves while a cluster of young girls are getting too silly and will be shushed soon.

In the middle of everything sits the most beautiful bride-to-be I've ever seen. She's stunning. In a navy blue sari with rich bullion gold embroidery and tiny mirror spangles she sits serenely, hands laid out before her on a pillow. Her thick black hair is thrown over one shoulder, and a navy scarf gracefully frames her face. She's dripping with gold—earrings, bracelets, a *tikka chutti* parting her hair—but I've been told this is just for the *mehndi* party. Just wait 'til the wedding! Tonight's Girls' Night is lavish but more intimate and low-key than tomorrow's marathon wedding. Tonight is all about the bride. Her bridesmaids adjust her scarf or fan her or push back her bracelets—little unnecessary ways to cosset her.

Amid the festivity, the henna artist quietly, carefully draws the mehndi designs on the bride's hands. She has already finished her feet and palms, where the groom's name hides in a paisley tail to be found tomorrow. Now she works on the last part: a meandering showpiece that covers fingers, hands, wrists, and arms. Lacy bands encircle each finger like russet knuckle rings. Round lotus flowers bloom over her hands, shooting eddied tendrils down each finger. She embellishes each motif elaborately with layers of frills and fronds and lines and dots until the design looks like auburn lace.

When she finally finishes, the artist sits back and examines her work, and the women gather around to admire. All eyes are on the bride. "What do you think, do you like it?" she asks the bride. Her mother-in-law answers for her. "She's beautiful," she says. And everyone nods and smiles in agreement.

This bracelet gives you the ease of adding and removing a rich henna design for just a night! Build this design by starting with the large marquis filigrees first. While you can easily change the sizing on this bracelet, err on the smaller size: a smaller size will keep the whole hand bracelet in place, so it won't slip around too much.

MATERIALS

9 antiqued brass 10mm round filigrees

4 antiqued brass 26×24 rounded diamond filigrees

5 antiqued brass 14mm square filigrees

2 antiqued brass 37×28 marquis filigrees

3" (7.5 cm) antiqued brass 4×2mm texture cable chain

31 antiqued brass 5mm jump rings

2 antiqued brass 4mm jump rings

1 antiqued brass 10mm lobster clasp

TOOLS

1.5mm steel hole punch

Two pairs of pliers (for opening and closing jump rings)

FINISHED SIZE

Hand motif measures 2¾" wide × 3½" high (7 × 9 cm). Bracelet measures 7" (18 cm) around.

1. With metal hole punch, punch a hole in unpunched end of 1 of the large marquis filigrees (**Figures 1 and 2**).

2. With two pairs of pliers, open all jump rings.

3. According to photos, connect filigrees together with 5mm jump rings, starting with large center motif, then continuing to bracelet (**Figures 3 and 4**). With pliers, close jump rings as you go.

4. Adjusting as necessary, with two pairs of pliers, attach one end of chain to small round filigree at top of hand motif with 4mm jump ring (**Figure 5**). Close ring. Repeat for second chain end and second 4mm jump ring into same hole.

5. Adjusting as necessary, with two pairs of pliers, attach one 5mm ring to last round filigree of one end of bracelet. Close ring. Repeat for second end of bracelet, but attach lobster clasp to ring. To wear a traditional hand bracelet, slip the chain over your middle finger (like a ring) and allow the larger motif to decorate the top of your hand. To secure this piece, wrap the bracelet portion around your wrist, and clasp on the underside of your wrist.

Fig. 1

Fig. 2

Fig. 3

Fig. 4

Fig. 5

GUJARAT: MEHNDI HAND BRACELET ~ 71

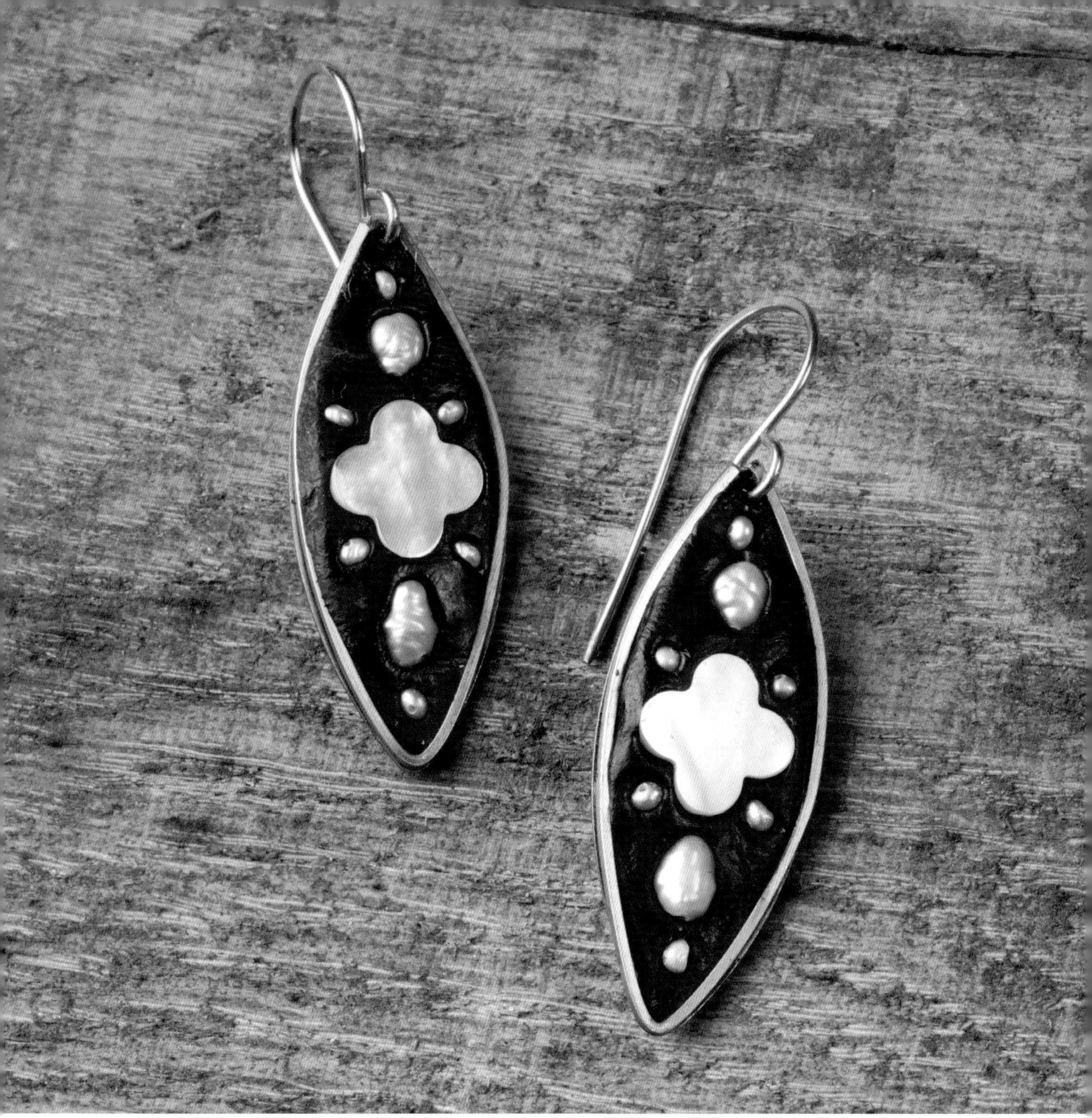
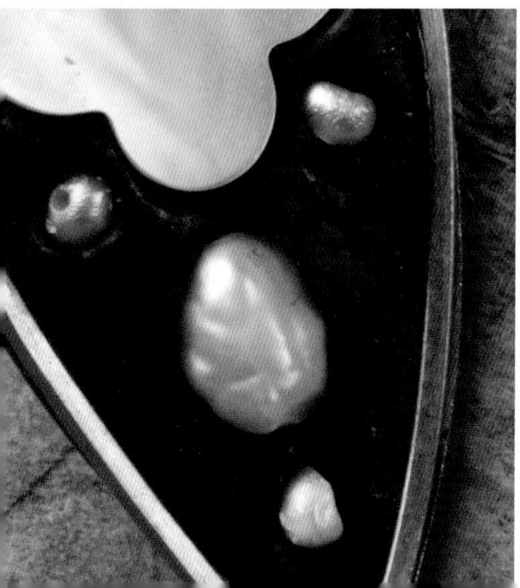
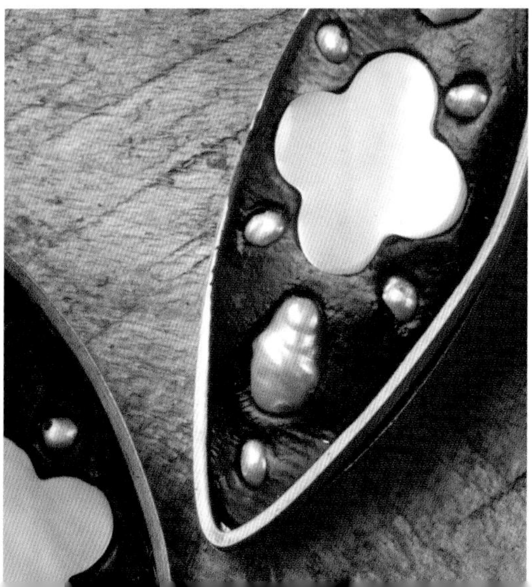
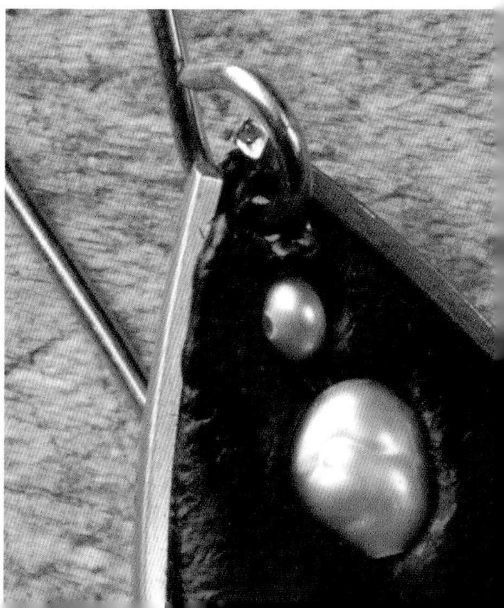

UDAIPUR
Inlaid Pearl Earrings

As the sun rises over Lake Pichola, local women in bright saris walk down the *ghat* to wash. Squatting down where the water meets the steps, they wash their hair, squeeze it dry, and braid it for another day of selling tamarinds and chilis in the market. The water gently laps, and the morning light bathes the city with a dazzling, hazy glow.

I watch the scene unfold every morning from my little whitewashed room. The 500-rupee room is quaint and unassuming, but like everything else her in Udaipur, it's beautiful. A *haveli* window frames my view, and I want to stay and enjoy the peace, but there's too much to see here. Udaipur is ridiculously picturesque. Sweeping hillside vistas and hanging gardens, with lush patios to take it all in. This lake town is often compared to Venice for how the scenic city and waterways marry into such a romantic union. It's almost too pretty here.

In keeping with Udaipur's splendor, artisans here produce some of the most splendid handiwork in all of India. It is over-the-top design-wise, from its embroidery traditions to its highly detailed mosaic work. I've fallen the hardest for the inlaid bone furniture made here. It's opulent and graphic and dizzyingly ornate. Several artisans work on one piece for three months (thus the big prices they fetch in the West). Using bones from fallen camels, artisans cut thousands of diamonds, paisleys, flowers, circles, and flourishes, then set each tiny shape in its hand-carved wooden home on the piece. The work is laborious. But the effect is... gorgeous. Well, it's almost too beautiful.

These earrings are a pared-down version of the richly embellished bone inlay work from Udaipur. I scoured sources for the right elements to make this design perfect. Black epoxy clay makes an easy surface to "inlay" and gives a basic background to allow the elements to pop. Pearl replaces bone, and the glowing pearls work well off the matte black and then play well with the gold tone of the findings. If the graphic black-and-white palette isn't your favorite, the sky's the limit for other colors and beads to use. Look for other shaped beads with a smaller scale. For an easier version of these earrings, choose ready-made bezel pendants, and skip the wire frame step entirely.

MATERIALS

2 brass 35×14mm marquise dangles

8" (20.5 cm) square 21-gauge raw brass wire

Black two-part epoxy clay

2 mother-of-pearl (MOP) 10mm quatrefoils

4 freshwater 4×5mm pearl nuggets

12 freshwater 1×2mm seed pearls

2 raw brass 25×12mm ear wires

TOOLS

Paper clip

Wire cutters

Flat-nose pliers

Tweezers

Two pairs of pliers (for opening and closing jump rings)

FINISHED SIZE

2" (5 cm) long.

1. With wire cutters, cut wire into two 4" (10 cm) sections.
2. With flat-nose pliers, bend wire in center at an angle that mirrors bottom point of marquise. With fingers, form one end of wire to mirror curve of marquise (**Figure 1**). Repeat for second end of wire.
3. According to package directions, mix black epoxy clay to make one quarter-sized ball (**Figure 2**).
4. Take a small amount of epoxy clay and press evenly into the curved side of brass marquise dangle (**Figure 3**). Add more as needed.
5. With tweezers, set pearls, quatrefoils, and nuggets into epoxy clay as shown. Press pearls down so they are flush with epoxy clay surface (**Figure 4**).
6. Press wire from Step 2 into epoxy clay at outer edge of marquise (**Figure 5**). With wire cutters, cut ends of wire to make a neat join at top of marquise.
7. Open a paper clip. With end, poke a hole into epoxy clay through brass marquise hole (**Figure 6**) and smooth edges.
8. Repeat Steps 2–7 for second earring.
9. Let epoxy cure according to package directions.
10. With pliers, open up loops of ear wires. Attach one inlaid marquise dangle to ear wire (**Figure 7**). With pliers, close loop. Repeat for second dangle and second ear wire.

Fig. 1

Fig. 2

Fig. 3

Fig. 4

Fig. 5

Fig. 6

Fig. 7

Udaipur: Inlaid Pearl Earrings ~ 75

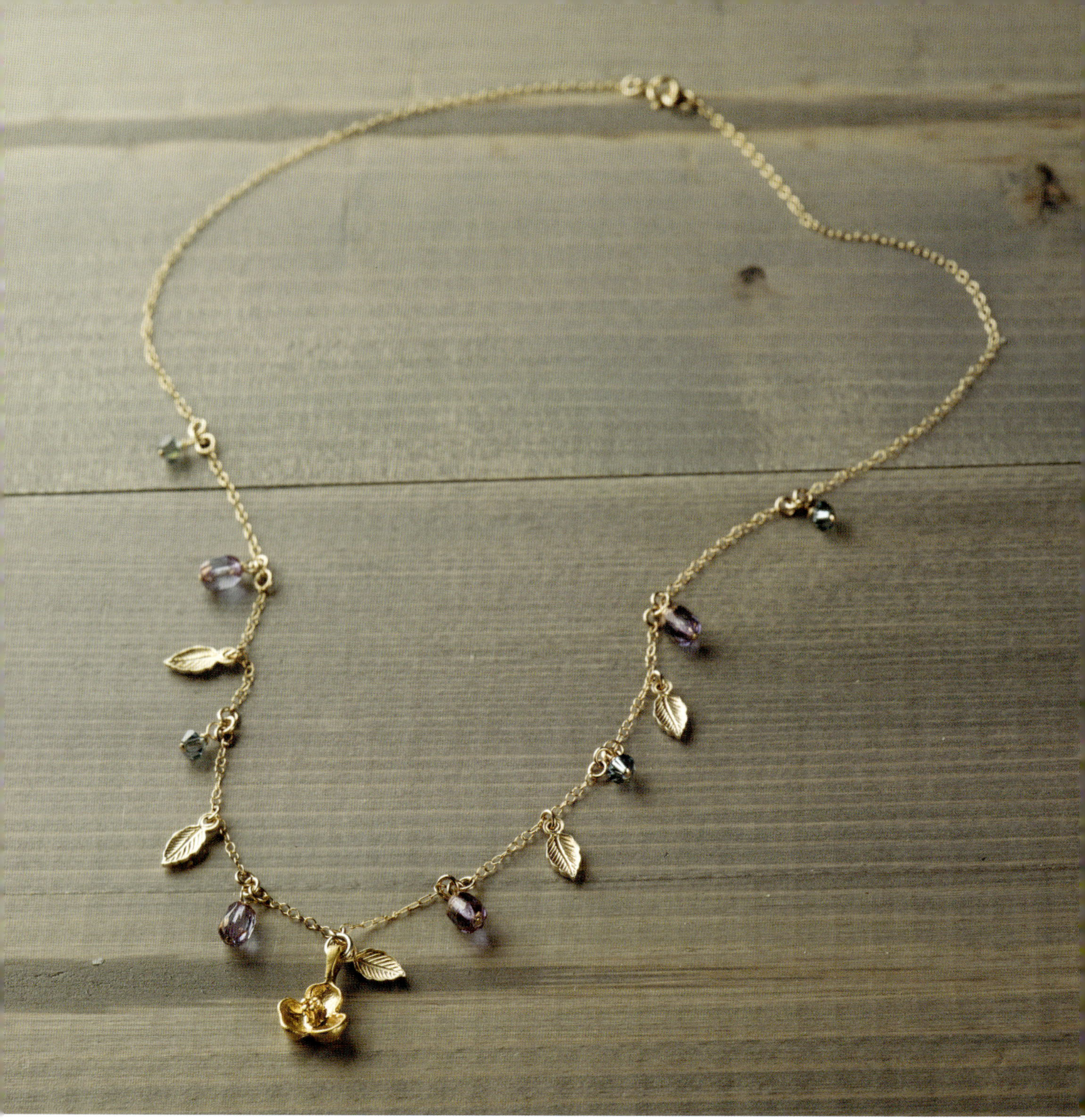
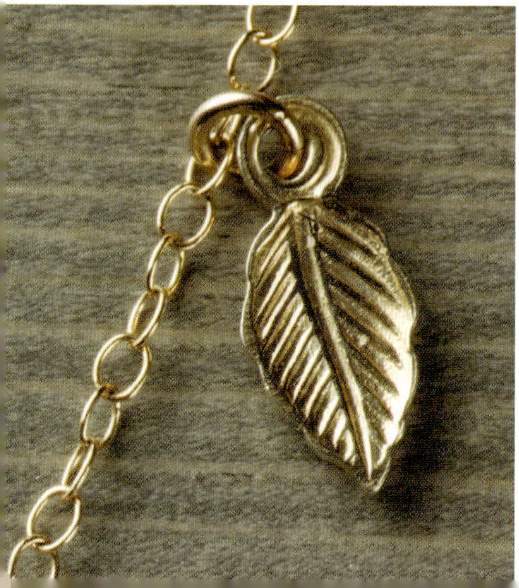
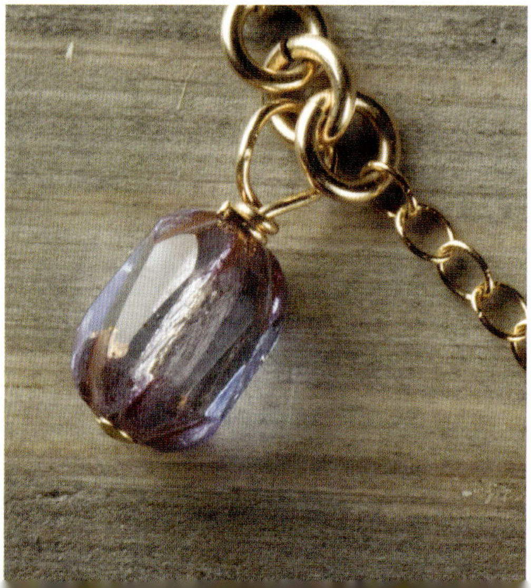
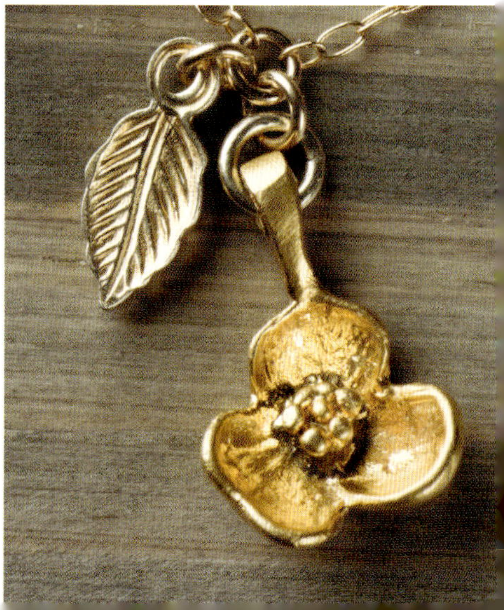

MUMBAI
Sari Gold Necklace

Soft sell this is not. I really feel like calling this guy "fabric vendor" doesn't cut it. With his heavy black mustache and a fiercely piercing stare, I think "fabric bully" or "fabric henchman" is a more appropriate description.

It all started innocently enough. Me, a weak-willed woman in the sari district, walking though the shops, trying to decide where to start. The fashion sights were dazzling, and everywhere I looked I fell in love again: the saturated colors, the draping, the dripping gold embroidery. Even the outdated mannequins in bad wigs couldn't detract from the beauty of all these saris. It was a wonderful sensory experience, just nearing overload. But then, from the doorway of one shop, the Fabric Bully grabbed my arm. "Miss, miss, come see, I have what you want! Come see, come see!" and pulled me into his fabric shop.

His shop is a wonderland, really, but I'm not feeling it right now. I'm drinking the chai he forced on me and just trying to figure out how to get out of here. Every time I make a move for the door he blocks my way and gets down more rolls of sari fabric. He unfurls each one with a proud pageantry, all while staring menacingly across the counter. And I wonder, "He's pretty short, I wonder if I could take him?" Probably not. No, my best option is to just submit and buy something, so I start to scan the shelves. They're packed. But I'm determined. The rolls of fabric are dazzling; fluid and silky-smooth with a delicate gold metallic border. Each color a confection: mango, purple, saffron, peacock, carnation, scarlet, strawberry.

I spy rolls of golden trim and seize my chance. "I'll take this!" I assert, grabbing a fat roll of ribbon. Happy to be walking out of the shop, I inspect my purchase. The wide lavender gauzy ribbon is loaded with sequins and beads and bullion embroidery. So decadent, but so graceful. It's just beautiful.

It's my beautiful Golden Ticket outta there.

This necklace captures the opulence of saris, but their delicate designs, too. And thanks to the low bead count of the design, this necklace is easy to upgrade by replacing the glass and crystals with gemstones, even some AA grade beauties.

MATERIALS

4 light amethyst 6×4mm cathedral-cut glass barrels

4 green tourmaline 3mm crystal bicones

5 gold-filled 11×5mm leaf charms

1 vermeil 15×10mm flower charm

8 gold-filled 24-gauge 1" (2.5 cm) head pins

18" (45.5 cm) gold-filled 1.5mm round chain

31 gold-filled 3mm open round jump rings

1 gold-filled 4mm open round jump ring

1 gold-filled 5mm open round jump ring

1 gold-filled 5mm spring clasp

TOOLS

Round-nose pliers

Wire cutters

Crimping pliers

Two pairs of pliers (for opening and closing jump rings)

FINISHED SIZE

18" (45.5 cm) long.

1. String 1 light amethyst glass barrel on 1 gold-filled head pin. Form a wrapped loop (see page 135; **Figures 1–3**) and cut end with wire cutters. Tighten end with crimping pliers. Repeat three more times to make 4 wrapped-amethyst glass dangles.

2. Repeat Step 1 using green tourmaline crystal bicones, to make 4 wrapped dangles.

3. With wire cutters, cut two ½" (1.3 cm) lengths of chain.

4. Link lengths of chain with one 3mm jump ring. With pliers, close ring. This will be the center of the necklace.

5. With pliers, open 4mm jump ring. Attach to the flower charm. With pliers, close ring.

6. With one 3mm jump ring, add 1 leaf charm to center ring. With pliers, close ring. With one 3mm jump ring, add flower charm to center ring. With pliers, close ring.

7. Cut six 1" (2.5 cm) lengths of chain.

8. Attach two of these lengths together with three 3mm jump rings. Attach 1 green tourmaline crystal dangle to the center jump ring (**Figures 4 and 5**).

9. Repeat Step 8 with 1 green tourmaline crystal dangle.

10. On either end of each chain created in Steps 8 and 9, attach three 3mm jump rings in a row. Attach 1 amethyst dangle to the center jump ring of each of these three-ring groups.

11. Working out from the center, attach one beaded chain created in Step 10. At the end of the chain, attach a 1" (2.5 cm) length of chain, then three 3mm jump rings. Attach 1 green tourmaline crystal dangle to the center jump ring. Repeat for the second side of the necklace.

12. Cut the remaining chain in half. Attach each half to the ends of the assembled chain

13. With a 3mm jump ring, attach 1 leaf charm halfway between the first amethyst dangle and the first green tourmaline crystal dangle, then between the first green tourmaline crystal dangle and the second amethyst dangle. Repeat for the second side of the necklace.

14. Open one 3mm jump ring. With ring, attach spring clasp to one end of chain. With pliers, close ring.

15. Open one 5mm jump ring. Attach to second end of chain. With pliers, close ring.

Fig. 1

Fig. 2

Fig. 3

Fig. 4

Fig. 5

Mumbai: Sari Gold Necklace ~ 79

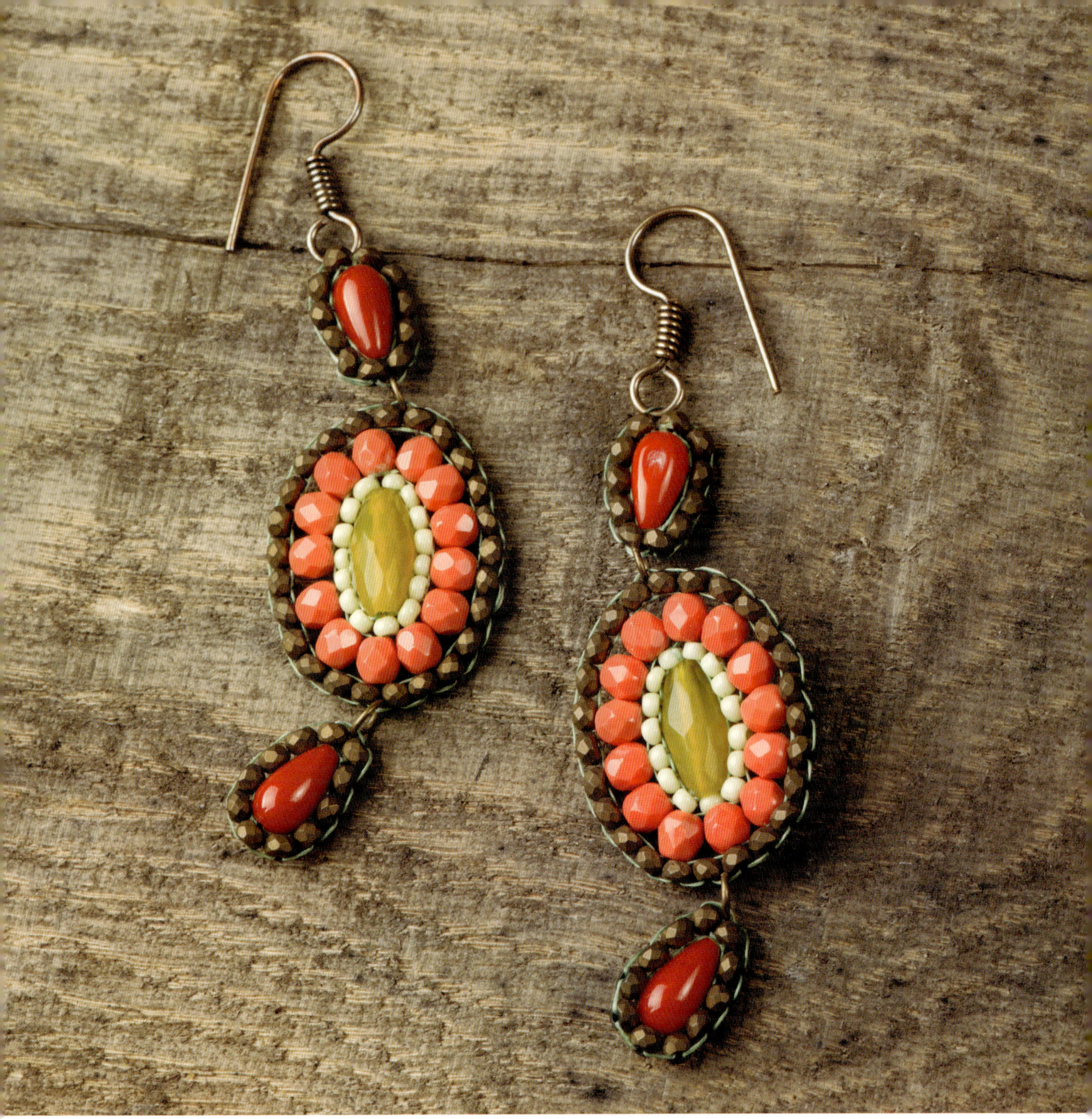

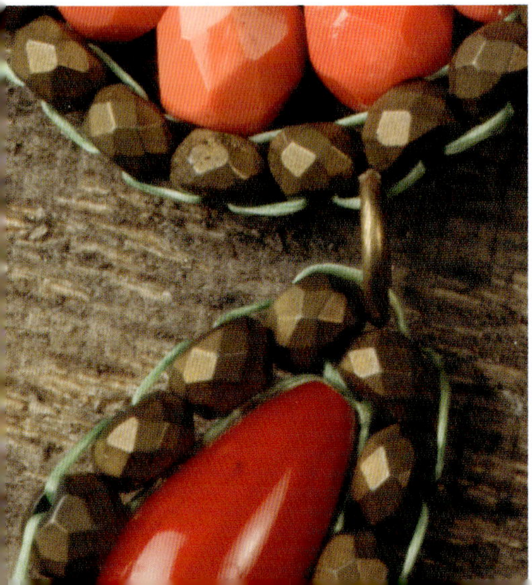

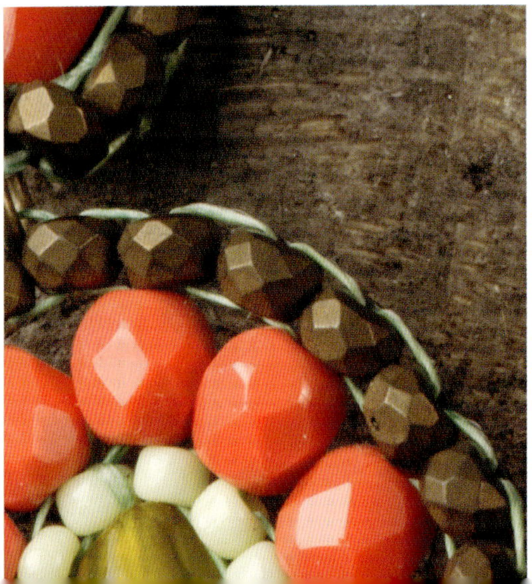

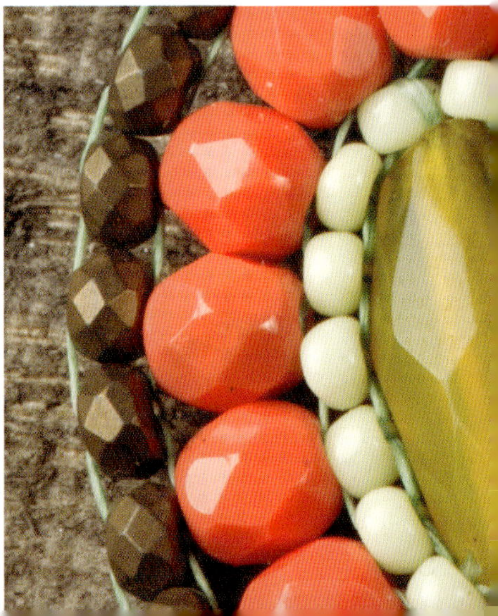

BAGRU
Print Block Earrings

In a small stall on a dusty street in Bagru, Ajay works with mallet and chisel like his father and grandfather before him. The mallet strikes the chisel with rhythmic clinks as he works, precisely carving a floral pattern into the hard block of sheesham wood. For twelve hours a day, Ajay carves wooden print blocks here in Bagru, a desert city in northern India and epicenter of this thriving artisanal industry.

The print block started this morning with a careful line drawing that Ajay transferred to the planed-smooth wood blank. The design—a buxom bouquet of flowers with stems and leaves that curl into a paisley shape—is traditionally inspired, but current, too, as it will grace tablecloths and pillows from high-end retailers in the West. Ajay squats behind a small table where he works, with an arsenal of tiny chisels strewn before him. In swift, cadenced movements, he angles the chisel in place, thumps the chisel with the wooden mallet, and flicks away the tiny wood shrapnel from the cut. Again and again and again. Surely and evenly he composes the design. All day long. With his straight chisel, he metes out the smooth, fluid curves of the paisley's long lines. And with his curved chisel, he *tap tap taps* a tiny, flawless circle set in a little flower bud. As I watch him work, I cannot see any flaws. I marvel at how, if I weren't watching him make this piece, I could only assume it was machine made. In the line of production, from block carving, to printing, to dyeing, Ajay is simply called "carpenter," working the job assigned to his caste hundreds of years ago. But you can see he's an artist. His floral paisley is an opulent composition, an intrepid and heady design, while his well-practiced cuts are impossibly precise.

When Ajay finishes the print block, it goes to a printer who will hand stamp the fabric, and then the fabric goes to the dyer. Tomorrow the process starts again. I don't know if Ajay sees himself as a worker, an artisan, or an artist.

I know the answer without a doubt. This is an artist.

The design of these earrings is a colorful take on print-block patterns, but the idea is the same: lots of little details combining for a decadent design. Print blocks are most commonly seen with the design painted white, or left bare, and I think these earrings would also be divine in a similarly monochromatic palette. Use all white beads (or any single color) for a less flashy, but still showy, pair of earrings.

MATERIALS

2 yellow 15×8mm faceted jade barrels

94 bronze 3×2mm pyrite rondelles

30 light chartreuse 11º seed beads

26 coral pink 6mm opaque glass faceted rounds

4 red coral 10×5mm teardrops

4 antiqued brass 4mm open round jump rings

2 oxidized copper 25×18mm ear wires

Beading thread

G-S Hypo Cement adhesive

TOOLS

Scissors

Beading needle

Flat-nose pliers

FINISHED SIZE

3" long × 1" wide (7.5 × 2.5 cm).

1. To make main component: leaving a 6" (15 cm) tail, pass needle through yellow jade barrel once, and again, and again in the same direction, making two floats of thread (**Figure 1**). Position these two threads along one edge of barrel bead. These will be your beading "base threads."

2. String 2 chartreuse seed beads on needle and position them so they are both sitting square on rim of jade barrel (**Figures 2**). (The first bead will be sitting as it was strung, and the second bead will be sitting upside down from how it was strung. The thread should be connecting the 2 beads on the outside ends.) Holding the 2 seed beads here, pass needle under the base threads, from back to front. Now pass needle through the second seed bead, starting at end sitting on rim of jade barrel.

3. String a third seed bead onto needle and position bead right next to second bead. (This bead and every subsequent bead will be sitting upside down from how it was strung.) Holding seed bead here, pass needle under base threads, from back to front. Now pass needle through seed bead, starting at end sitting on rim of jade barrel. Repeat this step four or five more times until 8 or 9 seed beads are strung around roughly one half of jade barrel (**Figure 3**).

4. Pass needle through jade barrel once, and again, and again in the same direction, making two new floats of thread. Position these two threads along other side of jade barrel. They should run 180 degrees along other half of rim of bead. These will be your "base threads" for the second half. You should be back at the start.

5. Pass needle through first bead from bead end to outside end.

6. Turning your work if necessary, repeat Step 3 for remaining 8 or 9 seed beads, ending with your thread coming out the very first seed beads (**Figure 4**).

7. To begin second ring, string 2 opaque coral faceted rounds on needle and position them so they are both sitting square on first row of seed beads (**Figures 5 and 6**). Holding coral faceted rounds here, pass needle under base threads, from back to front, then pass needle through second coral faceted round. Continue in this manner, stringing 13 coral faceted rounds around, passing thread through connecting threads from previous ring.

8. For third ring, repeat Step 7 using 25 bronze pyrite rondelles.

9. With beading needle, secure thread by tying half-hitch knots (see page 137) over 5 five beads. Pass thread through bead and trim end close with scissors.

10. Repeat Steps 1–9 for second main component.

11. To make red coral teardrop components: repeat Steps 1–6 and Step 9 using a red coral teardrop bead as the base bead and 11 bronze pyrite rondelles for the first row of beads. Repeat three more times, to make four red coral teardrop components.

12. If necessary, on a flat surface, run a line of adhesive around all center components and position first bead rows so they are flush. Let dry.

13. Find center of oval and attach 1 teardrop (pointed end) with one 4mm jump ring, through floats of thread on outside of component. Close with pliers. Repeat for second end of oval and second teardrop. Repeat for second earring.

14. With two pairs of flat-nose pliers, open loop of ear wire. Find center of 1 teardrop (round end) and attach to ear wire, through floats of thread on outside of component. Close with pliers.

Fig. 1

Fig. 2

Fig. 3

Fig. 4

Fig. 5

Fig. 6

Bagru: Print Block Earrings ~ 83

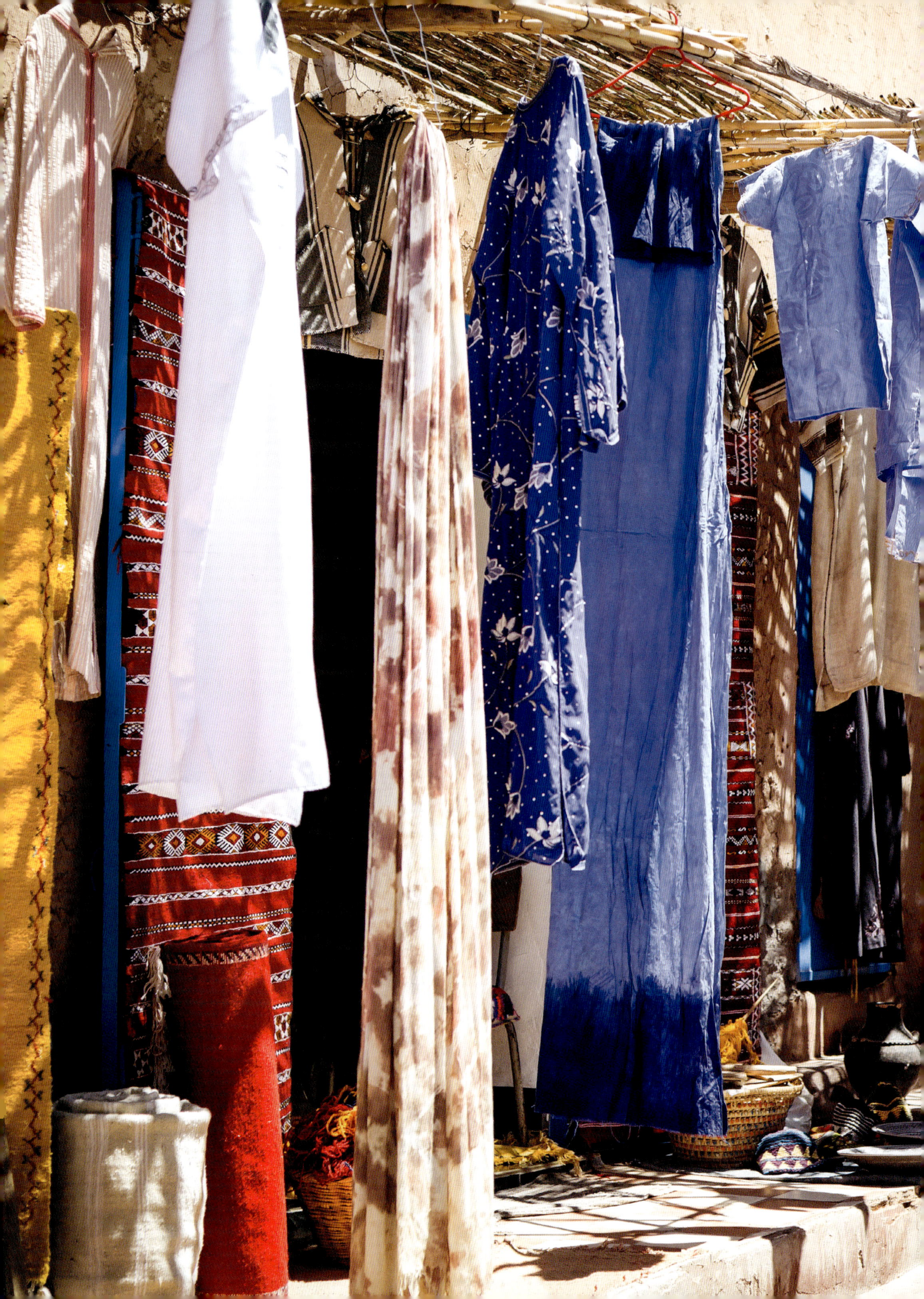

Chapter Four

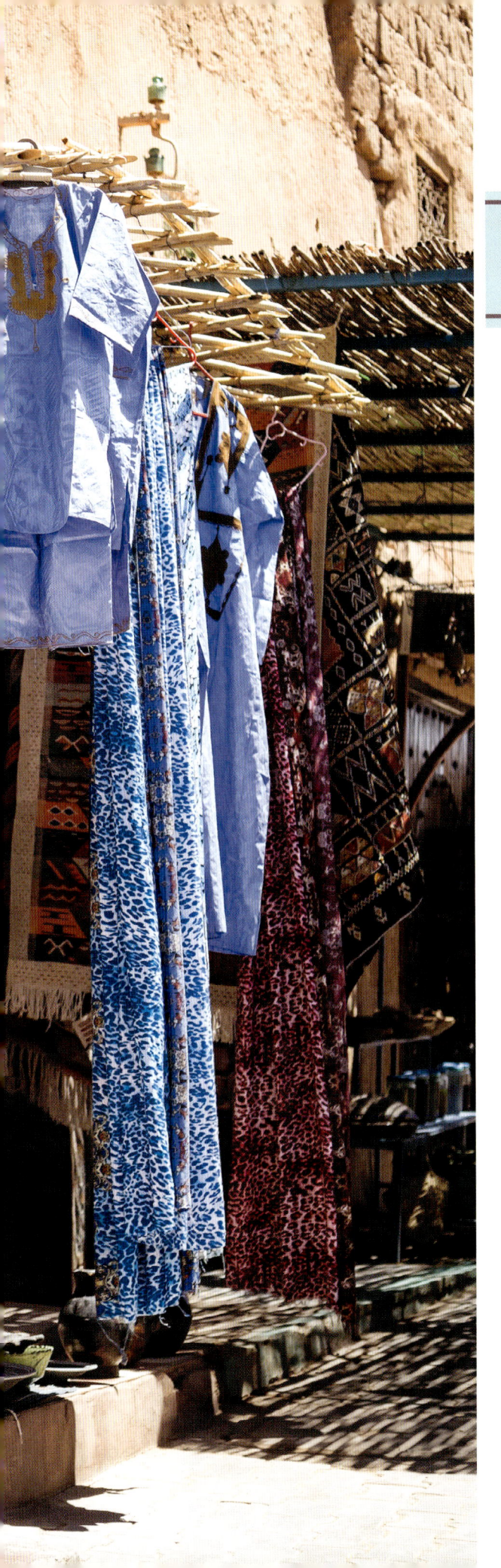

AFRICA

I love African design for its bold, brazen style and its unapologetic pride. African design packs meaning and history into its recognizable style, which operates as a unifier across the continent. And it's so beautiful! We all know the primary colors of the African design: green, red, black, gold. This pan-African palette appears everywhere, from nearly every African flag to beads, fabric, and graffiti. These colors represent hope and harmony and stand witness to a history of spilled blood. Add to this palette bold, large-scale patterns. While the actual patterns certainly vary among countries and tribes, African patterns consistently pack meaning with the print. African women even assign wise proverbs to fabric prints, making their fashion a fashion *statement*! African style represents African identity, and that's what I love about it most. Design with purpose, boldly representing a people and their history.

© GettyImages.com/adam smigielski

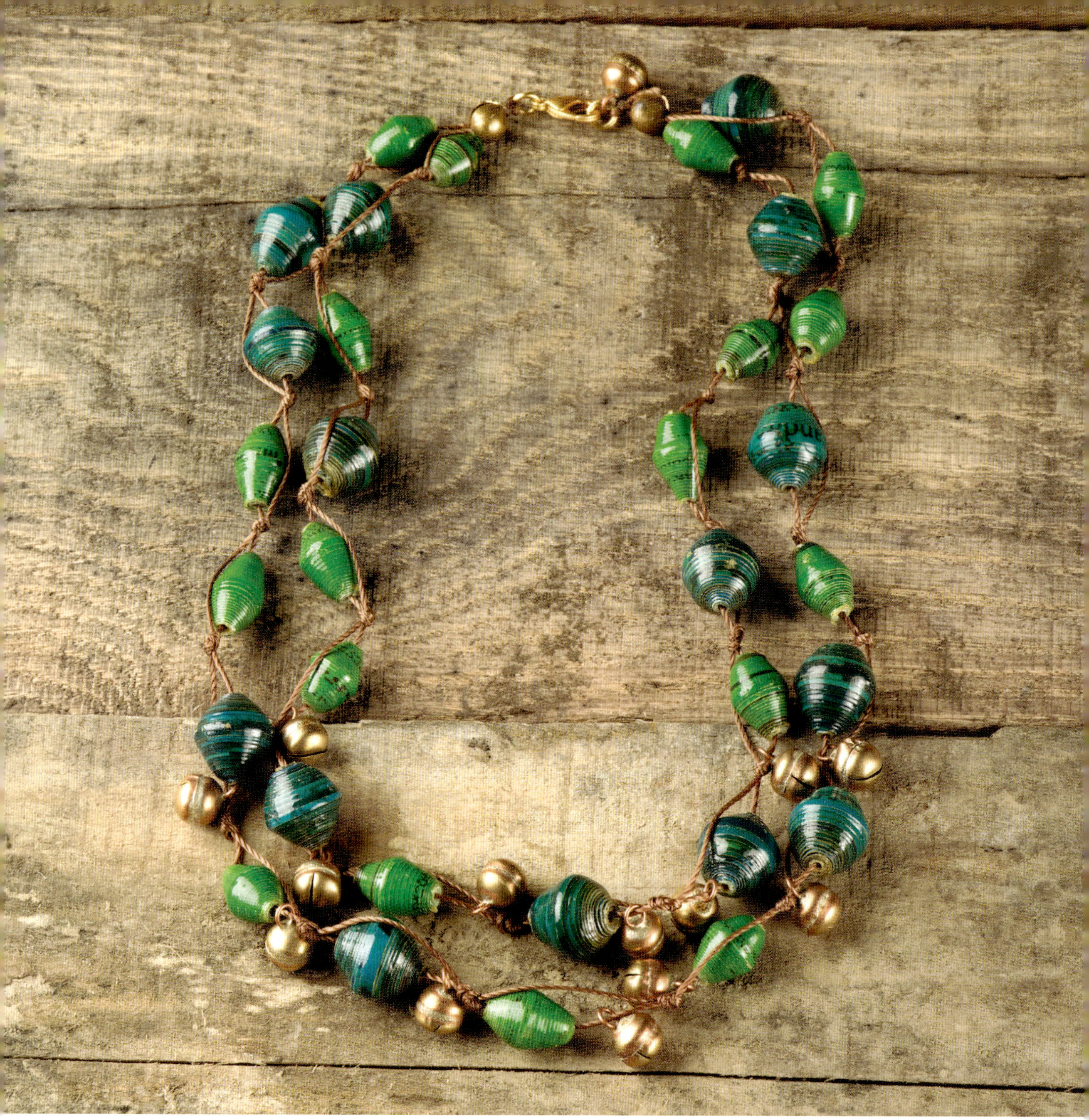

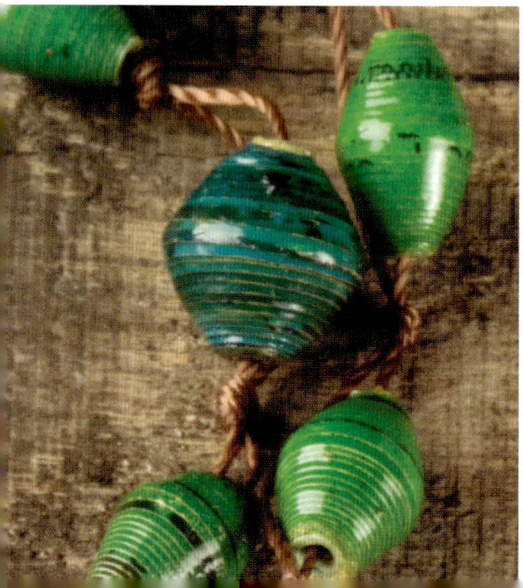

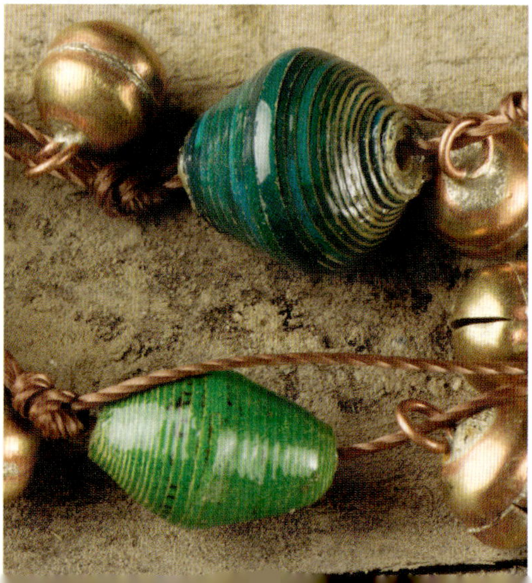

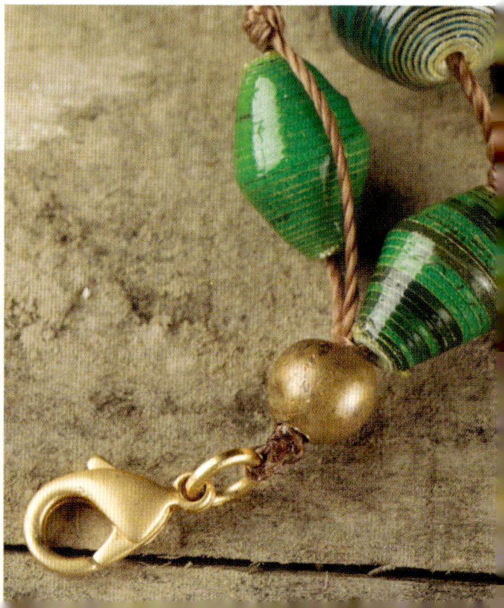

UGANDA
Paper Bead Necklace

Wide palmettos cast dancing shadows on the hot dirt. Under the shade of a corrugated roof, the women gather, chattering and laughing, busting chops in a language I don't understand. Millie is the manager and ambassador of the operation. She is tall and confident and wears a boldly printed green dress with puffed sleeves and a matching wrap on her head. She strikes me as the "mayor."

"These women are all displaced from the war. They started making beads from paper because that's what was available, but they didn't have a way to sell them. But we connected with buyers in the West. It is a very good arrangement! Before, these women did not have money to take care of their families. Now, they make a good income and have money to buy food and clothes for their children!" She is proud of this micro-economy and I see why: this market has given these women a means to provide for their families, all while disconnected from their homes and former trades. And all from recycled paper! It's like something from nothing.

Josephine works with a sleeping baby strapped to her back in a sling. Squatting next to her, I watch each quick step. She takes a triangle of magazine paper and places the widest end of one triangle on a wire mandrel, then rolls the paper quickly and evenly. Just before reaching the end, she squeezes a tiny drop of glue onto the paper, then carefully rolls the pointed paper tip in place and smoothes it with her fingers. She paints four long, broad strokes of clear varnish, covering the bead completely. Then she drops the wire into a cup in front of her to dry. Her deft movements produce each bead in less than a minute.

Around the table, the women are all working and talking quickly, with laughter erupting here and there. The paper beads on their wire stems fill the drying cups, like flower buds. Their colors pop beneath the sticky-shiny lacquer. Each bead is nuanced, bearing the mark of its maker's aesthetic, with different color choices, different sizes, different shapes.

Each one is a tiny work of art; each one a testament of renewal.

This beaded necklace is light and airy, so the beauty of each bead can shine, while Thai bell drops intermix for a fun accent. While the bells are subtle, you can easily omit them if you don't like your jewelry to jingle.

MATERIALS

18 kelly green 12×10mm rolled-paper bicones (A)

15 teal green 14×12mm rolled-paper bicones (B)

14 gold 10×8mm brass round bell drops (C)

2 gold-plated 6mm crimp covers

1 gold-plated 10mm lobster clasp

17' (5 m) brown .5mm polyester beading thread

2 gold-plated 5mm open round jump rings

G-S Hypo Cement adhesive

TOOLS

Sewing needle

Scissors

Crimping pliers

Two pairs of pliers (for opening and closing jump rings)

FINISHED SIZE

19" (48.5 cm) around.

Note: The color palette of the beads in the styled photos differs from that in the instructional photos. Paper beads come in myriad colors, so choose the palette you like best!

1. With scissors, cut beading thread into four 50" (127 cm) lengths.

2. Holding two lengths of thread together, tie an overhand knot (see page 136) about 4" (10 cm) from one end. On one length, on opposite end from knot, thread beading thread with needle. This will be the length that you will bead onto.

3. Onto thread with needle, string 1 kelly green bicone (A). Holding both threads together, tie an overhand knot about 1" (2.5 cm) from the starting knot, trapping the bead in between the two knots.

4. In the same manner, string beads and knot in between in the following sequence: B, A, A, B, AC, BC, CB, CA, CB, CA, A , B, A, B, A (**Figure 1**).

5. Repeat Steps 2–4 for remaining two threads, using the following bead sequence: B, A, A, B, A, BC, BC, AC, CA, CB, CA, CB, A, A, B, B, A. The two beaded lengths will be slightly different lengths.

6. Holding the two starting knots of both beaded lengths together, tie an overhand knot very close to the starting knots. Thread the four strands through 1 gold jump ring (**Figure 2**). Tie a square knot (see page 137) over the first knots (**Figure 3**). Glue a dot of adhesive to secure (**Figure 4**). Let dry. Repeat with second jump ring for the other ends of beaded lengths.

7. When adhesive is dry, trim thread ends very close. Cover knots with crimp covers. With crimping pliers, close crimp covers (**Figure 5**).

8. With two pairs of pliers, open up 1 jump ring and add lobster clasp. Close ring with two pairs of pliers. With two pairs of pliers, open up second jump ring and add 1 bell drop. Close ring with two pairs of pliers.

Fig. 1

Fig. 2

Fig. 3

Fig. 4

Fig. 5

Uganda: Paper Bead Necklace ~ 89

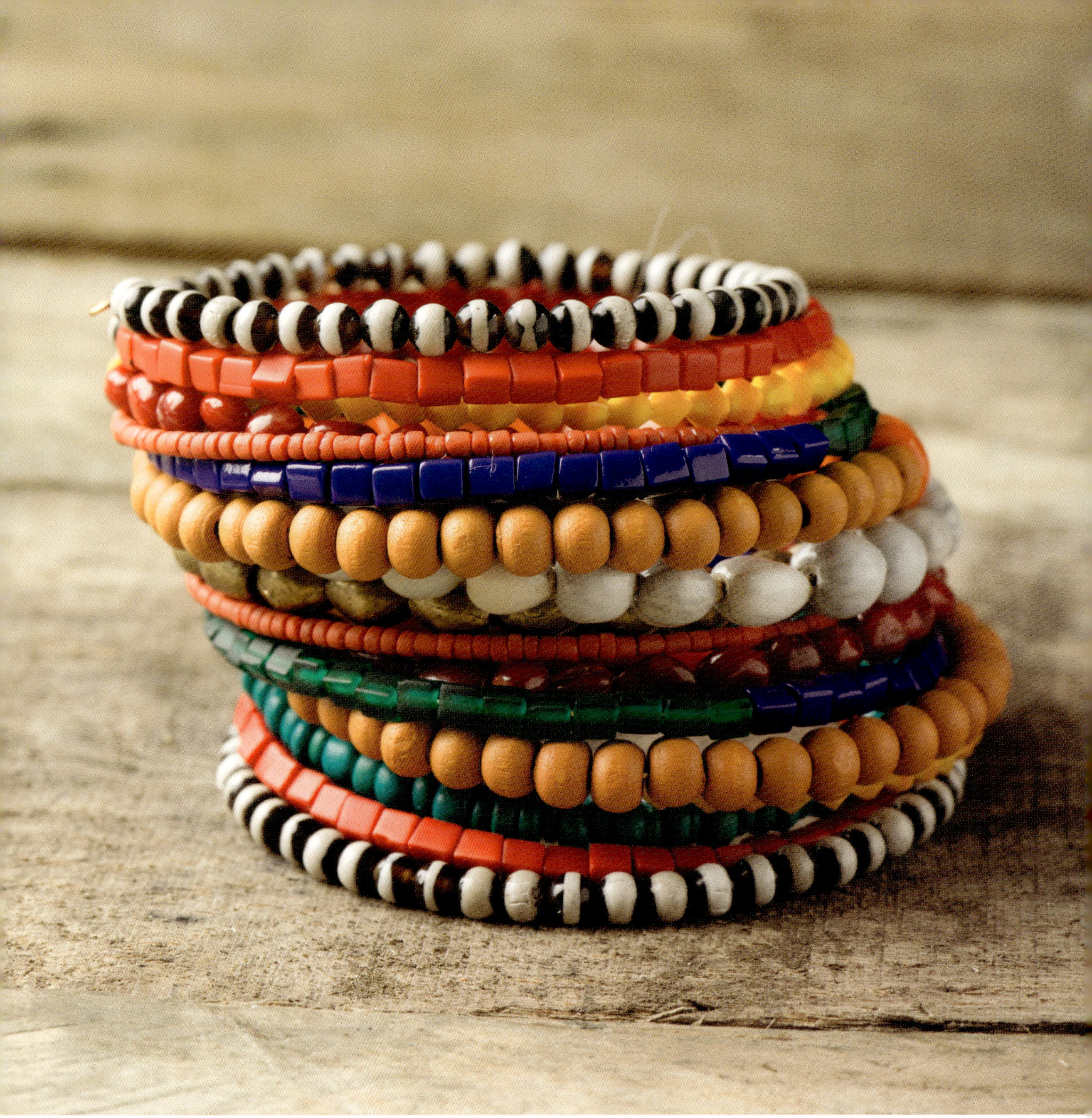
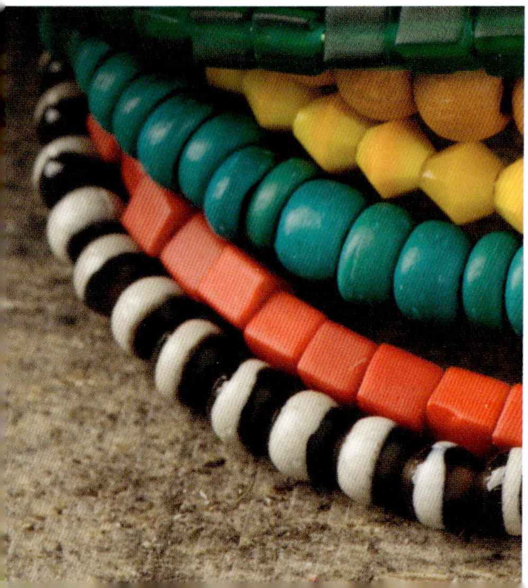
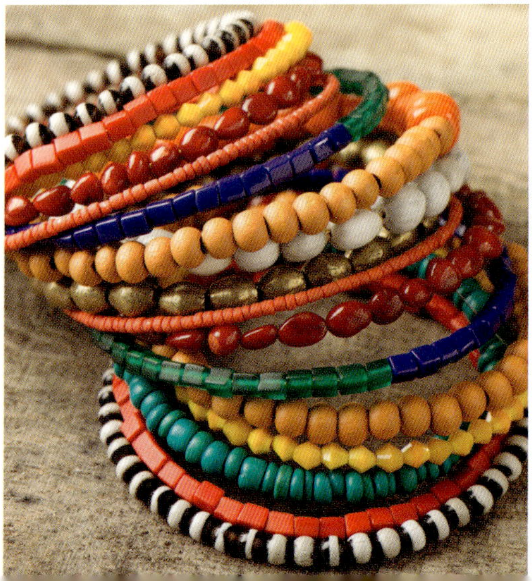
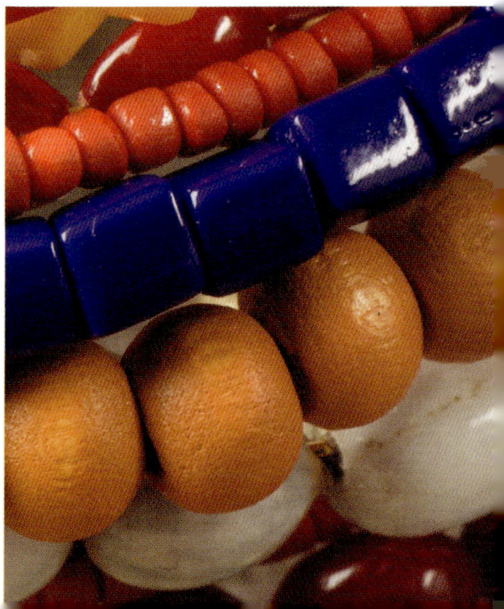

KENYA
Maasai Cuff Bracelet

As the Land Rover pulls up to the *kraal's* thorny fence, the whole village comes to greet me, and I am soon surrounded by a pressing group of children up to my waist. With grateful nods, I take the gourd of tea with milk offered to me, and we all smile and nod at each other, awkwardly, warmly, until I have finished.

It is late in the afternoon; the women of the village gather under the shelter of a twiggy acacia tree. Their shaved heads are coffee-bean black and their earlobes heavy with multicolored beaded earrings. Each women is wearing tons and *tons* of necklaces. Some sit on the ground near napping babies, others sit on low stools as they work. It is a special time, beading together under this tree. Beading is a chore here just like milking cows and preparing food, but they have finished up their other tasks quickly so they can spend extra time here, together. This is their time to be creative, to hone craftsmanship, to show off a little. To make something beautiful. The Maasai have an ancient beading tradition (who can say that?), and it is evident in their expert work.

Across the mat, Tigisi beads a large flat collar, a densely patterned bib with concentric rows of beads. Watching her work, I am struck by her attention to pattern and color and by her expert skill. She works the disc as a map of her village: large triangles piece together representing each family's *inkajijik*, or "home," in position. Around the edge she works a black-and-white pattern that represents the protective fence that surrounds the entire village. Using colors that have meaning to her and her community, Tigisi selects the palette for her piece: black is the color of her people, and white is the color of cow's milk, their sustenance. Orange represents hospitality and red the Maasai's strength and unity. Tigisi is making this glorious necklace for her daughter to wear on just one day, a month from now. On her wedding day, Tigisi's daughter will don her mother's masterful handiwork, and her village will surround her.

Maasai women wear many, many necklaces as status symbols. The rows and rows of this Maasai Cuff can be *your* status symbol. The color palette is traditional, and the black-and-white outer loops represent the kraal fence, just as on Maasai necklaces.

MATERIALS

94 black-and-white 5mm dzi agate rounds

106 matte red 4mm cubes

102 sunflower faceted 4mm bicones

62 red coral 6mm nuggets

212 matte red 2mm glass heishi

54 matte transparent green 4mm cubes

54 cobalt blue 4mm cubes

65 light orange 5×7mm wooden rondelles

12 orange 7×9mm glass crows

23 white 9×7mm Job's tears

27 African brass 9×7mm rice beads

84 teal coconut 2×5mm rondelles

24 loops 60mm gold memory wire

TOOLS

Memory-wire cutters

Round-nose pliers

FINISHED SIZE

2½" wide × 3" high (6.5 × 7.5 cm).

1. Onto memory wire, string:
   47 black-and-white dzi agate rounds
   53 matte red cubes
   84 teal coconut rondelles
   46 sunflower faceted bicones
   40 light orange wooden rondelles
   26 cobalt blue cubes
   23 matte transparent green cubes
   30 red coral nuggets
   119 matte red glass heishi
   27 African brass rice beads
   23 white Job's tears
   12 orange glass crows
   25 light orange wooden rondelles
   27 matte transparent green cubes
   23 cobalt blue cubes
   106 matte red glass heishi
   31 red coral nuggets
   51 sunflower faceted bicones
   53 matte red cubes
   45 black-and-white dzi agate rounds

2. Making sure that beads are pushed together, and leaving no large gaps, with memory-wire cutters, cut memory wire ½" (1.3 cm) from last bead. With round-nose pliers, make a simple loop (see page 134; **Figure 1**).

3. With memory-wire cutters, cut memory wire ½" (1.3 cm) from last bead on other end. With round-nose pliers, make a simple loop.

Fig. 1

Kenya: Maasai Cuff Bracelet ~ 93

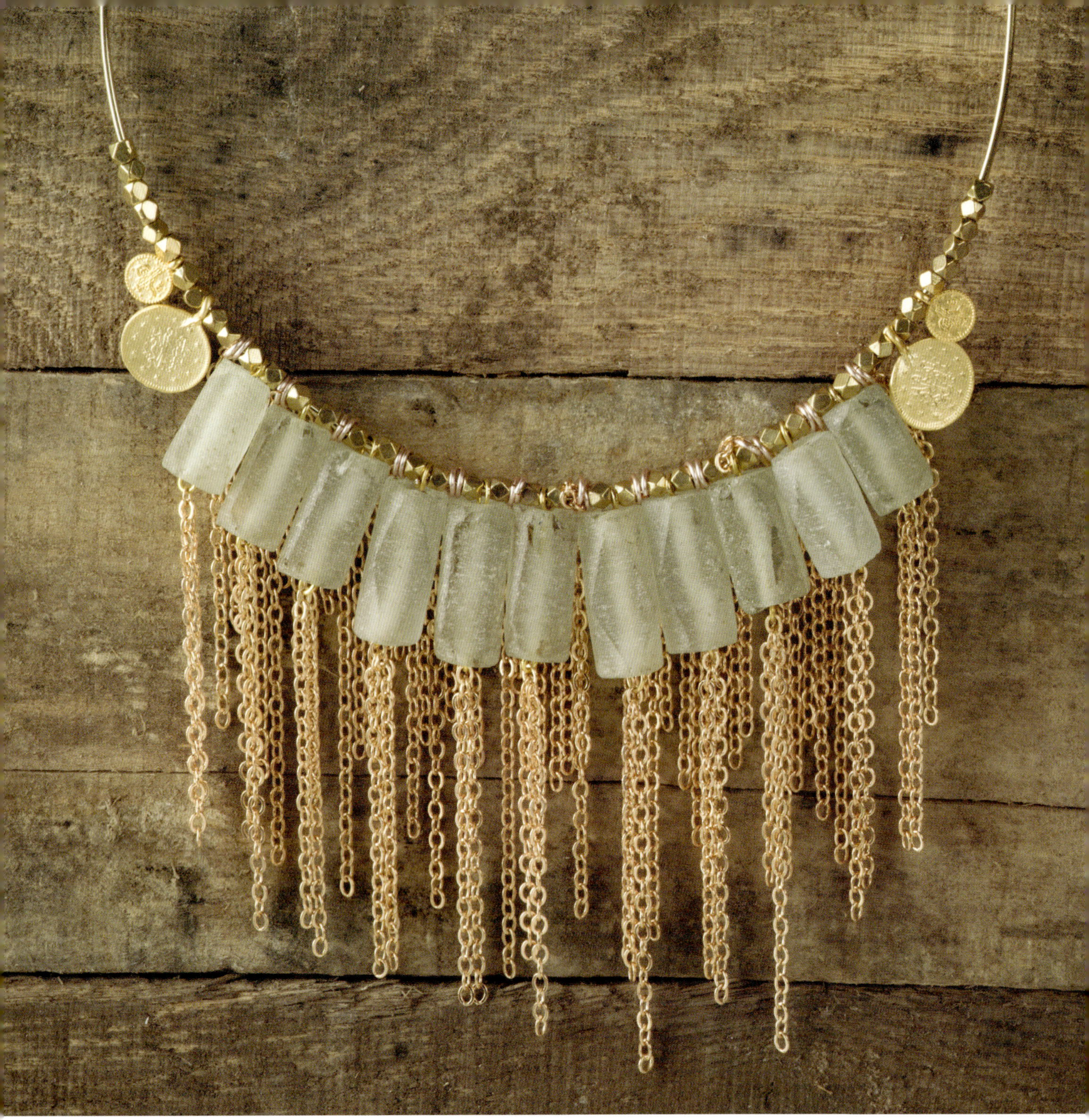
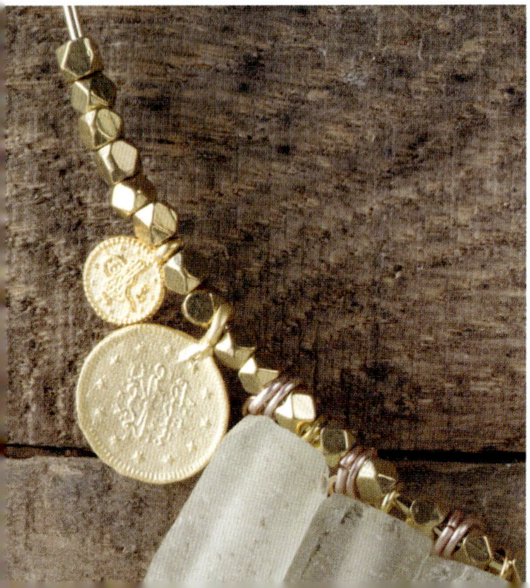
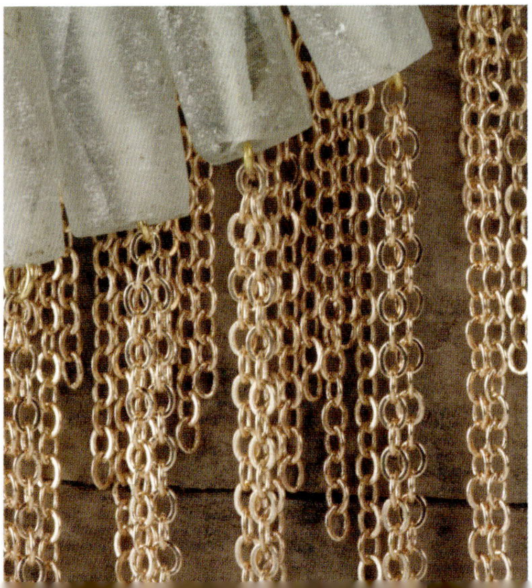
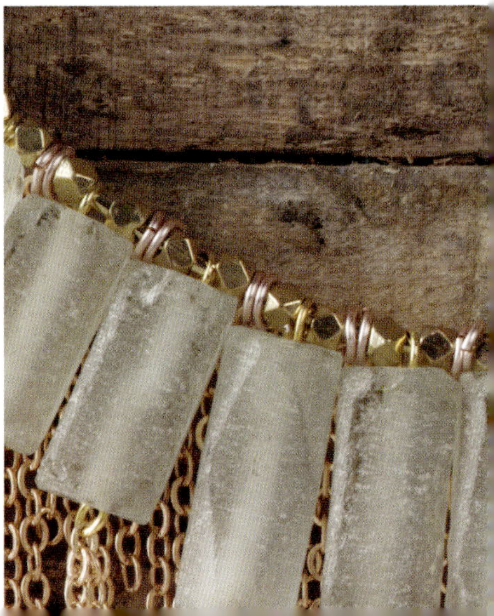

EGYPT
Modern Pharaoh's Collar

Daylight is fading as I look out across Cairo. A brown sprawl of houses, rooftops with satellite dishes. Streams of people are walking on the streets below: commuters, mothers holding children's hands and talking on the phone. Dudes in T-shirts looking aimless. Past the city, the pyramids rise out of the desert, ancient sentinels. A sandy haze blurs their unmistakable form, giving them a dreamy, ethereal mystique. Striking against a hushed aqua sky, they hover weightless, their bases shrouded as twilight fades.

Museums here are filled with Egyptian art and artifacts. That iconic style we all recognize as "Egyptian": scarabs, jewel tones, hieroglyphics, and gold. A decidedly Pharaonic style that jumped right off a papyrus somewhere and into every history book I've ever read. But I'm having to negotiate old Egypt with the culture around me now. Cairo today has its own style. Modern, gritty, and hip. With ancient-urban roots, sometimes traditionally Egyptian and sometimes Western, the different facets of Cairo come together to make something new. With the pyramids as a backdrop, this city pulses to its own jumbled mix tape.

Bringing together the varied sides of Cairo, this necklace nicely employs diverse elements to make a trendy piece with a style all its own. I chose the tumbled glass rectangles because they characterize the timeworn beauty of the pyramids at twilight: the matte finish of the tumbled glass looks sand-worn to me, and the pale aqua hue is a faded desert sky. The rest of this design is Pharaonic, hearkening back to Egypt's ancient roots. The statement-sized scale of the piece gives a nod to wide collars that Pharaohs wore; it's a wearable, subtler take on the look. And the necklace is dripping with gold. Gold was prized and flaunted by the Pharaohs, and now we can rock it for a night out.

MATERIALS

1 gold-plated 5½" (14 cm) wire neck ring

11 aqua tumbled glass 10×18mm–15×25mm faceted rectangles

42 gold-plated 3.3mm cornerless cubes

2 matte gold 18mm sultan seal charms

2 matte gold 10mm sultan seal charms

24 gold-plated 5mm jump rings

11 gold-plated 2" (5 cm) eye pins

12' (3.5 m) round 3mm gold chain

TOOLS

Flat-nose pliers

Wire cutters

Two pliers (for opening and closing jump rings)

FINISHED SIZE

5½" (14 cm) diameter.

1. With wire cutters, cut chain into thirty-five 4" (10 cm) lengths.

2. With pliers, open loops of eye pins. Choose a random midpoint on one chain length and attach link to loop of eye pin (**Figure 1**). Repeat for remaining 10 eye pins and ten chain lengths.

3. Onto 1 eye pin, string 1 tumbled-glass rectangle. With wire cutters, cut eye pin to 10mm past bead and form a simple loop (see page 134; **Figure 2**). Repeat ten times for each eye pin.

4. With two pairs of pliers, open twenty-four 5mm jump rings. Choose a random midpoint on one chain length and attach link to 1 jump ring (**Figure 3**). Repeat for remaining chain lengths and remaining jump rings.

5. Unscrew ball end of neck ring and string the following onto wire (**Figure 4**): 6 gold cornerless cubes, 1 small sultan charm, 2 gold cornerless cubes, 1 large sultan charm, 2 gold cornerless cubes, [2 chain dangles, 1 tumbled-glass dangle] eleven times, 2 gold cornerless cubes, 1 large sultan charm, 2 gold cornerless cubes, 1 small sultan charm, and 6 gold cornerless cubes. Screw on ball end of neck ring.

6. Bend neck ring to fit, if necessary.

Fig. 1

Fig. 2

Fig. 3

Fig. 4

EGYPT: MODERN PHARAOH'S COLLAR ~ 97

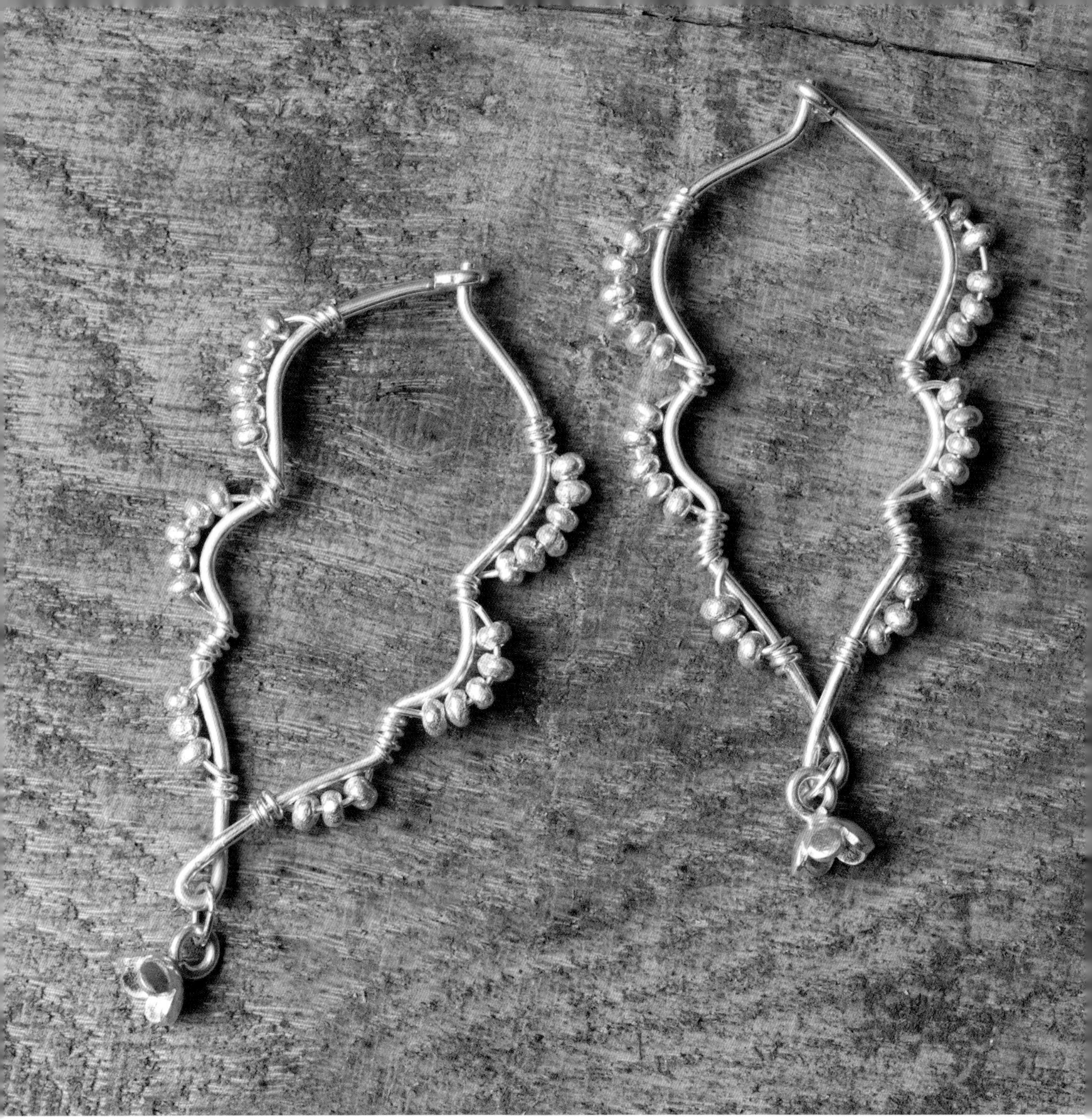

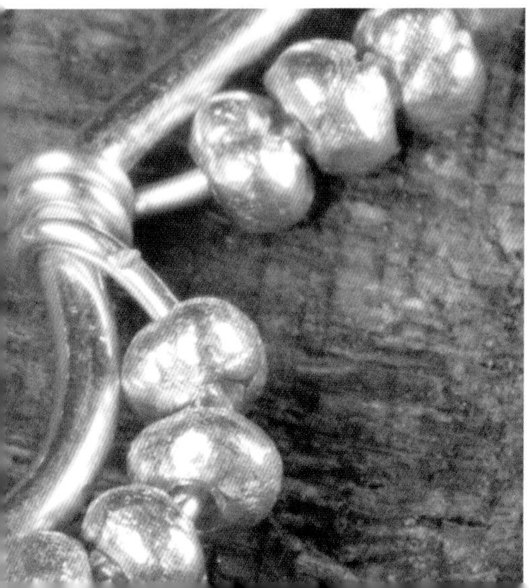

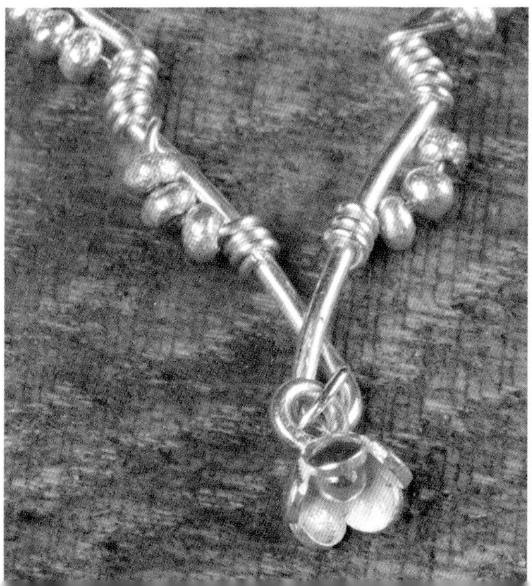

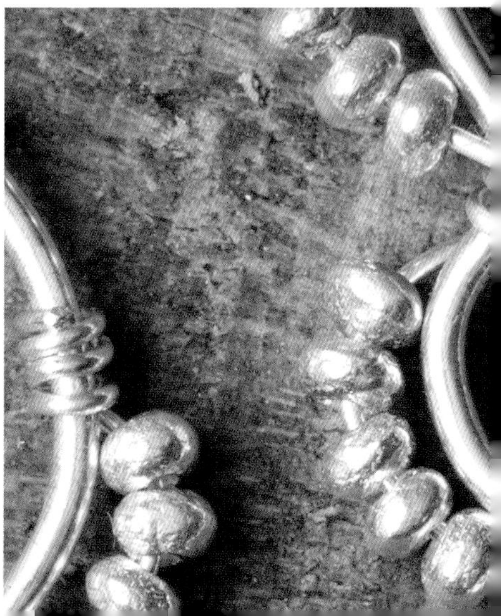

MOROCCO
Tea Glass Earrings

Upon entering a home, or before sitting down to eat, or after we eat, or even browsing in a shop for more than three minutes, someone offers me a cup of mint tea. It's a generous act that sums up Moroccan hospitality so well. And it really doesn't matter that I'm not much of a tea drinker. Drinking this mint tea, or *it-tay*, as it's called here, is too culturally important to negotiate, and it would be rude to refuse.

And I'm starting to get a little dependent on the whole tea thing now, too. Tea breaks throughout the day recalibrate my usual speed of dash-then-crash, which really wasn't doing me any favors anyway.

Lost in the *souk*, I stop for a tea break. Amid the chaos of donkeys laden with carpets and goods, and hard-sell hagglers, I find myself in an oasis of beauty. At my little café table a tea set waits on a brass tray. The worn silver teapot is formal, but curvier than European teapots—it's Maghreb-style. I can smell the tea, its mint and absinthe mingling with the gunpowder tea leaves like two old lovers. Fiddleheads of steams twist and swivel up from the glass. It's downright sexy. As my tea cools a bit, I inspect my tea glass. It is the most beautiful part of this pretty scene. Opulent gold scroll designs drip from the rim onto the magenta pink glass. The designs are effusive—romantic and wild—like wisteria spilling over a trellis. Delicate swizzles curl around the spade shape, making a curvy filigree. The design is gracefully pleasing, yet stimulating, and quintessentially Moroccan.

Just like these tea breaks I'm coming to love.

The Moorish shape of these earrings, with the delicate beaded picots, make an interesting interpretation of the lovely Moroccan tea glass designs. A bold design, with dainty embellishment. These earrings are made with sterling silver materials, so these are as luxe as they look. Go for a gold-filled version, but expect to pay more for materials—they would be divine, but a materials splurge, for sure. Or choose silver-plated base metal for a more economical version; just make sure metal allergies aren't an issue for the wearer. I worked these earrings in steps and took breaks as I went. If I couldn't manipulate the wire form like I wanted, I set the project down for a bit. Wrestling with wire can get a little tedious, and I didn't want to overwork the wire in frustration.

MATERIALS

12" (30.5 cm) half-hard 16-gauge sterling silver wire

24" (61 cm) half-hard 22-gauge sterling silver wire

56 Thai silver 2×3mm rondelles

2 silver oval jump rings

2 sterling silver 8mm flower charms

TOOLS

Wire cutters

Flat-nose pliers

Round-nose pliers

Crimping pliers

Two pairs of pliers (for opening and closing jump rings)

Pencil

Permanent marker

Cup bur

Hammer

Bench block

FINISHED SIZE

2" long × 1¼" wide (5 × 3.2 cm).

Note: To make two identical earrings, shape the two earring forms at the same time. Do one step of the design on one earring and repeat it for the second earring. Do not complete one earring and then make the second; it is easier to make the two earrings identical if you can adjust the earrings to match along the way.

1. With wire cutters, cut 16-gauge wire into two 6" (15 cm) lengths.

2. With round-nose pliers, form a loop in the center of one wire, pulling end away in a wide V shape (**Figure 1**). Repeat for second wire.

3. Following pattern below, with flat-nose pliers, bend wire once and again back to form the "stair step" in the design. Repeat on other side of V (**Figure 2**). Repeat for second wire.

4. Using a pencil, form one wire into a slight semicircle (**Figure 3**). With flat-nose pliers, bend wire back to complete semicircle. Repeat on other side (**Figure 4**). Repeat for second wire.

5. Using a permanent marker, form one wire into a larger slight semicircle. Repeat on other side (**Figure 5**). Repeat for second wire.

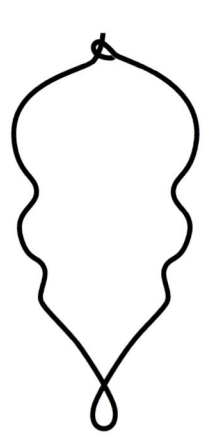

Tea Glass Earrings pattern

Fig. 1

Fig. 2

Fig. 3

Fig. 4

Fig. 5

Morocco: Tea Glass Earrings ~ 101

6. Using flat-nose pliers, bend one side of wire at the top (**Figure 6**). With wire cutters, cut wire about 5mm from bend. File wire ends with cup bur (**Figure 7**). Repeat for second wire.

7. The ends of the two wires should cross. Using flat-nose pliers, bend second wire perpendicularly at about the place where first wire bends (**Figure 8**). With wire cutters, cut wire about 10mm from bend. With round-nose pliers, form a simple loop (see page 134) as a catch for back of earring (**Figure 9**). Bend as necessary with flat-nose pliers so wire bend fits easily into loop.

8. Keeping loop catch off end of block, hammer wire form, avoiding bottom loop.

9. With wire cutters, cut 22-gauge wire into four 6" (15 cm) lengths.

10. Starting at bottom loop, attach one length of wire, leaving ½" (1.3 cm) length. Following photo, wrap wire around form three times, string 3 rondelles onto wire (**Figure 10**), and return wire to same side of form, then wrap wire five times around form. In same manner, string 5 rondelles onto wire, wrap wire two times, string 6 rondelles, and wrap wire twice.

11. With flat-nose pliers, pull wire tight and cut end close with wire cutters. With crimping pliers, press wire end close to form. Repeat for beginning of wire.

12. Repeat Steps 10 and 11 three more times until each side of each form is embellished with wire and beads.

13. With two pairs of pliers, open 2 oval jump rings. Attach 1 silver flower charm to 1 jump ring and attach to bottom loop of one form (**Figure 11**). With two pairs of pliers, close jump ring. Repeat for second silver flower and second form.

Fig. 6

Fig. 7

Fig. 8

Fig. 9

Fig. 10

Fig. 11

Morocco: Tea Glass Earrings ~ 103

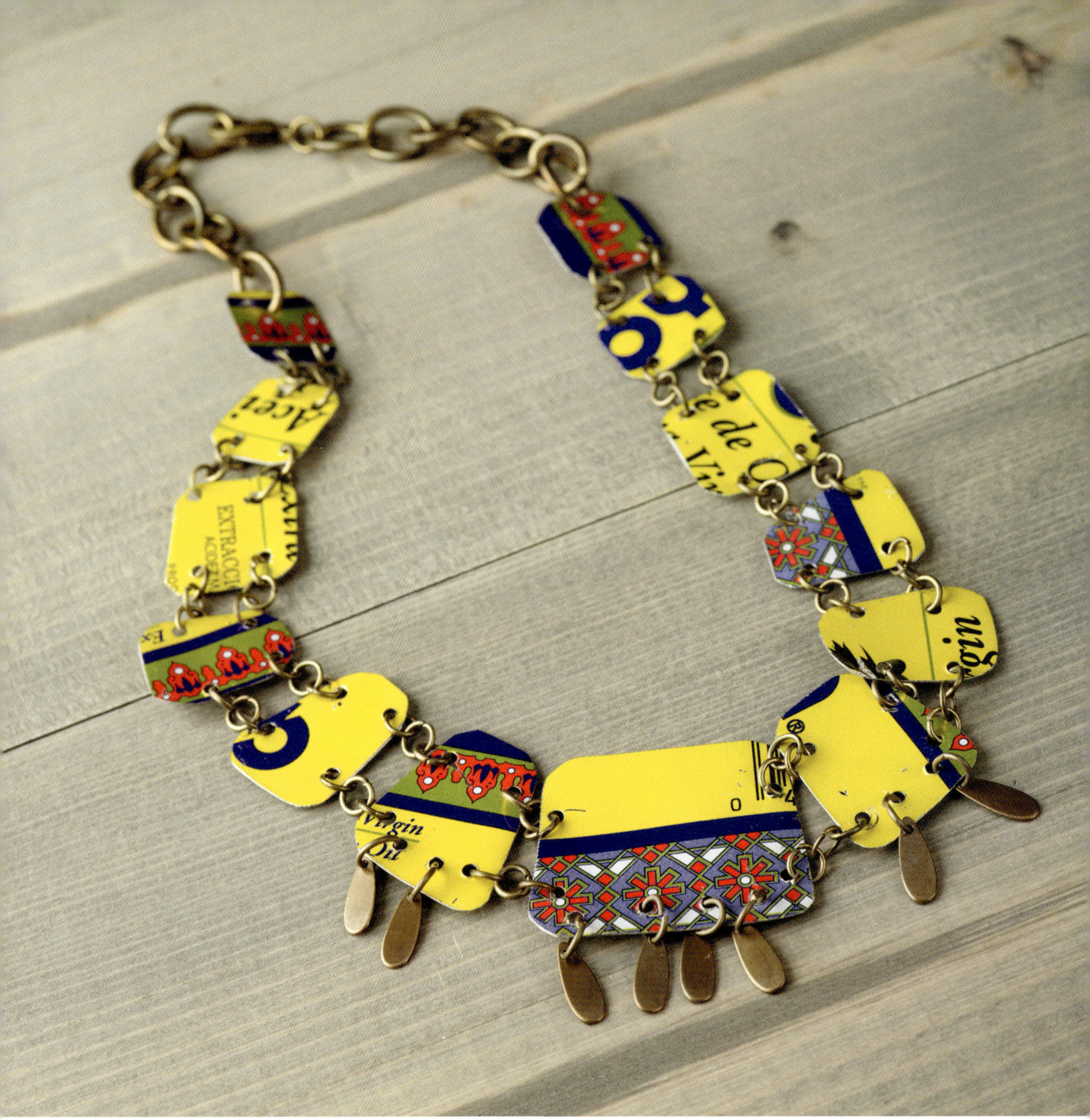

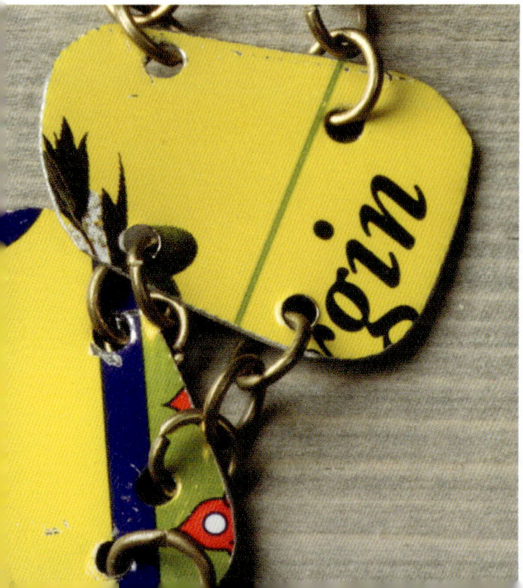

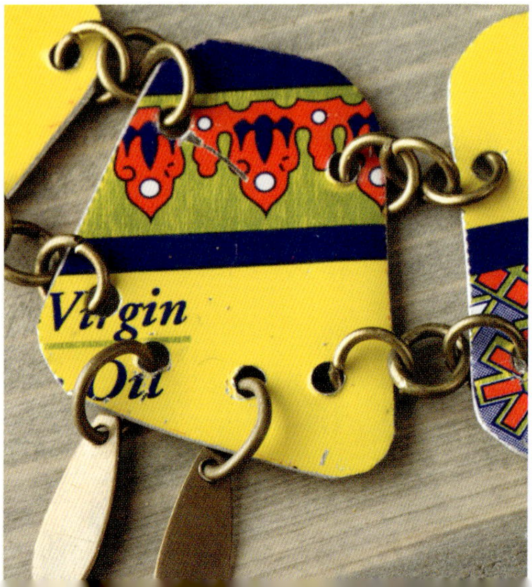
Virgin

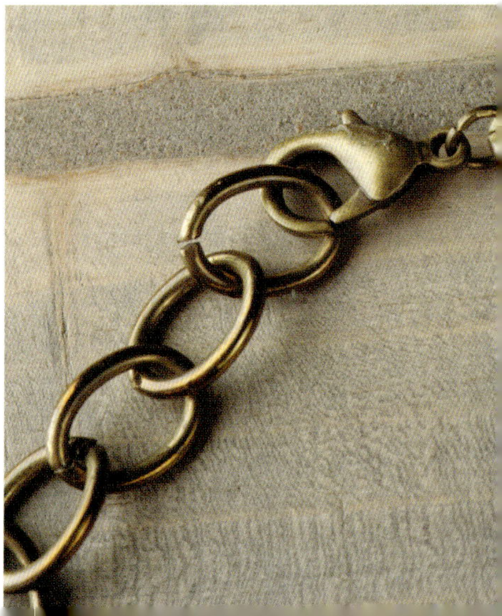

SENEGAL
Recycled Tin Necklace

Elhadji works quickly, surely. His studio is a small tent in the market, and he sits at a low table, an upturned bucket for his stool. Next to him on his right sits a plastic laundry basket full of rinsed pop cans, their tops and bottoms removed. Next to him on his left: me, sitting at his elbow, watching him work.

Wielding a rugged pair of pliers in his right hand, Elhadji works a long length of heavy-gauge wire. The wire is hard to manipulate, I know, but he seems to make easy work of it, bending it into curves and bends and then sometimes sharp, defined angles with the pliers. Before long he is finished with this step: an armature of a sandpiper, with its plump body and skinny bird legs. There is no break as Elhadji picks up a pop can and a rusted pair of kitchen scissors from the basket. With long, careful draws of the blades, he cuts a shallow angle around the top of the can that barely spirals downward. As he cuts, a thin ribbon of red-and-white printed metal grows long, like an apple peeled on an Appalachian porch. He works more slowly on this step, cutting the strip with a uniform width. A quarter of an inch maybe? When he's done cutting he begins to wrap the cut metal strip around the armature, and I smile as I recognize the basic basketweaving technique that he uses. Traditional basketweaving to make a quirky pop-can bird! Should I be surprised? Elhadji is an innovator, a creative soul who isn't hindered by limited resources, but inspired and tested by them.

When the piece is done, he sets it off to the side of the table, carefully facing the little bird toward the market as if presenting it to court. Then he cuts a long piece of wire from a bale, and starts the next piece.

Pieces made from recycled materials have a look all their own. Boisterous and colorful, often on the verge of tacky. They're not for everyone, to be sure! But for those of us who like the gallant use of recycled materials as they are, this necklace is a great piece to try. Feel free to use different types of printed metal (chew tobacco tins, for example), but know that heavier-gauge metal will require a jeweler's saw for cutting, and a heavier-grit sandpaper to slough off metal burs.

MATERIALS

Printed metal can

5" (12.5 cm) antiqued brass 10×12mm oval unsoldered link chain

1 antiqued brass 15×12mm lobster clasp

72 antiqued brass 5mm open round jump rings

8 antiqued brass 5×7mm open oval jump rings

8 antiqued brass 12×5mm paddle charms

TOOLS

Tin snips or heavy-duty scissors

Can opener

Metal punch

Two pairs of pliers (for opening and closing jump rings)

Flat-nose pliers

Wire cutters

#220 sandpaper

Permanent marker

FINISHED SIZE

21" (53.5 cm) long.

Note: Make sure to buy cans that are made with printed metal—not shrink-wrap labels. Find interesting printed tin cans at a global food store; some brands of olive oil, soy sauce, tea, and coffee still come in printed metal cans. Another good option are vintage cans. Do avoid most soda or beer cans made today, though, as they are not rigid enough for this project.

1. With can opener, remove top of can and empty contents. Repeat for can bottom. Wash and dry cans.

2. With tin snips, cut down side of can and smooth metal so it lies flat.

3. Copy or trace tin tile shapes from templates on page 109.

4. With permanent marker, trace tile shapes onto metal, taking care to choose the most appealing parts of can (**Figure 1**).

5. With tin snips, cut out tiles. With sandpaper, smooth edges of each piece.

6. With permanent marker, transfer dots onto each tile piece to mark hole placement.

7. With metal punch, punch holes (**Figure 2**). Remove any metal chads with wire cutters. With flat-nose pliers, press flat any rough metal edges.

8. Lay tin tiles out in order (**Figure 3**). Attach one 5mm jump ring to every hole except 3 tiles and single holes punched on end of last 2 tiles (**Figure 4**). Close attached rings with pliers.

9. With pliers, link attached jump rings with a connecting 5mm jump ring. With pliers, close rings (**Figure 5**).

10. With wire cutters, cut chain into two 2½" (6.5 cm) lengths. With pliers, open end link of one length of chain and attach to one end tin tile. Close with pliers. Repeat for second length of chain and second end tin tile.

11. With pliers, open one free end link of chain and attach lobster clasp. Close link with pliers.

12. Attach 1 paddle to one bottom hole with 1 oval jump ring. Close with pliers. Repeat for remaining paddles and oval jump rings.

Fig. 1

Fig. 2

Fig. 3

Fig. 4

Fig. 5

SENEGAL: RECYCLED TIN NECKLACE ~ 107

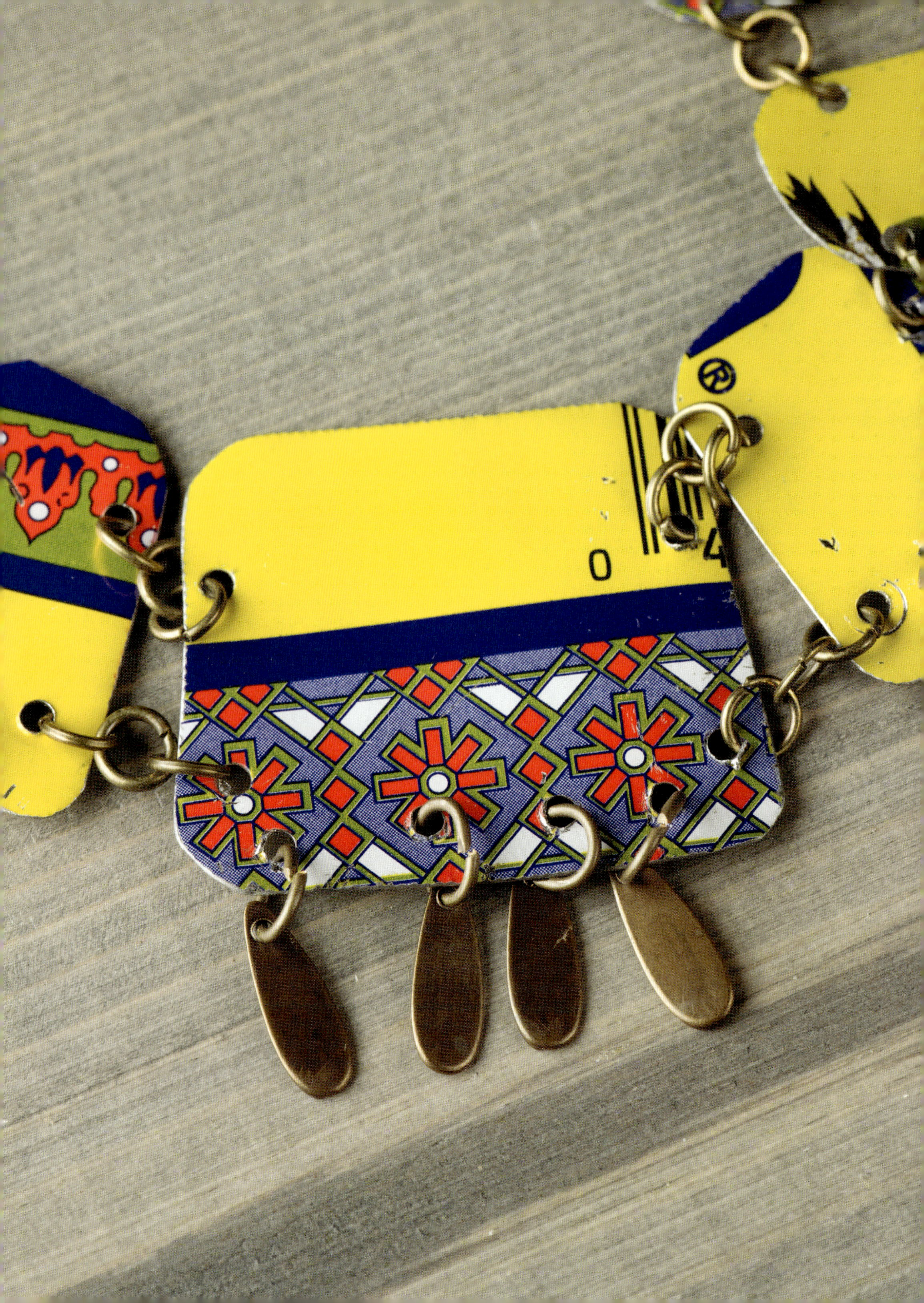

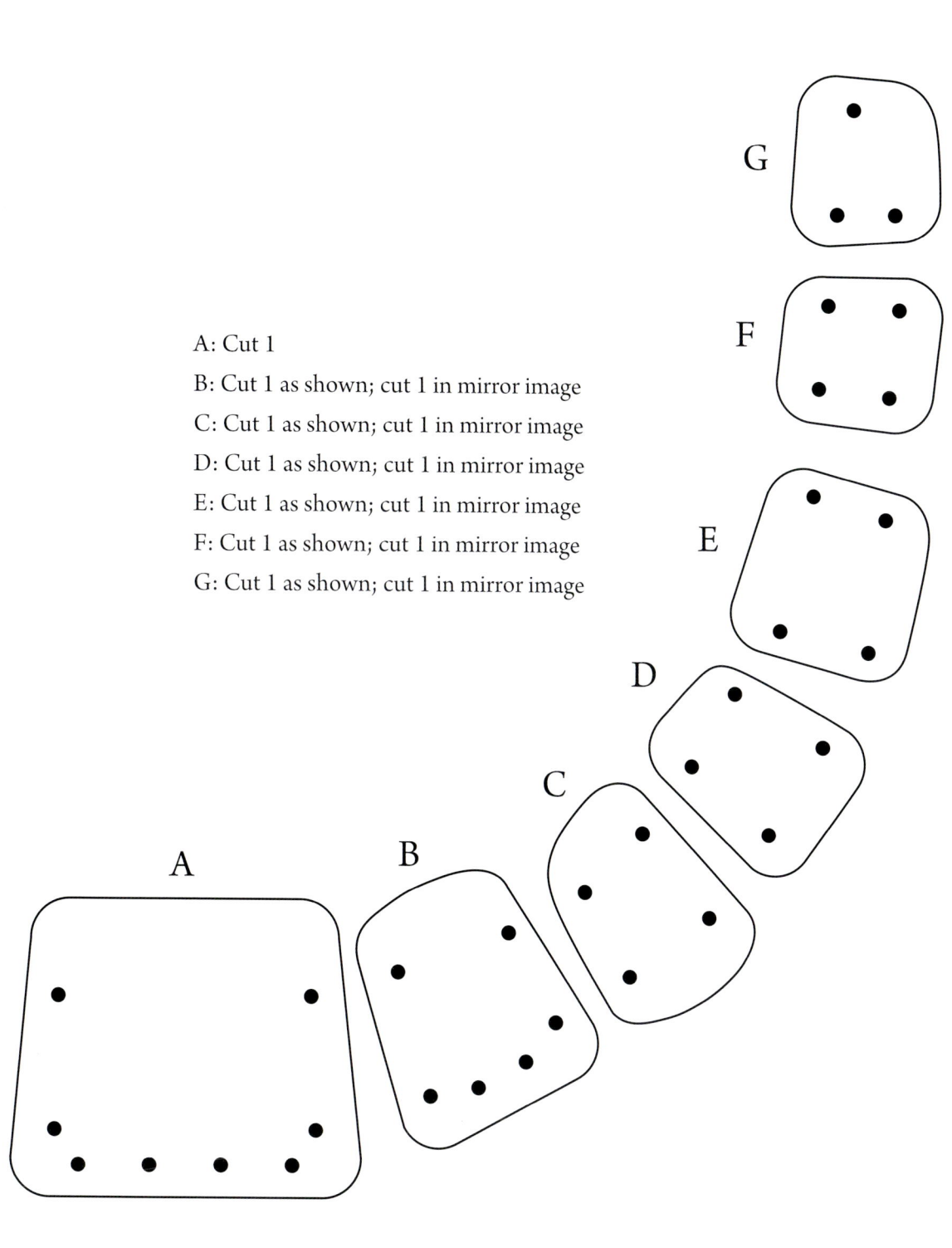

A: Cut 1
B: Cut 1 as shown; cut 1 in mirror image
C: Cut 1 as shown; cut 1 in mirror image
D: Cut 1 as shown; cut 1 in mirror image
E: Cut 1 as shown; cut 1 in mirror image
F: Cut 1 as shown; cut 1 in mirror image
G: Cut 1 as shown; cut 1 in mirror image

Recycled Tin Necklace templates

SENEGAL: RECYCLED TIN NECKLACE ◆ 109

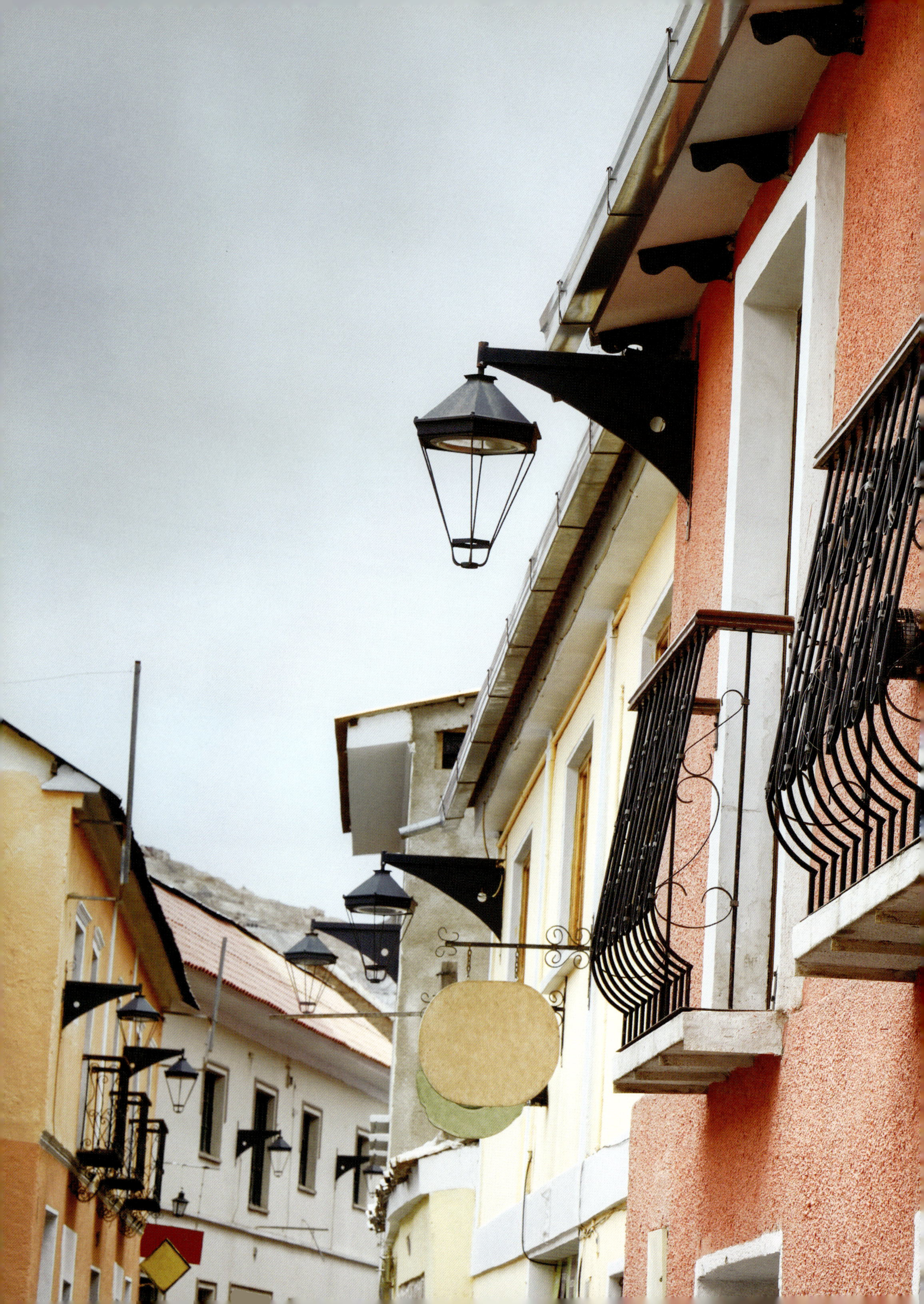

Chapter Five

LATIN AMERICA

Mixed together in Latin American culture are two predominant ethnic identities: the Iberian (Spanish) and the indigenous (Amerindian). Almost as soon as the Spanish arrived in the New World, these two cultures began to intermix, birthing a new Hispanic culture. There are still enclaves of distinctly Spanish or distinctly Amerindian identity, but Latin America today evinces a myriad of mixed cultures. Exploring Latin American design, you can see the imprint of Iberian influence here: Spanish lace, Catholic imagery and icons; and indigenous influence there: highland wool, boisterous colorwork, and weaving. The two once-distinct cultures now interplay together to form a spectrum of Latin American style. On one end we see design heavily influenced by the indigenous, and on the other, more Iberian design. Vibrantly colorful and beautiful from end to end.

© GettyImages.com/dani3315

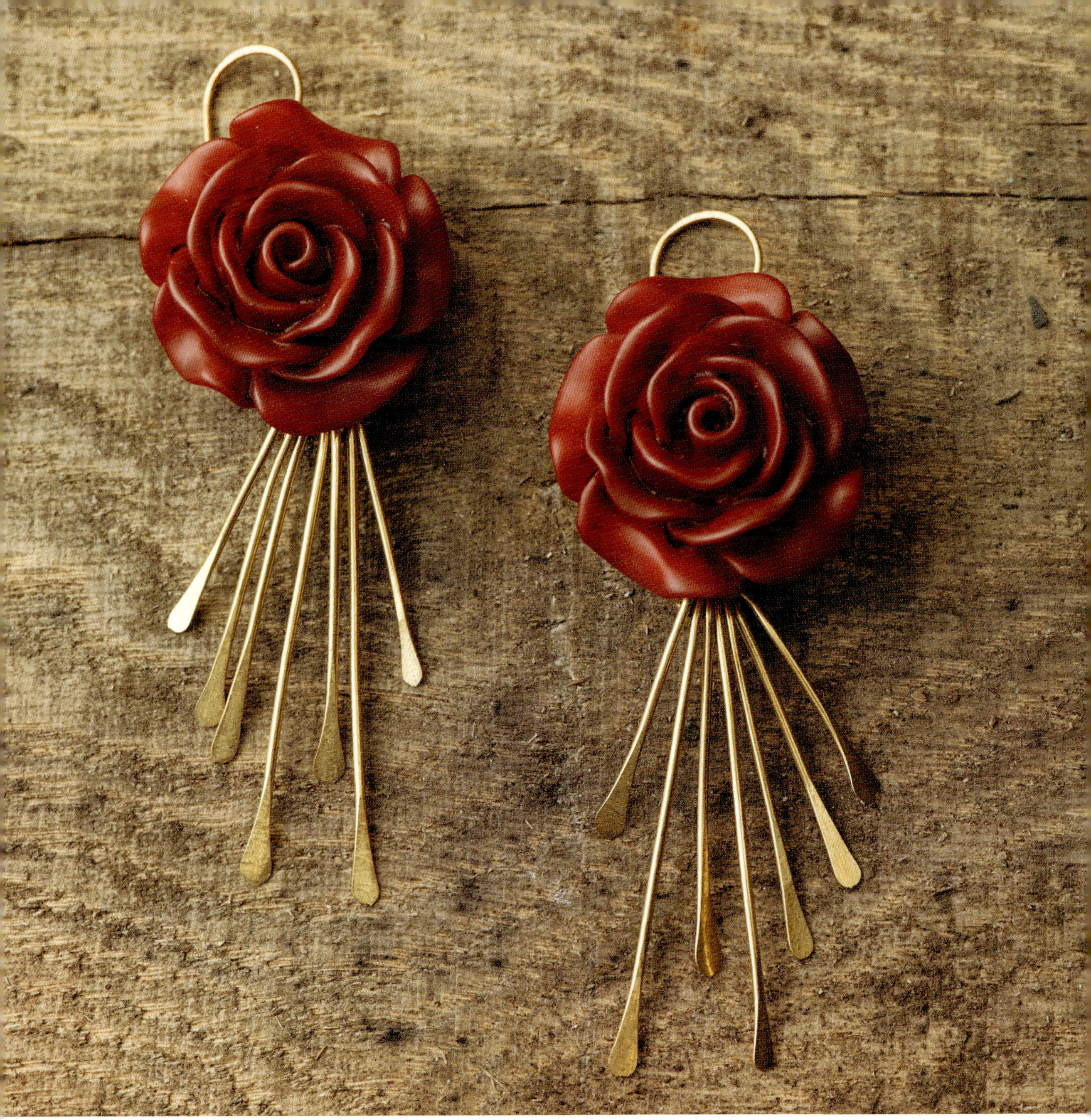

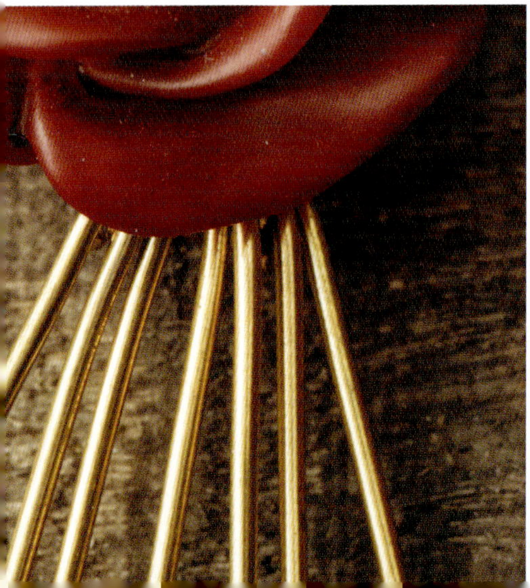

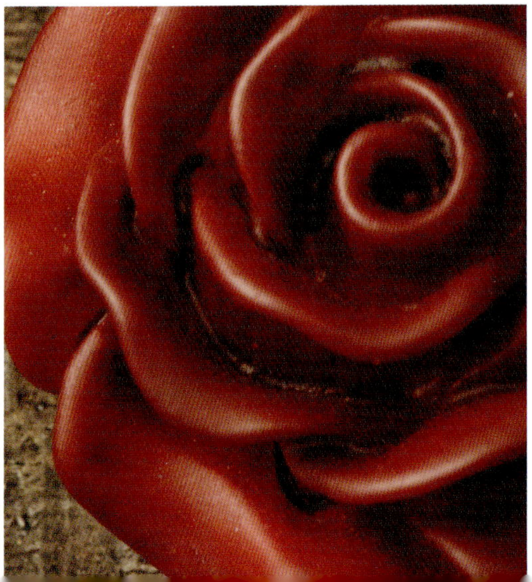

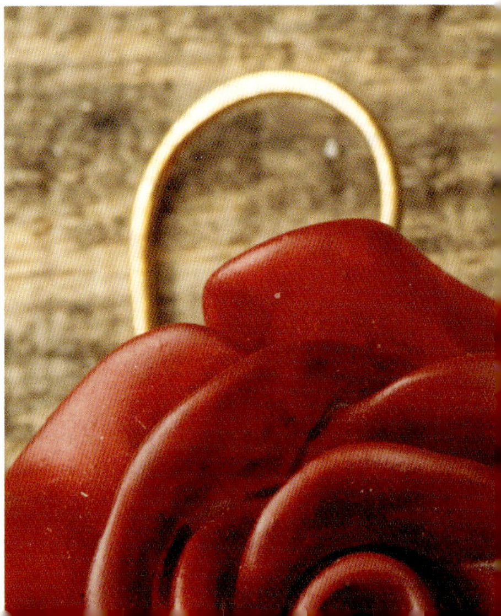

MEXICO
Frida Kahlo Earrings

In a house painted Kodachrome blue, a canary-yellow floor stretches under my feet in the dining room. I am in La Casa Azul, paying my dues to Frida Kahlo, the iconic Mexican artist who lived and painted and died here. There's an eerie feeling as I walk slowly through the rooms filled with her lovely effects. Everywhere, something vivid. Vibrant. It's such a pretty museum-house but a little haunted, too.

After leaving the house and buying the necessary Frida souvenirs—one wool Frida worry doll (my new pincushion for my sewing box) and one Frida pillbox—I decide I need a break from all the color and chaos. I buy a big *torta* and cold *chela* from a street vendor and perch on a garden wall, beer by my side, sandwich in my hands, mindlessly people-watching as I sit in the sun.

Sated with all things Frida, it's hard to process my thoughts right now. I came here with a love of Frida, the icon. Frida, the renegade feminatrix. But Frida's dismal life of illness stands in odd contrast to her "floribundant" image. Bright folkloric costumes; theatrical hairdos; big, bold jewelry! I'm puzzled by the disconnect. I wonder, how consciously did she craft her overstated image? In the end, I suppose it doesn't really matter; we all craft a persona for the world to know us by. Frida's façade was just wonderfully colorful, that's all.

These earrings are bold and slightly over-the-top, just like Frida. The focal point—huge resin red roses—are a nod to Frida's iconic, oversized floral headbands. You can certainly scale this element down if you like—smaller rose beads are out there—but the large scale is in keeping with Frida's attention-grabbing style. To lessen the plastic-y look of the roses, I painted them with a matte varnish that I tinted with marsala red paint. This gives the roses a velvety appearance and keeps them from looking like a Cracker Jack prize. Finally, the hammered brass paddles give more drama by adding nearly two more inches of length to these already long earrings. Construction-wise, these earrings are a little fussy, so don't be discouraged if it takes more than one try to get them right. You'll want the roses to be snugly secured by the loops at the top and bottom, so they face forward (and don't spin around). Remember: it's just wire—easy come, easy go.

MATERIALS

2 red resin 28mm rose beads

20 brass 18-gauge 3" (7.5 cm) paddles

2 brass 25mm ear wires

6" (15 cm) square brass 21-gauge wire

Matte acrylic varnish

Dark red acrylic paint (Deco Art "Dark Cherry" used here)

TOOLS

Paintbrush and palette

Toothpick

Round-nose pliers

Flat-nose pliers

Two pairs of pliers (for wire wrapping and opening and closing jump rings)

Crimping pliers

Wire cutters

FINISHED SIZE

3" (7.5 cm) long.

---

1. On palette, mix a quarter-size dollop of varnish with two drops of red acrylic paint and stir with toothpick. Paint rose and let dry (**Figure 1**). Paint second coat. Let dry and let cure for at least 24 hours.

2. With wire cutters, cut brass paddles into the following lengths: four 50mm lengths (A), four 40mm lengths (B), two 35mm lengths (C), two 30mm lengths (D), and two 28mm lengths (E) (**Figure 2**).

3. With round-nose pliers, make a simple loop (see page 134) at wire end of each paddle, making sure that loop is perpendicular to paddle (**Figure 3**).

4. With wire cutters, cut square brass wire into two 3" (7.5 cm) lengths.

5. Using flat-nose pliers and one length of square brass wire, make a shallow triangular simple loop—with a ⅜" (10 mm) base—about 1½" (3.8 cm) from one end (**Figure 4**). Repeat for the second length of square brass wire.

6. Onto one triangular loop, place 7 brass paddles in the following order: E, C, B, A, B, A, D, making sure all loops face away. With two pairs of pliers, wrap shorter wire tail around top of triangle (**Figure 5**). Cut end of tail with wire cutters and tighten close with crimping pliers. Repeat for second triangular loop, but reverse paddle order: D, A, B, A, B, C, E.

7. Thread wire through resin rose and situate triangle loop so it is parallel to face of rose (**Figure 6**). With flat-nose pliers, make a 90-degree bend as close as possible to rose and cut with wire cutters, leaving a 10mm end. With round-nose pliers, complete the simple loop, making loop as tight as possible to rose. Repeat for second wire and second rose.

8. With pliers, open ear wires. Add 1 ear wire to simple loop and close ear wire with pliers. Repeat for second ear wire and second rose.

114 ⸺ GLOBAL STYLE JEWELRY

Fig. 1   *Fig. 2*

Fig. 3   *Fig. 4*

Fig. 5   *Fig. 6*

Mexico: Frida Kahlo Earrings ∼ 115

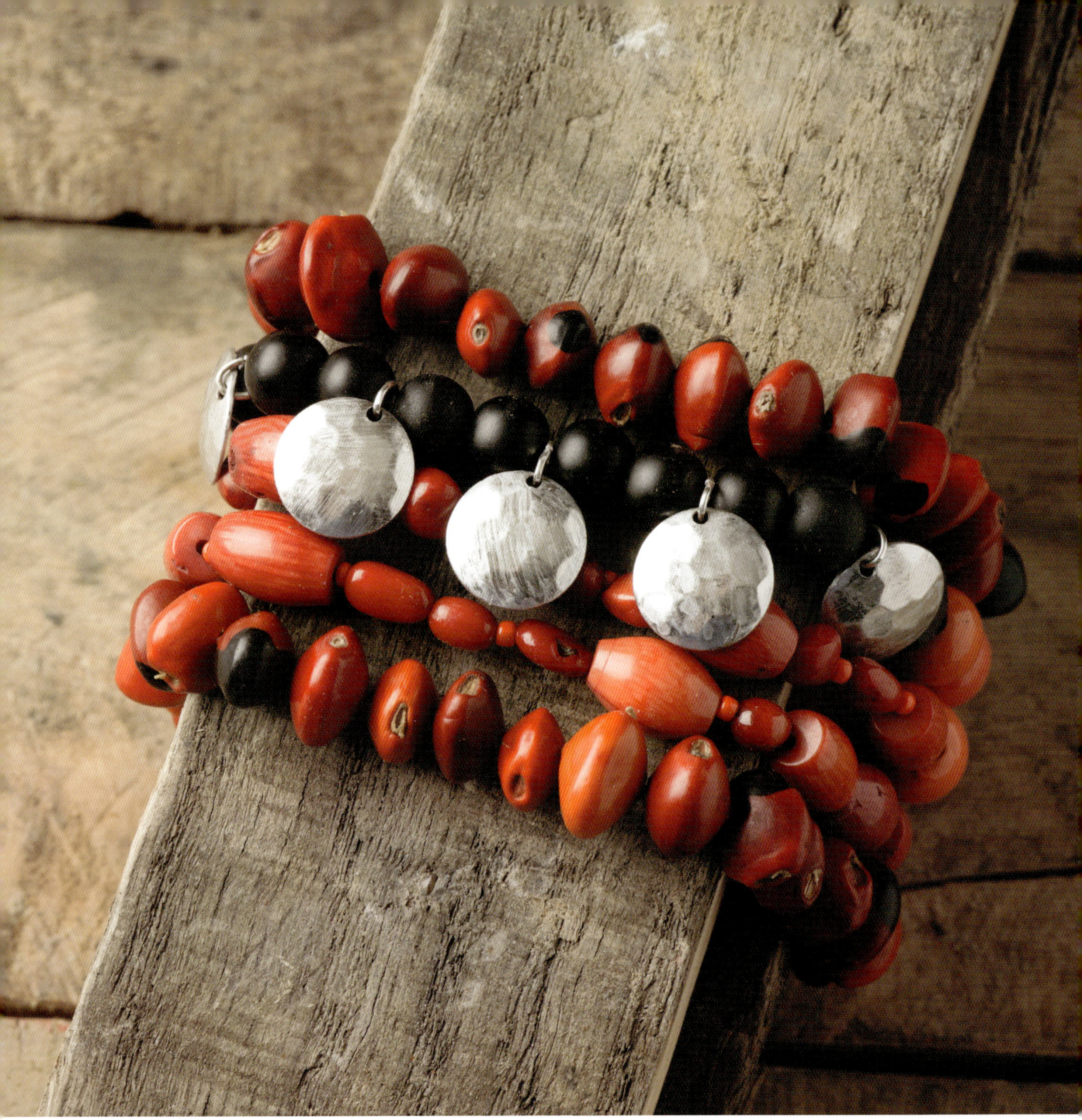
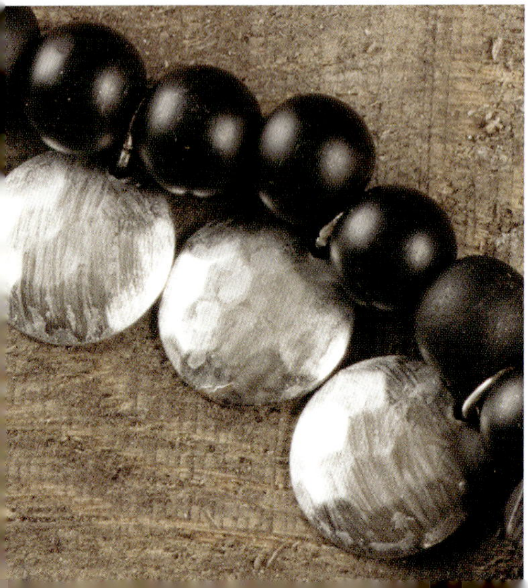
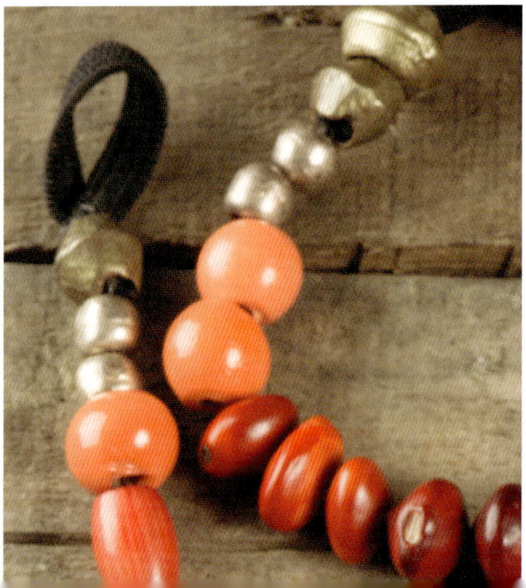
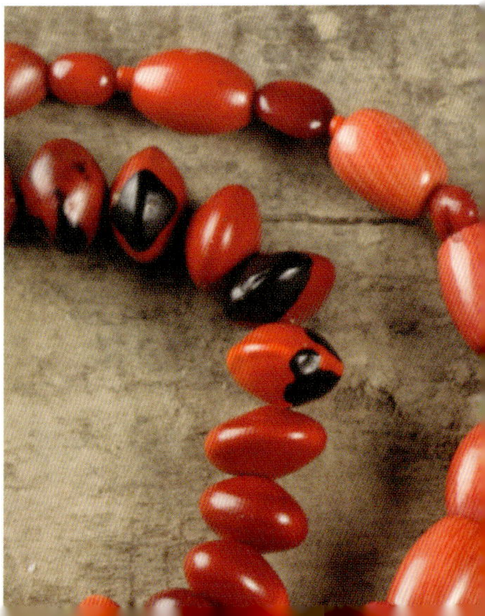

WESTERN AMAZONIA
Shipibo Wrap Bracelet

After trekking and camping the Inca Trail outside of Cuzco, we travel down to Puerto Maldonado. Here, in the lowlands of Peru, we enter the Amazon Basin. It is lush and hot and humid, but finally, finally, after ten days in the mountains, I can draw a full breath.

Walking through town, I see a Shipibo woman selling the coolest embroidered textiles. They're like nothing I've ever seen before, and after two days I am able to find someone who speaks Shipibo and can help me ask her about them. "She says that when she was growing up, all the women worked on a piece together. Now she makes these herself and sells them to tourists," he translates. Tracing my finger over the design, I am struck by how simple the concept is: it's a labyrinth. A warren of little lines and easy angles. And the colors! So simple. This one is just charcoal lines on a paprika-orange background. The two simple colors are stunning together, with a candid contrast that makes an intrepid design. And the maze-like, serpentine pattern is hypnotic.

"It reminds me of a circuit board!" I exclaim. My translator frowns quizzically, disapprovingly. "Well, not so much like a circuit board," I recant. I clear my throat. "Would you ask her where the designs come from?" After a brief exchange he relays, "She says it is from *ayahuasca*." "What's that?" I ask. "Ayahuasca is a plant in the tea they drink." Oh. I don't understand how a plant explains the design, but I don't want to waste any more of my translator's time and patience. Seeing my confusion, he quietly, kindly, divulges, "It's a . . . psychedelic tea." Oh! I get it now.

The long wrap design of this bracelet is very straightforward, with lots of cool elements. *Huayruro* seeds echo the red/black palette found in Shipibo textiles, while the silver disc pendants look a lot like the septum (nose) rings that some Shipibo men wear. As a very subtle detail, I worked a Morse code message into the red coral bead portion. It reads, "terra incognita," which means "unknown land" in Latin. This phrase appears on ancient maps to show regions unexplored and unknown, and Western Amazonia, to this day, is such a land. The coral barrels stand in for the "dashes," while the coral nuggets make nice "dots."

MATERIALS

54 red-and-black 10×6mm huayruro seeds

15 salmon 10mm Turkish glass rounds

10 matte black 8mm druks

4 silver seamed 6mm African rounds

2 cast brass 10×8 bicones

1 cast brass 12×8mm donut

2 black bone 10mm cornerless cubes

17 red coral 12×8mm barrels (A)

15 red coral 6mm nuggets (B)

14 orange opaque 11º seed beads (C)

5 silver hammered 16mm discs

5 silver 6×4mm oval jump rings

1 black 35×12mm wooden toggle

8" (20 cm) black ¼" (6 mm) elastic

48" (122 cm) black FireLine braided bead thread

G-S Hypo Cement adhesive

TOOLS

Scissors

Beading needle

Two pliers (for opening and closing jump rings)

FINISHED SIZE

38" (96.5 cm) long. Wraps five times for bracelet or once or twice for necklace.

1. With scissors, cut elastic into two 4" (10 cm) lengths. Make a loop with one length and tie with an overhand knot (see page 136). Loop should be about ½" (1.3 cm) across. Trim ends, leaving 5/32" (4mm) tails.

2. With second length, repeat Step 1, but first thread elastic through both holes of toggle, then make loop, and tie and cut (**Figure 1**).

3. With two pairs of pliers, open 5 oval jump rings. Add 1 hammered disc to 1 jump ring and close with pliers to make one pendant. Repeat four times for remaining discs.

4. Thread beading needle with length of thread. Pass thread through knot of elastic loop several times to secure, ending with thread exiting knot by the cut ends (**Figure 2**).

5. String onto thread:

   1 cast brass bicone, 2 silver African rounds, 1 glass round

   A, C, B, C, B, A, B, C, B, A, B, C, B, A, 2C, 2B, C, A, B, C, A, B, A, B, C, 3A, C, 2A, B, C, A, B, C, 2B, C, A, C, 3A

   6 ceramic rounds, 28 huayruro seeds, 3 glass rounds

   1 black bone cube, 1 black druk, 1 hammered disc pendant (2 black druks, 1 hammered pendant) four times, 1 black druk, and 1 black bone cube

   3 ceramic rounds, 26 huayruro seeds, 2 glass rounds, 2 silver African rounds, 1 cast brass bicone, 1 cast brass donut

6. Leaving ½" (1.3 cm) of slack on beaded portion, pass thread through knot of elastic loop with toggle several times to secure, entering knot by cut ends. Tie a few tiny knots and cut thread.

7. Position cast brass bicone near elastic loop to cover elastic knot (**Figure 3**). Secure with a few drops of adhesive and let dry. Position cast brass donut near elastic loop on toggle end to cover elastic knot (**Figure 4**). Secure with a few drops of adhesive and let dry.

Fig. 1

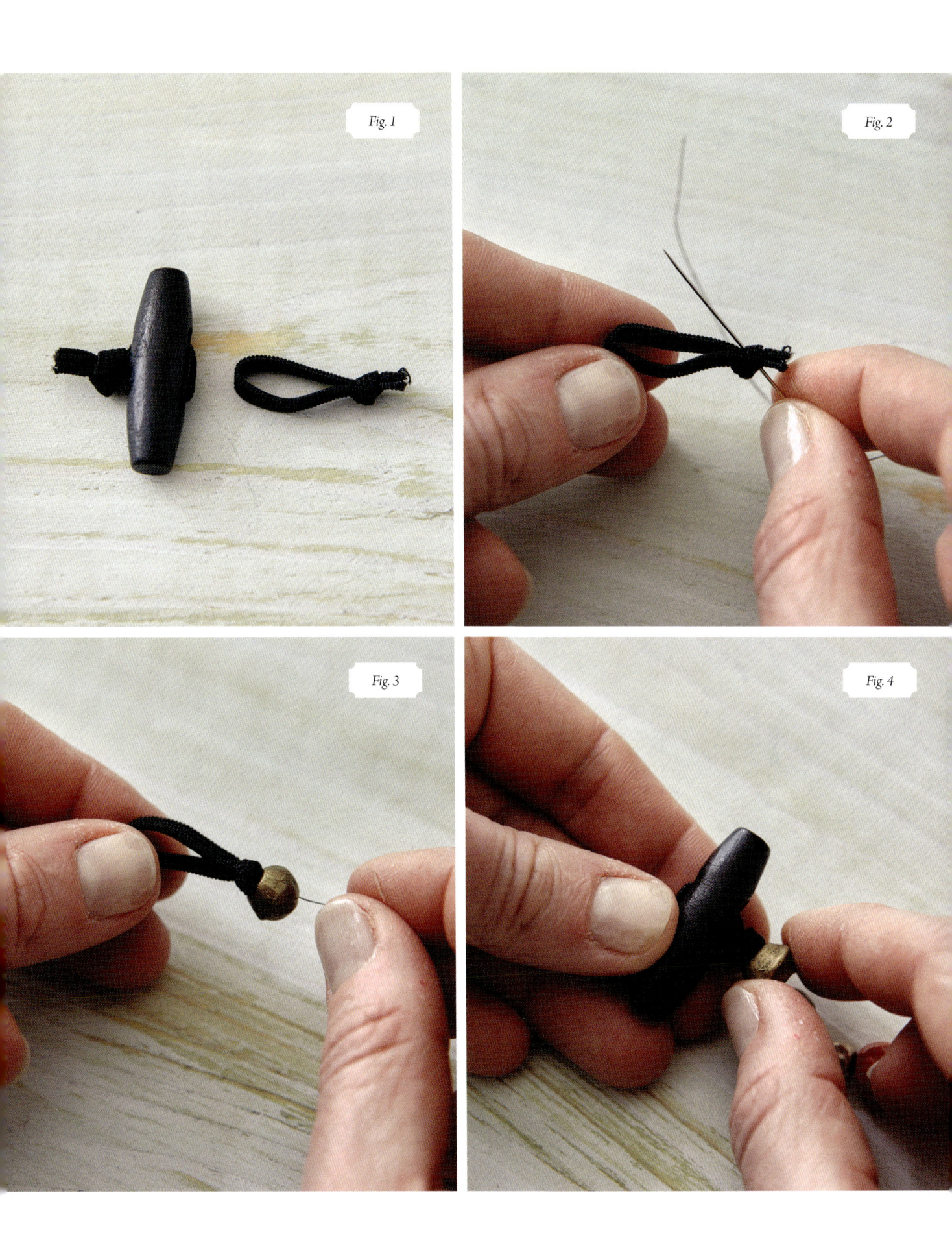

Fig. 2

Fig. 3

Fig. 4

WESTERN AMAZONIA: SHIPIBO WRAP BRACELET ∽ 119

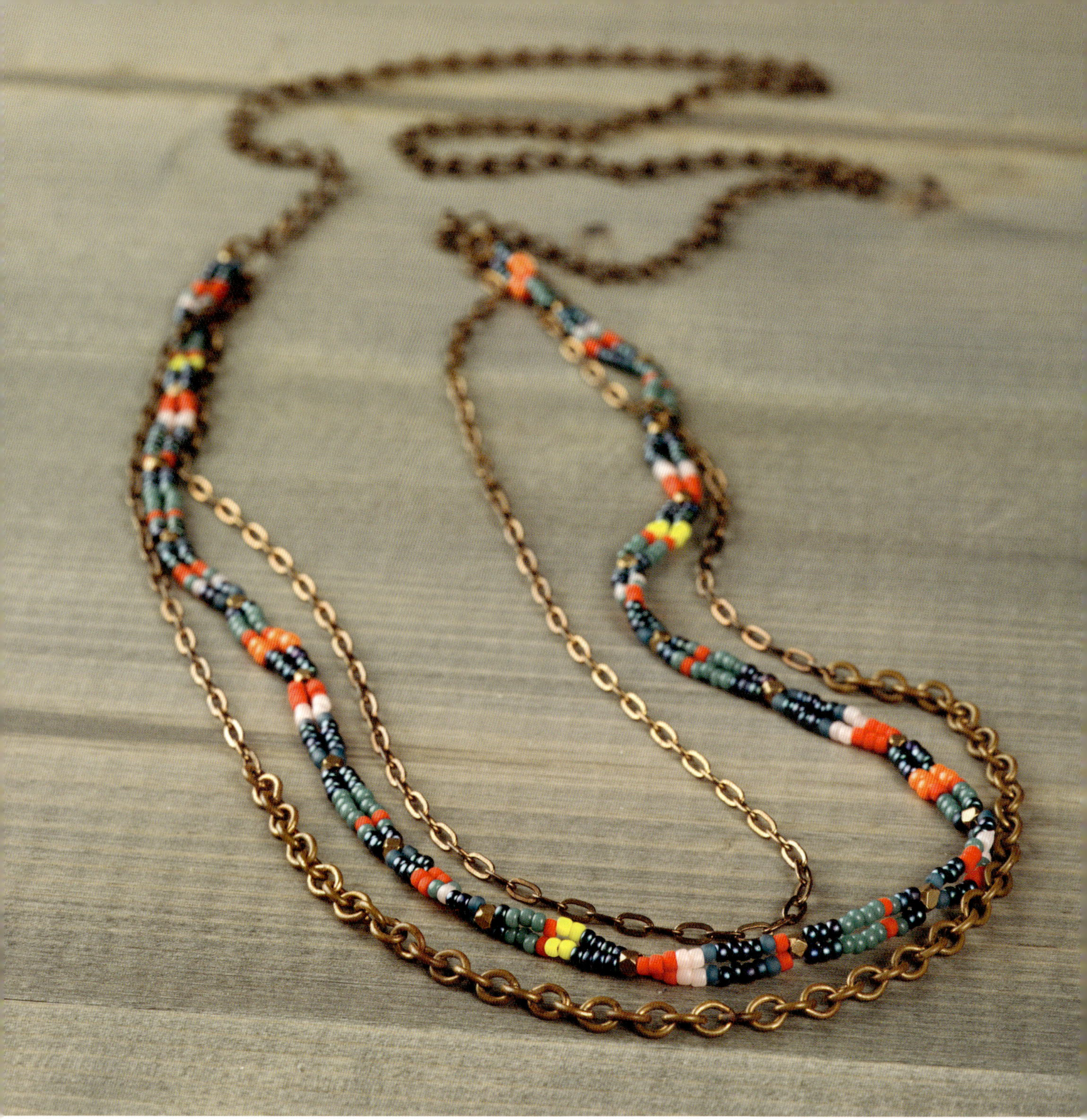

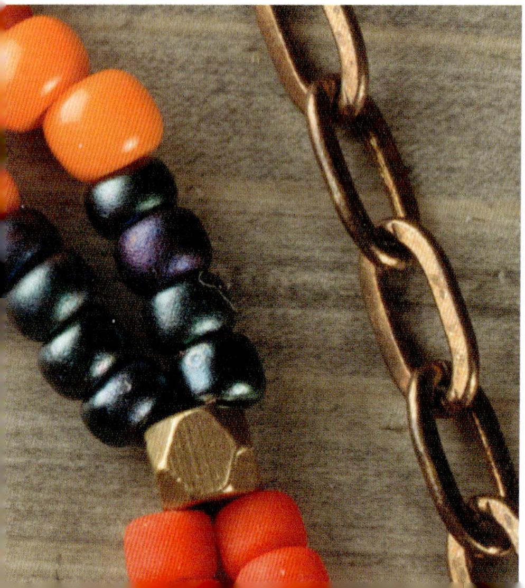

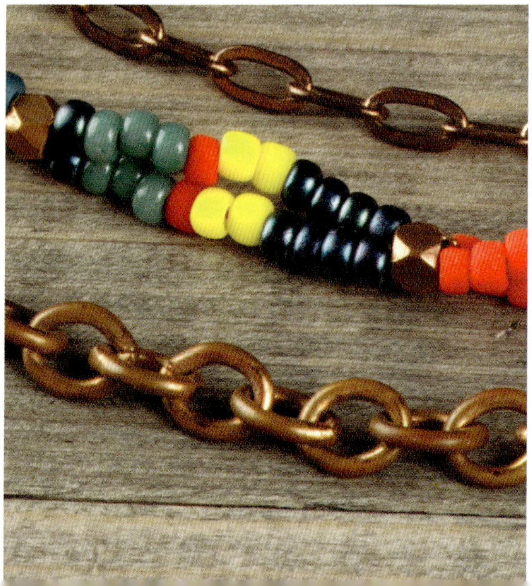

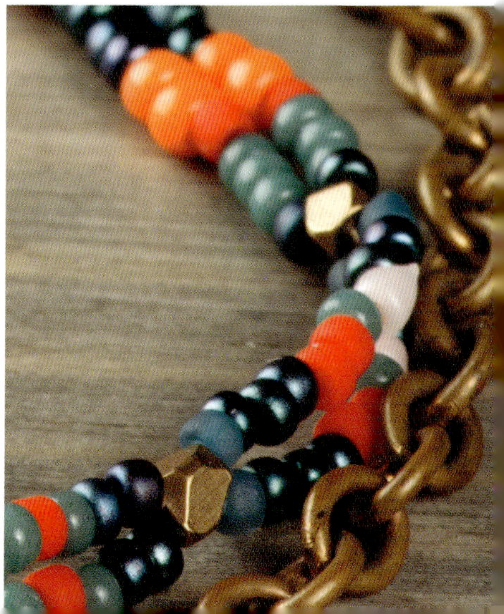

GUATEMALA
Mayan Weaving Necklace

As the motorboat powers across, blue volcanoes loom on the other side of this highland lake, misty clouds shrouding their unseen peaks. I am crossing Lago Atitlán to meet Jimena del Rosario Morales, the master weaver who will teach me traditional Guatemalan weaving. She is a small, older woman dressed traditionally in a colorful skirt and heavily embroidered *huipil* blouse. Her shiny black hair is piled high and wrapped in a red woven *cinta* ribbon.

A smoky smell wafts from inside the concrete-block home, while dogs and a rooster amble around the yard. I ask her if she made the beautiful blouse she's wearing. "Sí, sí!" she answers with a hint of exasperation, as if to say, "Who else would have made it?!" The blouse is a dazzling masterpiece, elaborately woven with technicolored stripes, and figures of chevrons and diamonds and birds, and dark stripes. She shows me some red thread that she has already dyed, and I wonder what dye makes such a rich red. *"Y lo que hace que este color? Este rojo?"* I ask. "Cochineal," she answers.

On the backstrap loom that hangs from a tree, Jimena weaves a pattern busy with color with intricate designs of animals and stripes and zigzags. Borders of diamonds and chevrons rise up along each side, while the field in between boasts new patterns and pictures every inch or so. With nimble fingers that know the pattern, Jimena picks up warp threads, just a few at a time, and passes a weft thread underneath. Quickly and meticulously she works this line of her pattern across the hundreds of warp threads. Tiny little floats of threads color the pattern as it rises up the warp threads like a painted phoenix. At the end of the row, she unceremoniously beats down the threads with the beater. Then she begins a new line, one with a new design, with new thread counts. How on earth does she remember all this?!

Because of its intrinsic busyness, I feel a little goes a long way when interpreting Guatemalan weaving for jewelry. Two strands of seed beads represent a stripy section of weaving and interpret the complex design well. Pops of red and chartreuse and orange play well with the more sedate blue-teal palette and the warmth of the chain. Customize the design concept to suit your taste. Use a different color palette, or use just one color of seed beads for a simple but stunning look.

MATERIALS

210 metallic iris blue 11º seed beads (A)

12 opaque orange 11º seed beads (B)

98 opaque teal 11º seed beads (C)

44 turquoise-lined transparent matte iolite 11º seed beads (D)

80 opaque matte red 11º seed beads (E)

32 matte transparent Ceylon pink 11º seed beads (F)

12 matte opaque dandelion yellow 11º seed beads (G)

23 antiqued brass 2.5mm cornerless cubes (H)

60" (152.5 cm) red beading thread

24" (61 cm) antiqued brass 4.5×2mm flat-link chain

17" (43 cm) antiqued brass bicycle chain

7" (18 cm) antiqued brass 4×5mm round oval chain

2 antiqued brass 4mm jump rings

G-S Hypo Cement adhesive

TOOLS

Tape

Wire cutters

Scissors

Two pairs of pliers (for opening and closing jump rings and links)

FINISHED SIZE

31"–34" (79–86.5 cm).

Notes: Whenever a 2.5mm antiqued brass cornerless cube appears in the pattern, both threads will pass through this one bead, while all seed bead sections are worked as two individual strands.

When laying out the beaded strand to attach to the chain, let it twist a few times naturally.

1. With scissors, cut beading thread into two 30" (76 cm) sections. Tie an overhand knot (see page 136) about 4" (10 cm) from one end and tape to surface.

2. Taking note that glass seed beads are worked on individual strands of beading thread, and cornerless cubes are strung onto both threads together, string beads according to the following pattern. Repeat entire pattern three times:
   H
   D, 3A, 2E, C, F, 2A, D
   H
   A, 3C, E, 2G, 4A
   H
   4E, 2F, D, 4A, D, E
   H
   3A, 4C, E, C, 2A
   H
   D, 3A, 2E, C, F, 2A, D
   H
   A, 3C, E, 2B, 4A
   H
   3E, 2F, D, 4A, D
   H
   3A, 4C, E, C, 2A
   (**Figure 1**)

   When pattern is complete, tie an overhand knot and string one 2.5mm cornerless cube to cover knot (**Figure 2**).

3. Pass both threads of beaded section through one 4mm jump ring and tie a double knot close to cornerless cube. Thread ends through cornerless cube to cover knot. Repeat for second end of beaded section and second 4mm jump ring. Apply a drop of adhesive over knots. With scissors, cut close when dry.

Fig. 1

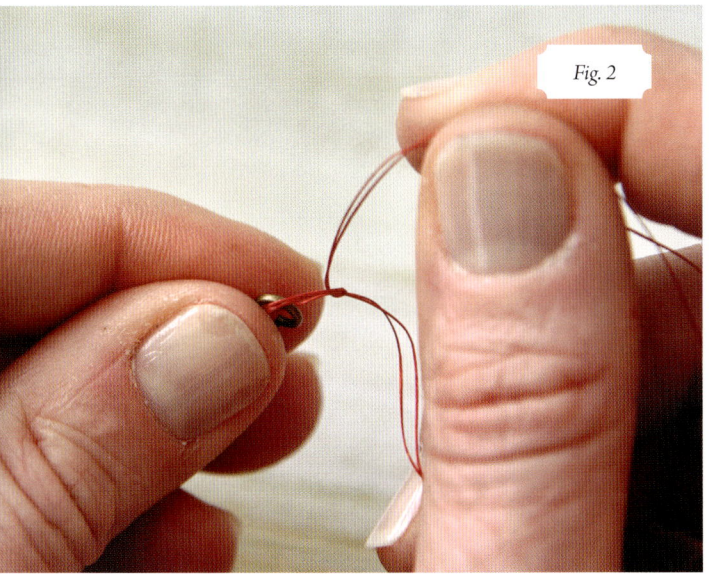

Fig. 2

Fig. 3

4. With wire cutters, cut flat-link chain into the following lengths: one 14" (35.5 cm) length and two 5" (12.5 cm) lengths.

5. With two pairs of pliers, open end links of round-link chain. Attach one end of round-link chain to one end of 5" (12.5 cm) flat-link chain length. Repeat for second end of round chain and second 5" length of flat-link chain so that round-link chain section is in the center of flat-link chain sections.

6. Lay out center sections in graduated order: 14" (35.5 cm) length of flat-link chain, beaded section, 17" (43cm) length of flat-link/round-link section.

7. With two pairs of pliers, open the end link of 14" (35.5 cm) flat-link length and 17" (43 cm) flat/round-link section and attach to 4mm jump ring, keeping layers in order (**Figure 3**). Close links. Repeat for second ends of chain lengths.

8. With two pairs of pliers, open one 4mm jump ring and attach to one end of 17" (43 cm) bicycle-link chain, keeping layers in order. Close ring. Repeat for second 4mm jump ring and end of bicycle-chain length.

GUATEMALA: MAYAN WEAVING NECKLACE ~ 123

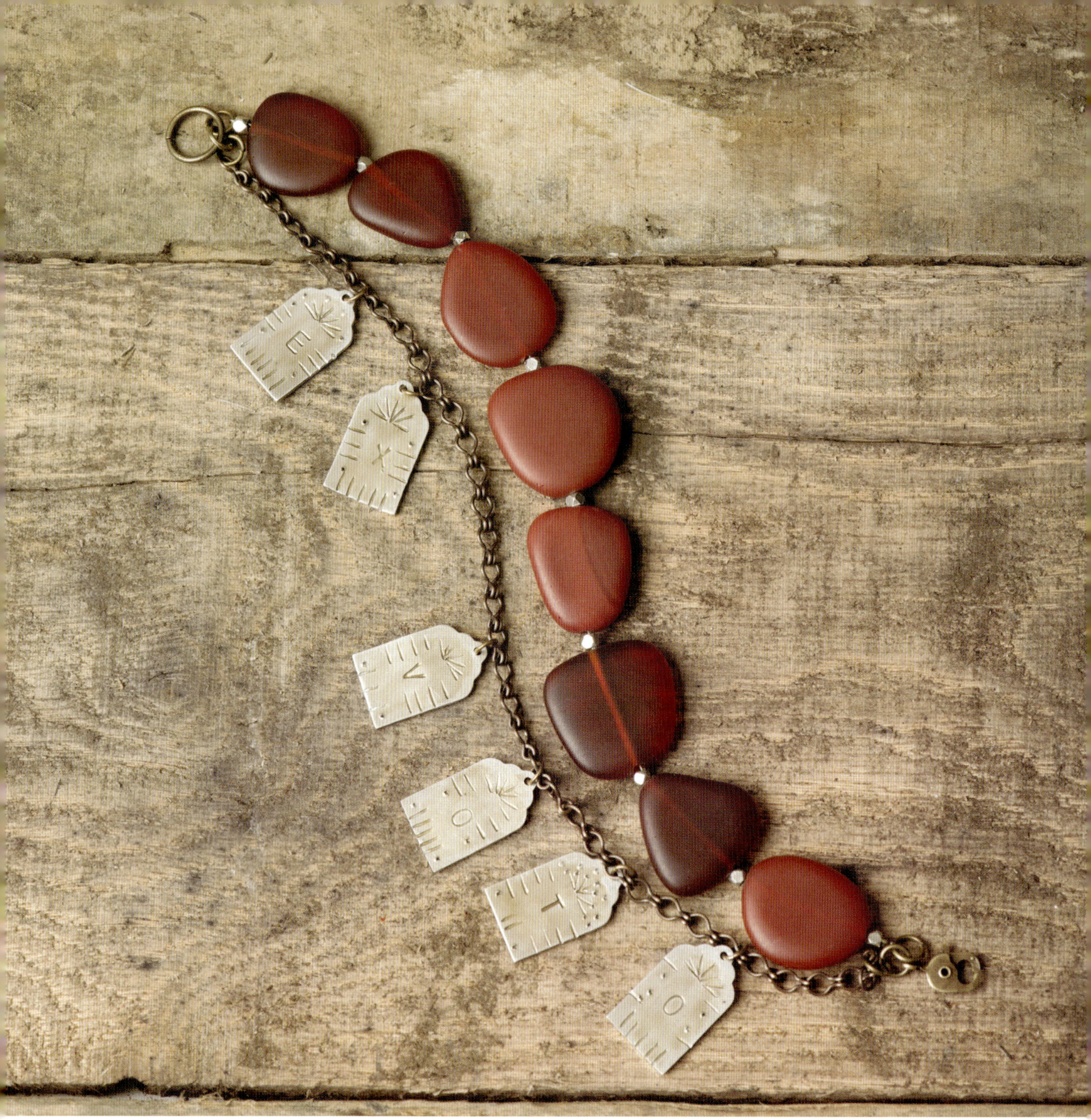

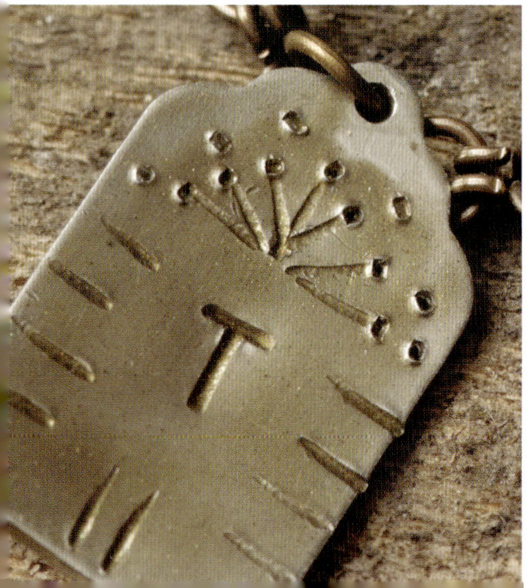

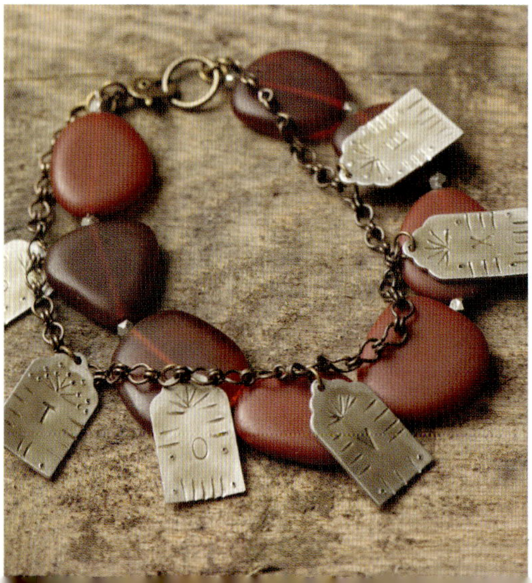

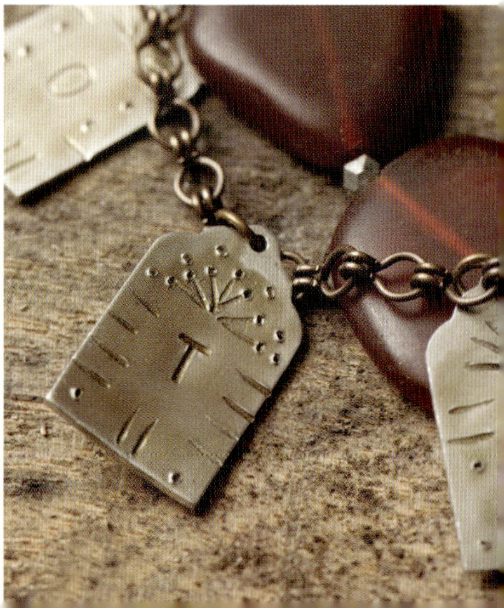

OAXACA
Retablo Charm Bracelet

Isabel brings me the *retablo* from the kitchen. It's a small tin shrine with scalloped demilune sides and a crown-like top, darkened with the patina of cooking smoke and fingerprints. In the center is an image of La Virgen de Guadalupe. Her figure is meek—head gently tilting down—while a wildly yellow, spiky corona radiates from her.

"My grandfather worked in the silver mines. He was engaged to the most beautiful girl in town, Carolina, who sold tortillas in the square. My grandfather loved her very much and used to walk her home every day. One day there was an accident at the mine, and my grandfather's mineshaft started to collapse. A beam fell on my grandfather's leg, trapping him. He called to his friend José to get help and tell Carolina that he would be late. But José loved Carolina too. So José did not get help but went to Carolina. As he walked her home, José told her that my grandfather had run off with another woman. Carolina wept bitterly.

"But meanwhile the *jefe* rescued my grandfather and got a doctor, who set my grandfather's broken leg. My grandfather lay in a bed for several weeks in the boss's house. But as his leg was healing, his heart was breaking for Carolina. Finally he could take it no longer, so he dragged himself a mile to the church, pulling his broken leg behind him. When he got to the church he fell on his face before La Virgen and cried, 'Heal my leg and heal my broken heart!' Suddenly his leg was healed, and when he looked up, there was a bouquet of poinsettias before him. He jumped up and ran to Carolina. He told her all that happened and gave her the flowers that La Virgen had given him. Then they walked to the church and got married that very day.

"This is the retablo that my grandfather bought the next day in devotion to La Virgen for healing his leg and giving him Carolina, my grandmother."

The six shrine-shaped charms on this bracelet spell out "EX VOTO"—a religious offering to a saint out of gratitude. After embellishing the shrine tags, I applied two uneven coats of translucent bronze nail polish to "warm up" the bright aluminum finish of the tags and make them look more like a real retablo. The red sea-glass strand is a nod to poinsettias, which are a traditional part of the La Virgen de Guadalupe story.

MATERIALS

8 red sea glass flat 20mm nugget beads

7" (18 cm) antiqued brass 5mm bicycle chain

1 antiqued brass 12mm pincher-style clasp

9 silver 2.5mm cornerless cubes

6 aluminum 21×12mm tag charms

6 antiqued brass 4mm open round jump rings

6 antiqued brass 5mm open round jump rings

1 antiqued brass 10mm open round jump ring

12" (30.5 cm) flexible beading wire

2 antiqued brass 2mm crimp beads

Translucent bronze nail polish

TOOLS

Small flat screwdriver

Nail

Hammer

5mm metal alphabet stamping set

Crimping pliers

Wire cutter

Two pairs of pliers (for opening and closing jump rings)

FINISHED SIZE

8" (20.5 cm) long.

1. Place 1 aluminum tag on bench block. With screwdriver and hammer, hammer line designs onto tag, following photo on page 124 (**Figure 1**). Repeat five more times for remaining aluminum tags.

2. With nail and hammer, hammer dot designs onto tag, following pattern (**Figure 2**). Repeat five more times for remaining aluminum tags.

3. With letter set and hammer, hammer E onto center of tag (**Figure 3**). Repeat with X, V, O, T, and O for remaining aluminum tags.

4. With nail polish brush, brush one irregular layer of nail polish onto tags (**Figure 4**). When dry, repeat for back side. Apply a second coat to both front and back of tags.

5. Space tags evenly on chain, leaving a space between the X and V. Attach tags with 4mm jump rings, making sure to attach tags to same side of chain.

6. Pass one end of flexible beading wire through crimp bead, through 1 antiqued brass 5mm jump ring, and back through crimp bead. Crimp with crimping pliers.

7. Onto flexible beading wire, string [1 silver 2.5mm cornerless cube and 1 flat red sea-glass nugget] eight times, ending with 1 silver 2.5mm cornerless cube.

8. Pass second end of flexible beading wire through crimp bead, through 1 antiqued brass 5mm jump ring, and back through crimp bead. Crimp with crimping pliers.

9. Attach one 5mm jump ring to each end of chain.

10. Align red glass-nugget and chain strands on work surface. With two pairs of pliers, open fifth 5mm jump ring and attach to last jump ring on one end of each strand. The fifth jump ring attaches the two strands together. Close jump ring. Repeat with sixth 5mm jump ring on other end of strands.

11. With two pliers, open fifth 5mm jump ring and attach to 10mm jump ring. With pliers, close ring. With two pliers, open sixth 5mm jump ring and attach to clasp. With pliers, close ring.

Fig. 1

Fig. 2

Fig. 3

Fig. 4

Oaxaca: Retablo Charm Bracelet ~ 127

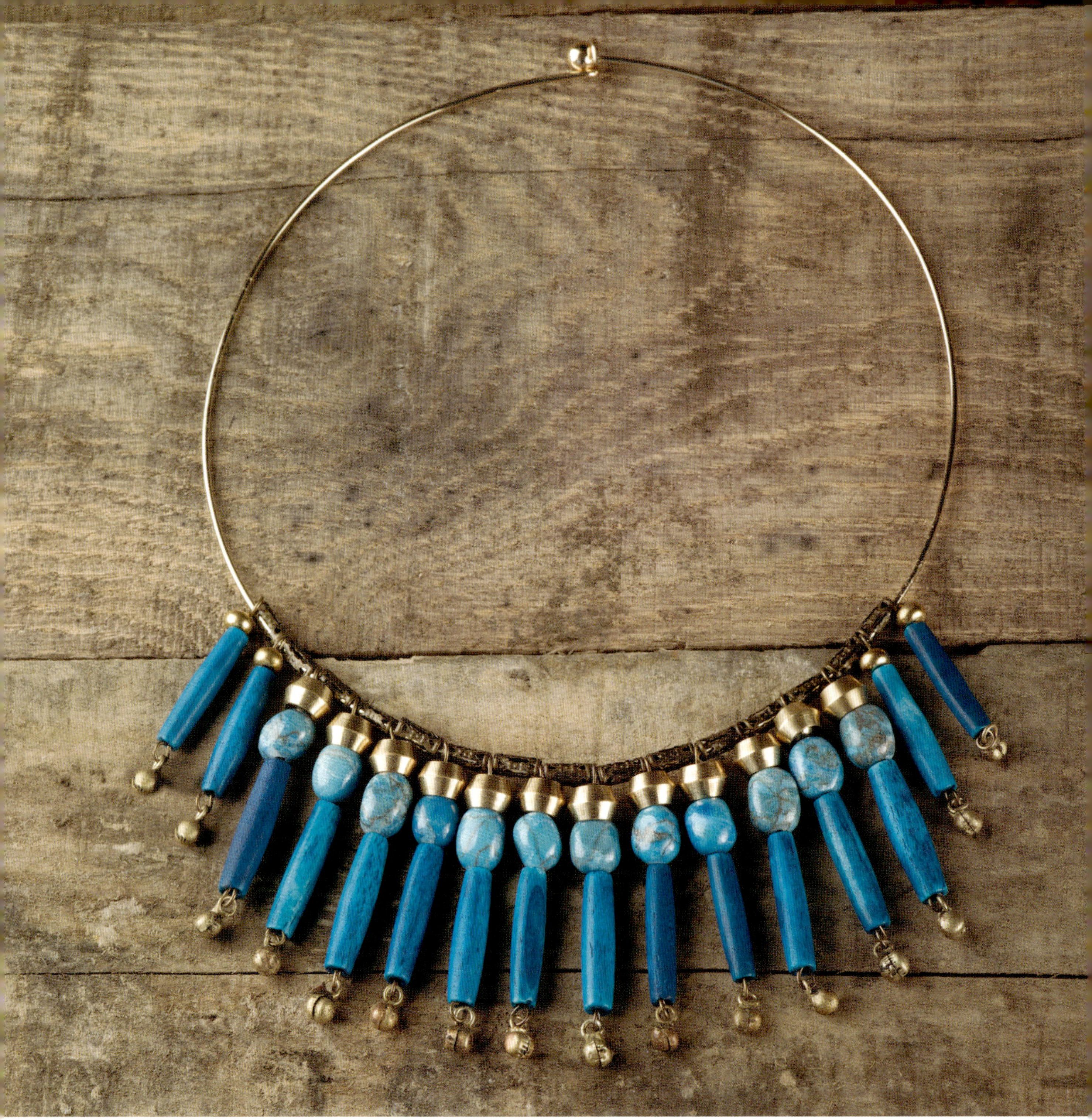
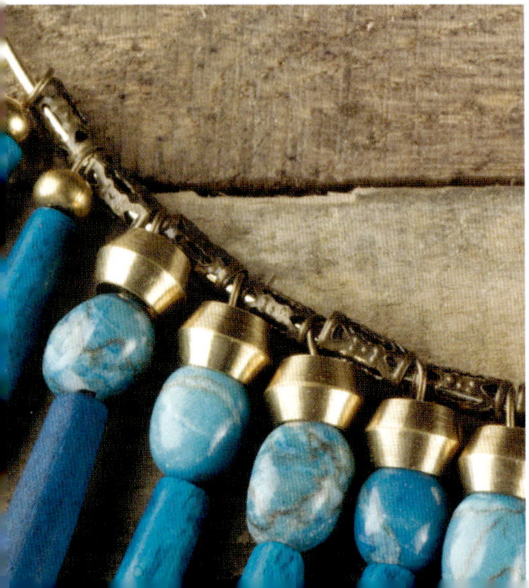
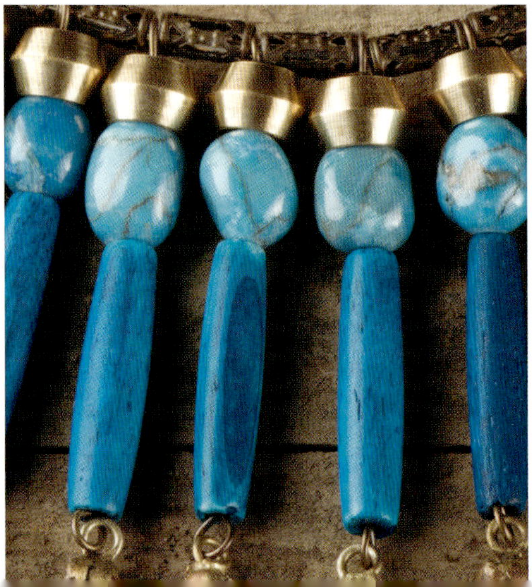
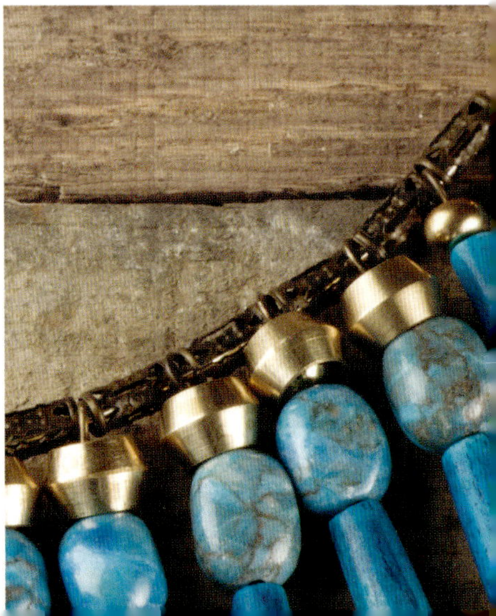

PERU
Incan Quipu Necklace

After bitter struggles and the ravage of disease, Spanish viceroy Francisco de Toledo executed Túpac Amaru, the last Incan emperor, in a public square in Vilcabamba in 1572. The great Incan Empire was defeated. With the conquest of the Incan people, the Spanish were now able to establish their own dominion and pursue their mission: amassing the fabled gold of *Nuevo Mundo*.

To colonize Peru, the Spanish systematically destroyed any strongholds of Incan culture and replaced them with Spanish customs. Temples became Catholic churches, and the Quechua language submitted to Spanish. And as they searched towns for stores of gold and riches, the Spanish also "cleaned house" to remove Incan holdovers. Like the knotted *quipus*, found in every home. But what the Spanish didn't know was that these quipus were actually an advanced accounting system that reported the wealth of the empire. Quipus, admittedly, don't look like much. A base string with strands and strands of colored cotton cords, knotted here and there. Maybe a decoration, or a belt? But through the precise placement and type of knots, the quipus accurately documented each Incan's economic worth. If the Spanish had only known! There before them was the treasury log of the Incans' vast wealth. Who knows how much gold the Incans were able to hold back from their conquerors?

At a festival in Cuzco, I watched Quechua processions and pageantry for two days from a café table. The women were dressed delightfully in traditional dress: woven shawls, layers of bright red skirts, and Incan *montera* hats. The men were dressed more Western than Quechua, I thought. But I noticed that several men had quipus slung over one shoulder, and I had to smile.

Sticking it to the man, Inca style.

This necklace is a simple interpretation of traditional quipus. The design is straightforward and very easy to elaborate on: experiment with beads, pendants, fibers, and chain. For this project, I took bone beads and dyed them with household dye. The effect is bold and bright, as bone takes the dye very well. And with a myriad of colors to choose from, you can pull together your own custom palette.

MATERIALS

16 bone 25×7mm tubes

12 turquoise 14mm nuggets

12 brass 8×10mm bicones

16 brass 5mm rounds

4 gold-plated 4×3mm rondelles

15 antiqued brass 10×4mm filigree tubes

16 antiqued brass 5mm clapperless bells

16 antiqued brass 3" (7.5 cm) eye pins

1 gold-plated 5½" (14 cm) neck ring

Fabric dye

Matte sealer

Disposable container

Newspaper

Note: 5mm brass rounds do not show in final design. They are used to stabilize the large holes of the brass bicones.

TOOLS

Round-nose pliers

Two pairs of flat-nose pliers (for opening and closing eye pins)

Wire cutters

FINISHED SIZE

5½" (14 cm) diameter.

---

1. In disposable container, prepare fabric dye according to package directions, diluting as desired. Place bone beads in dyebath and leave until color is as saturated as desired.

2. When dyed, remove from dyebath and rinse with water until water runs clear. Dry completely on terry towel (**Figure 1**). Place beads on newspaper. In a well-ventilated area, spray a coat of matte sealer on beads. Turn beads and spray until beads are completely sealed.

3. With two pairs of pliers, open loop on 1 eye pin. Attach antiqued brass bell (**Figure 2**). With pliers, close loop. Repeat for each eye pin.

4. To make long dangles: onto 1 eye pin, string 1 bone tube, 1 turquoise nugget, one 5mm brass round, and 1 brass bicone (**Figure 3**). (The brass round will not show but will help keep the bicone in place [**Figure 4**]). With wire cutters, cut pin 12mm past round. With round-nose pliers, form a simple loop (see page 134; **Figure 5**). Repeat to make 12 eye pins.

5. To make medium dangles: onto 1 eye pin, string 1 bone tube and 1 brass rondelle. With wire cutters, cut pin 12mm past rondelle. With round-nose pliers, form a simple loop. Repeat to make 4 eye pins.

6. Unscrew ball end of neck ring. String onto neck ring [1 medium dangle, 1 filigree tube] two times, [1 long dangle, 1 filigree tube] twelve times, 1 medium dangle, 1 filigree tube, and 1 medium dangle (**Figure 6**). Screw ball end back on neck ring.

7. Adjust shape of neck ring as needed.

Fig. 1

Fig. 2

Fig. 3

Fig. 4

Fig. 5

Fig. 6

Peru: Incan Quipu Necklace ⁓ 131

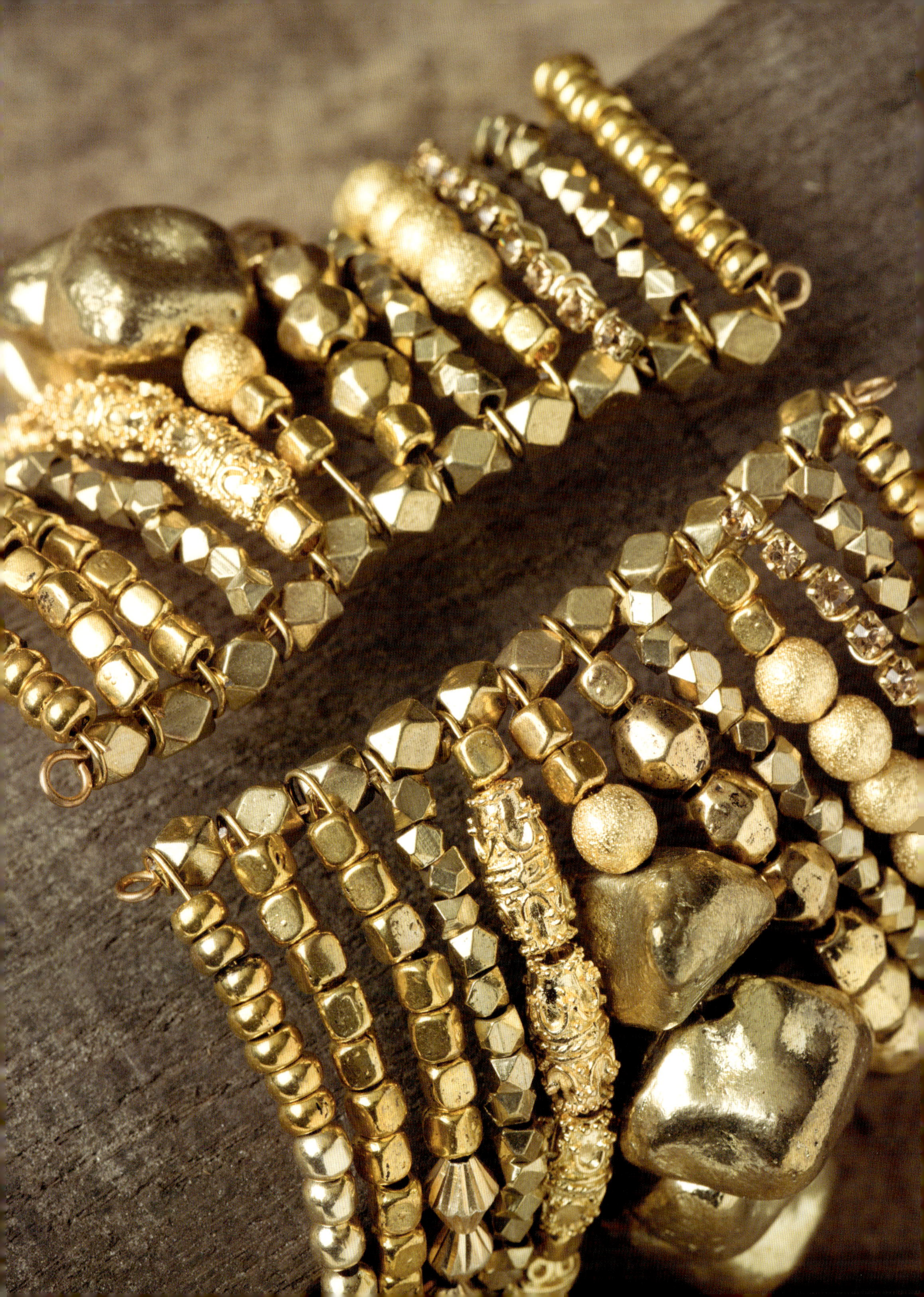

HELPFUL TECHNIQUES

There are a few techniques that are used throughout the projects. Here are some tips in case you're not familiar with them or need a reminder.

Opening and Closing Jump Rings

Using two pliers of your choice, hold the jump ring with the opening visible between the pliers. Gently open the jump ring by twisting the two ends apart (**Figure 1**). To close, gently twist the ends back together, adding a little bit of pressure so that the ends "click" as they pass each other and settle in place. Jump ring ends should make a smooth join. Don't open and close jump rings too often, as this will weaken the jump ring in time. Do not open jump rings by pulling them apart (**Figure 2**).

Fig. 1 — *Do*

Fig. 2 — *Don't*

Crimping Crimp Beads

After passing flexible beading wire through the crimp bead, through the project (usually a jump ring; **Figure 1**), and back through the crimp bead, position the crimp bead where you want it. With the flat part of crimping pliers, gently squeeze the crimp bead closed (**Figure 2**), making sure that flexible beading wire passes on each side of the crimp bead. With the pointed part of crimping pliers, firmly squeeze an indentation in the center of the crimp bead (**Figure 3**), making sure that flexible beading wire passes on either side of the indentation. With the C-shaped part of crimping pliers, slowly squeeze the crimp bead so it folds in half at the indentation (**Figure 4**). Squeeze the crimp bead a few times around.

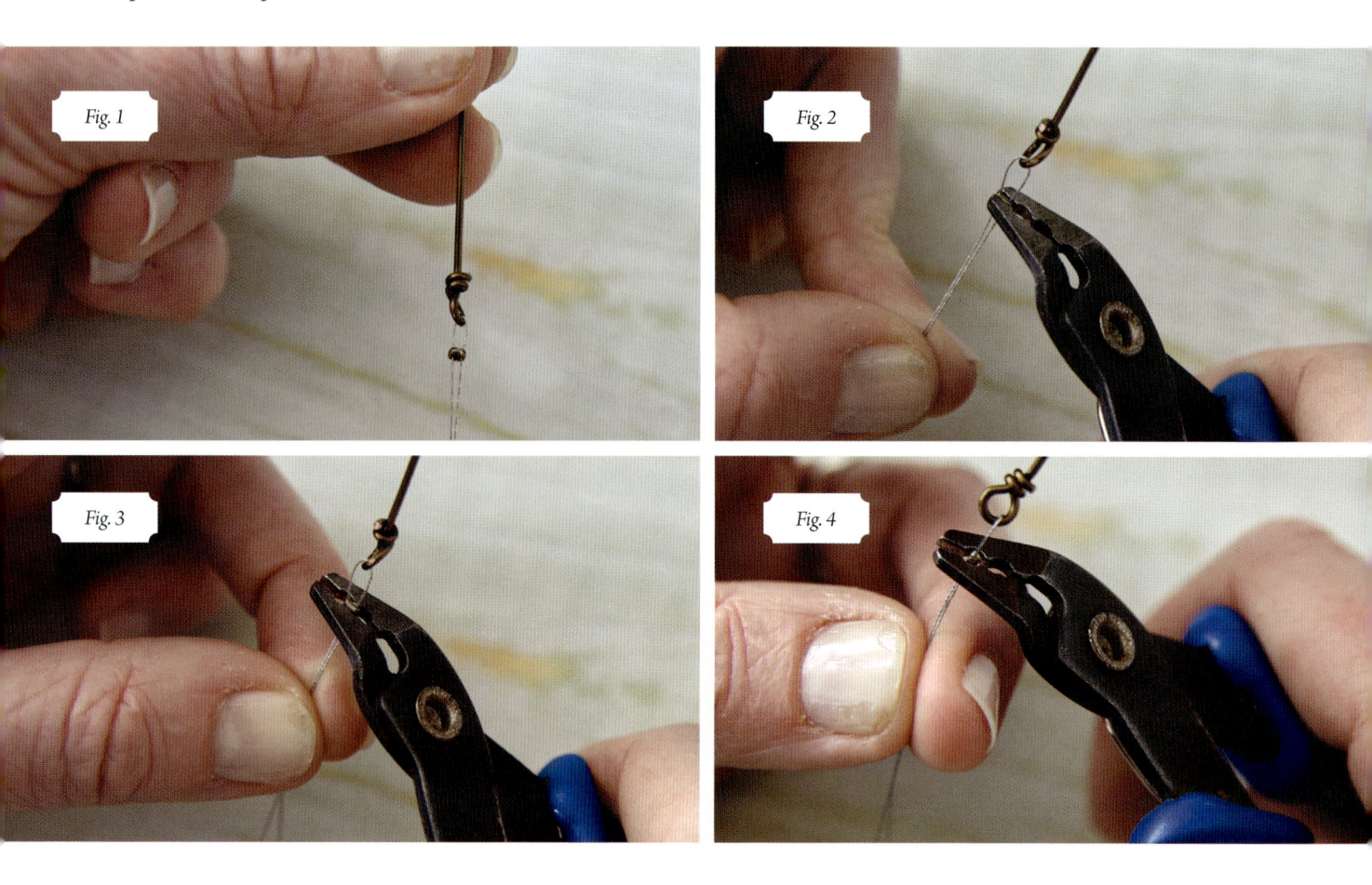

Fig. 1

Fig. 2

Fig. 3

Fig. 4

Simple Loop

With flat-nose or chain-nose pliers, make a 90-degree bend in the wire about ¼" (6 mm) from the end (**Figure 1**). Grasp the end of the wire with round-nose pliers and roll the wire until the tip meets the bend (**Figures 2 and 3**).

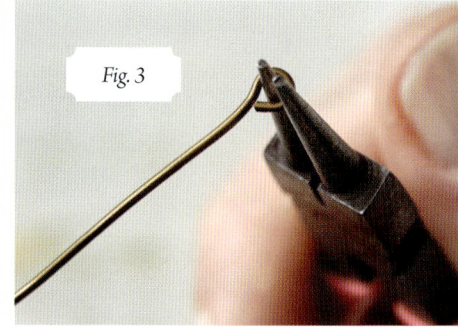

Fig. 1

Fig. 2

Fig. 3

Wrapped Loop

With flat-nose or chain-nose pliers, make a 90-degree bend in the wire about 1" (2.5 cm) from the end (**Figure 1**). Using round-nose pliers, bend the wire to create a long tail (**Figure 2**). Continuing to hold the loop with the round-nose pliers, use the flat-nose or chain-nose pliers to grasp the tail and wrap it around the wire below the loop. Wrap the wire twice or as many times as desired (**Figure 3**). Trim off any excess wire (**Figures 4 and 5**).

Fig. 1

Fig. 2

Fig. 3

Fig. 4

Fig. 5

HELPFUL TECHNIQUES ~ 135

Overhand Knot

This is one of the simplest and most versatile knots. I use it to start and finish most of my knotting projects. Make a loop with your cord. Take one end of the cord and pull it through the loop, so that it wraps around the cord (**Figure 1**). Pull the ends to tighten the knot (**Figure 2**).

For a double overhand knot, wrap the end around the cord once more before tightening.

Fig. 1

Fig. 2

Half-Hitch Knot

This is an easy knot that when done in a series creates a pretty cord. I used it in several projects. Take two lengths of cord, knot them together with an overhand knot, and tape the ends in place. Holding one strand in your left hand, take the other strand and loop it under the left-hand strand, around, and through the loop (**Figure 1**). Gently pull the right-hand strand to secure the knot (**Figure 2**). Continue creating half-hitch knots until you reach your desired length (**Figure 3**).

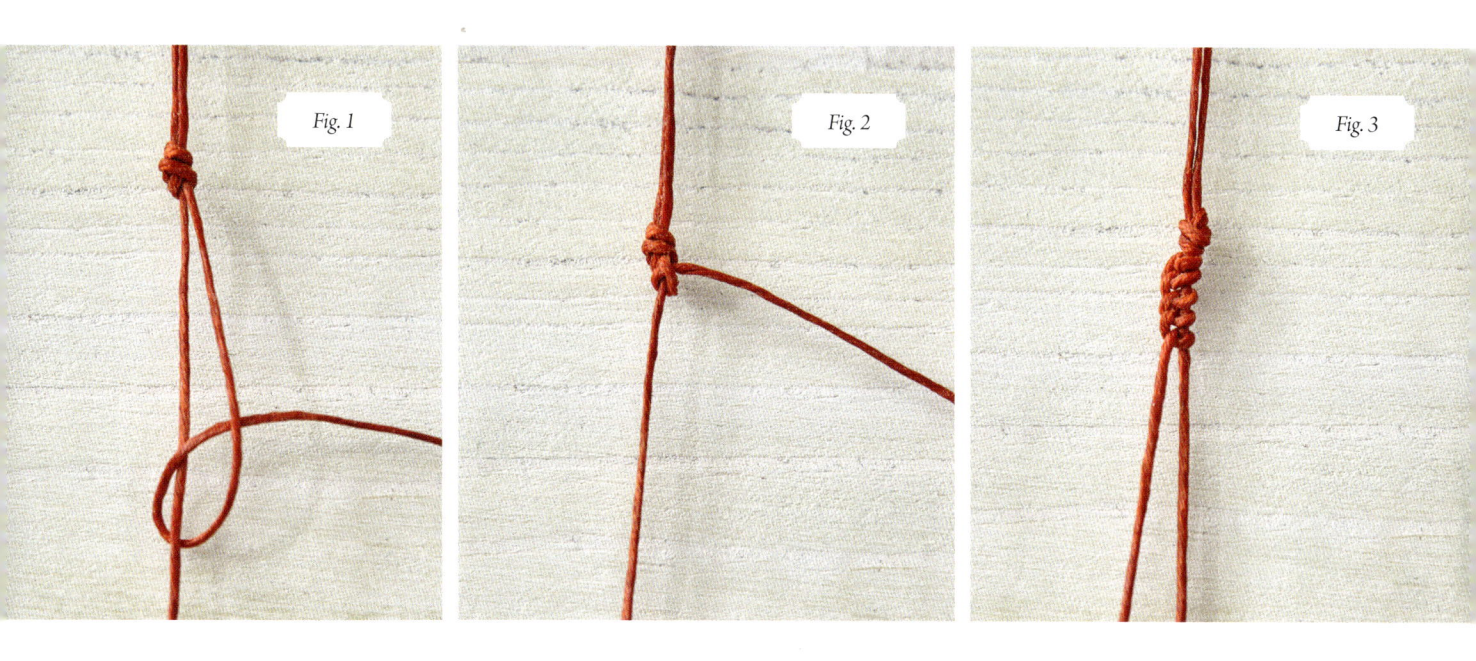

Fig. 1

Fig. 2

Fig. 3

Square Knot

Tie the right cord over the left. (**Figure 1**). Pull to tighten. Tie the left cord over the right. Pull to tighten. (**Figures 2 and 3**).

Fig. 1

Fig. 2

Fig. 3

Helpful Techniques ~ 137

RESOURCES

Celtic Knot Bracelet
Box clasp: DD From Scratch; cornerless cube beads: St. Katherine's Supply Co.; glass cubes and crimp beads: Fusion Beads; flexible beading wire: Beadalon.

Polish Pottery Earrings
Ear wires: Purity Beads; coin beads: Halcraft; heishi beads: Best Bobs; seed beads: Fusion Beads; beading thread: Beadalon.

Gaudí Tile Bracelet
Czech tiles: Raven's Journey; epoxy clay: Artbeads; bezel bracelet: Jewelry Shoppe.

Sølje Chain Maille Necklace
5/32" (4 mm) and 13/64" (5 mm) jump rings: Medieval Chainmaille; lobster clasp: Fusion Beads; chain: House of Gems; tag drops: Oz Brass Shop; 4mm jump rings: Bohemian Findings.

Vyshyvka Bracelet
Coral barrels: Stone Town; seed beads: Fusion Beads; MOP quatrefoils: DIYbeads888; cornerless cube beads and memory wire: St. Katherine's Supply Co.; Akha links: Hands of the Hills; coral rounds: Gemplus 24; brass wire: Vintaj.

Bangkok Street Necklace
Linen cord: On a Cord; all brass beads and bell: St. Katherine's Supply Co.

Raked Pebble Bracelet
Seed beads: Artbeads; rondelles: Black Bear Haversack Trading Post; clasp: Beads in Vogue; flexible beading wire and jump rings: Hobby Lobby; crimp beads: Jewelry Shoppe; quartz point: La Bead Oh; coin: The Coin Connoisseur; silver wire: Fusion Beads.

Iznik Tile Earrings
Aqua rectangles, gold-plated wire, and head pins: Hobby Lobby; cobalt square: Raven's Journey; coral barrels: Stone Town; aqua squares: Uncommon Beads; brass ID tags: Alyssabeths Vintage; ear wires: Fire Mountain Gems and Beads; raw brass square wire: Fusion Beads.

Apsara Cuff Bracelet
Rondelles, rounds, and cubes: JM Beads; bicones: Beads in Vogue; cornerless cubes and memory wire: St. Katherine's Supply Co.; textured barrels, textured rounds, and wire: Hobby Lobby; nuggets: Modern Tibet; faceted rounds: StoneAge2; stardust rounds: Stone Town; rhinestone cup chain: Eureka Crystal Beads.

Kilim Cross Earrings
Poppy jasper cubes: Uncommon Beads; gold cubes: Hobby Lobby; ear wires: apartment301; beading thread: Fusion Beads.

Azulejo Tile Necklace
Copper rings: Metamorph Supplies; lapis bicones: Afghan Tribal; jade heishi: Silk Road; seed beads and faceted rounds: Fusion Beads; cornerless cube beads and clasp: St. Katherine's Supply Co.; square brass wire: Fusion Beads; antiqued brass wire: Hobby Lobby; vintage chain: Bead Haven; jump rings: The Beady Eye.

Mehndi Hand Bracelet
All filigrees and chain: Vintage Jewelry Supplies; jump rings: The Beady Eye; lobster clasp: Hobby Lobby.

Inlaid Pearl Earrings
Marquise dangles: Yakutum; brass wire: Hobby Lobby; epoxy clay: Artbeads; quatrefoil MOP beads: DIYbeads888; pearl nuggets: Fusion Beads; seed pearls: LuxBeads; ear wires: Beading On A Budget.

Sari Gold Necklace
Cathedral glass barrels: Beadaholique; crystal bicones: Fusion Beads; gold leaf charms: The Designer's Gem; gold flower charm: Lustrous Things; head pins: Fusion Beads; chain, jump rings, and clasp: Plazko.

Print Block Earrings
Jade barrels: New Century International; bronze pyrite rondelles: Stone Town; seed beads: Cherry Blossom Surplus; coral faceted rounds: Fusion Beads; coral teardrops and beading thread: Hobby Lobby; ear wires: Silk Road.

Paper Bead Necklace
Paper bicones: Outreach Uganda; bell drops: St. Katherine's Supply Co.; crimp covers: Shipwreck Beads; lobster clasp: Hobby Lobby; beading thread: Fusion Beads; jump rings: The Beady Eye.

Maasai Cuff Bracelet
Dzi agate rounds: Queenly Global; red cubes: Wanan Beads; sunflower bicones: New Century International; rondelles and Job's tears: Fire Mountain Gems and Beads; blue cubes: Nancy Lynn Designs; green cubes: Fusion Beads; coral nuggets: Backgard; glass heishi: Silk Road; brass rice beads: Hands of the Hills; glass crows: Lyla Supplies; memory wire: St. Katherine's Supply Co.

Modern Pharaoh's Collar
Neck ring and jump rings: Hobby Lobby; tumbled glass rectangles: JP Imported Beads; cornerless cubes: St. Katherine's Supply Co.; charms: AZsupplies; eye pins: Fire Mountain Gems and Beads; chain: Yadana Beads.

Tea Glass Earrings
16-gauge wire: Artbeads; 22-gauge wire, silver rondelles, and jump rings: Fusion Beads; flower charms: Crafty Mothers.

Recycled Tin Necklace
Chain and lobster clasp: Fusion Beads; jump rings: The Beady Eye; paddle charms: Teapots & Telephones.

Frida Kahlo Earrings
Rose beads: Honey Bee Chic Boutique; brass paddles and ear wires: Beading On A Budget; wire: Hobby Lobby; varnish and acrylic paint: Deco Art.

Shipibo Wrap Bracelet
Huayruro seeds: Rafael Beads; Turkish glass rounds: Lyla Supplies; druks, seed beads, jump rings, and FireLine: Fusion Beads; silver seamed rounds, bicones, and donut: Afrobeadia; cornerless cubes: Wild Things Beads; coral barrels: Wendy Jewelry Supplies; coral nuggets: Beads Glory; hammered discs: Yummy Treasures; toggle: St. Katherine's Supply Co.; elastic: Hobby Lobby.

Mayan Weaving Necklace
Seed beads and thread: Fusion Beads; cornerless cubes: St. Katherine's Supply Co.; chain: Hobby Lobby; jump rings: The Beady Eye.

Retablo Charm Bracelet
Sea-glass nugget beads: Beads in the Sea; chain, flexible beading wire, and crimp beads: Hobby Lobby; clasp: Patina Queen Jewelry Studio; cornerless cubes: St. Katherine's Supply Co.; charms: Jewelry Shoppe; jump rings: The Beady Eye.

Incan Quipu Necklace
Bone tubes and brass bells: St. Katherine's Supply Co.; turquoise nuggets, rounds, and eye pins: Fire Mountain Gems and Beads; brass bicones: Yakutum; rondelles: Fusion Beads; filigree tubes: You Are Not the Boss of Me; neck ring and dye: Hobby Lobby; sealer: Krylon.

SUPPLIERS

Afghan Tribal Arts
afghantribalarts.etsy.com

Afrobedia
afrobeadia.etsy.com

Alyssabeths Vintage
alyssabethsvintage.etsy.com

apartment301
apartment301.com

Artbeads
artbeads.com

Ava's Bead Boutique
avasbeadboutique.etsy.com

AZsupplies
azsupplies.etsy.com

Backgard
backgard.etsy.com

Beadaholique
beadaholique.com

Beadalon
beadalon.com

Bead Haven
beadhaven.com

Beading On A Budget
beadingonabudget.etsy.com

Beads Glory
beadsglory.etsy.com

Beads in the Sea
beadsinthesea.etsy.com

Beads in Vogue
beadsinvogue.com

The Beady Eye
thebeadyeye.com

Best Bobs
bestbobs.etsy.com

Black Bear Haversack Trading Post
black-bear-haversack.com

Bohemian Findings
bohemianfindings.etsy.com

Cherry Blossom Surplus
cherryblossomsurplus.etsy.com

The Coin Connoisseur
thecoinconnoisseur.etsy.com

Crafty Mothers
craftymothers.etsy.com

DD From Scratch
ddfromscratch.etsy.com

DecoArt
decoart.com

The Designer's Gem
thedesignersgem.etsy.com

DIYbeads888
diybeads888.etsy.com

Eureka Crystal Beads
eurekacrystalbeads.com

Fire Mountain Gems and Beads
firemountaingems.com

Fusion Beads
fusionbeads.com

Gemplus 24
gemplus24.etsy.com

G-S Hypo Cement
gshypocement.com

Halcraft USA
halcraft.com

Hands of the Hills
hohbead.com

Hobby Lobby
hobbylobby.com

Honey Bee Chic Boutique
honeybeechicboutique.etsy.com

House of Gems
houseofgemsinc.etsy.com

Jewelry Shoppe
hobbylobby.com

JM Beads
jmbeads.com

JP Imported Beads
jpimportedbeads.com

Krylon
krylon.com

La Bead, Oh!
labeadoh.com

Lustrous Things
lustrousthings.etsy.com

LuxBeads
luxbeads.etsy.com

Lyla Supplies
lylasupplies.etsy.com

Medieval Chainmaille
medievalchainmaille.etsy.com

Metamorph Supplies
metamorphsupplies.etsy.com

Michaels
michaels.com

Modern Tibet
moderntibet.com

My Jewelry Shoppe
hobbylobby.com

Nancy Lynn Designs
nancylynndesigns.etsy.com

New Century International
facebook.com/New-Century-Beads-321190631351765

On a Cord
hobbylobby.com

Outreach Uganda
outreachuganda.org

Oz Brass Shop
ozbrassshop.etsy.com

Patina Queen Jewelry Studio
patinaqueen.etsy.com

Plazko
plazko.com

Purity Beads
puritysilverbeads.com

Queenly Global Trading
(972) 231-8829

Rafael Beads
rafaelbeads.etsy.com

Raven's Journey
theravenstore.com

Shipwreck Beads
shipwreckbeads.com

Silk Road Treasures
silkroadtreasures.com

St. Katherine's Supply Co.
stkatherines.etsy.com

StoneAge2
stoneage2.etsy.com

Stone Town San Diego
sdstonetown.etsy.com

Teapots & Telephones
teapotsandtelephones.etsy.com

Uncommon Beads
uncommonbeads.etsy.com

Vintage Jewelry Supplies
vintagejewelrysupplies.com

Vintaj
vintaj.com

Wanan Beads
wananbeads.etsy.com

Wendy Jewelry Supplies
wendyjewelrysupplies.etsy.com

Wild Things Beads
wildthingsbeads.com

Yadana Beads
yadanabeads.etsy.com

Yakutum
yakutum.etsy.com

You Are Not the Boss of Me
youarenotthebossofme.etsy.com

Yuki Designs
yukidesigns.etsy.com

Yummy Treasures Bead Shop
yummytreasures.etsy.com

About the Author

Anne Potter designs, writes, and creates in Illinois with her husband and five children. Besides enjoying the creative life and being a patient, loving mother, Anne also likes to run, bike, travel, attend flea markets, and watch sports. She also loves to eat. Follow Anne and the ups and downs of her creative life at:

www.annepotter.com
Facebook: @handmadebyannepotter
Instagram: @_annepotter_

Acknowledgments

Thank you to Artbeads, Fusion Beads, and Vintage Jewelry Supplies for your generous donation of supplies.

Thank you to Kerry Bogert, Lisa Espinosa, Michelle Bredeson, Ann Swanson, Bonnie Brooks, Nicola dosSantos, and Debbie Blair at Interweave for your tireless hours of quality work, for being so supportive at every step, and for giving me such freedom to create.

To Marilyn and Dick Jaeger and Bob and Louise Potter for your faithful encouragement and wisdom. I love you.

To Jon, Dan, and Josh Josh, the best big brothers ever. Thank you for giving me a childhood of arts and literature, Zeppelin, and grit.

To Dick and Zoe Warner for years of warm hospitality and the very best of the Trader Joe's cookie aisle.

To my girls, Whitney, Leah, Cathy, Nicole, Jill, Tammi, Holly, Deb, Jeanne, Cindy, Julie, and Becky, for faithful friendship, years of laughter, and prayer.

To Brock and Liz Angelo for your unwavering support, for sharing your vision with me, and for the funnest friendship all these years. Everyone should have friends like you!

And to Susanna. You are my sweetheart and the best president of any art club ever. I love you!

Dedication

In loving memory of Josh Lamken (1969–2016).

For Eric, Brian, Molly, Lia, Kevin, and Josie.

You are arrows in my quiver

Psalm 127:4

INDEX

beads 9
brass beads, Indian 9

chain 7
clasps 7
crimp beads 7
crimp covers 8
crimping 134
cubes, cornerless 9
cup bur 8
cutter, wire 8

eye pins 7

filigree 9

glass beads, recycled 9
    Turkish 9

half-hitch knot 137
hardness, wire 7

head pins 7
hole punch, metal 8

jump rings 8
    opening and closing 133

knots 136–137

linen thread, waxed 7
loops, simple 134
    wrapped 135

mandrel 9
memory wire 7

natural beads 9
neck wire 8
needles, beading 8

overhand knot 136

paintbrush 9
paper beads 9
pliers 8

seed beads 9
silk thread 7
simple loop, making 134
square knot 137
stamping supplies 8
stamping tags 8

tags, stamping 8
threads 7
Turkish glass 9
tweezers 9

wire 7
    neck 8
wire cutters 8
wrapped loop, making 135

Metric Conversion Chart		
To Convert	**To**	**Multiply By**
Inches	Centimeters	2.54
Centimeters	Inches	0.4
Feet	Centimeters	30.5
Centimeters	Feet	0.03
Yards	Meters	0.9
Meters	Yards	1.1

EXPLORE MORE INSPIRING
Jewelry Designs

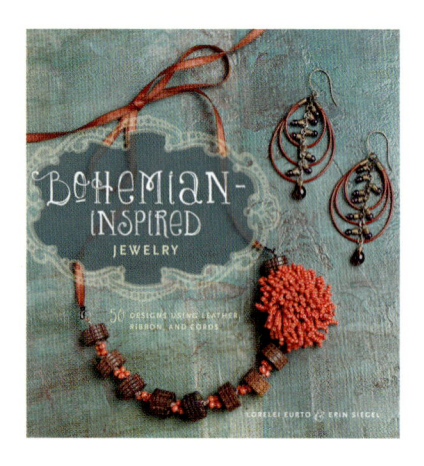

Bohemian-Inspired Jewelry

50 Designs Using Leather, Ribbon, and Cords

Lorelei Eurto and Erin Siegel

ISBN: 978-1-59668-498-0 | $22.99

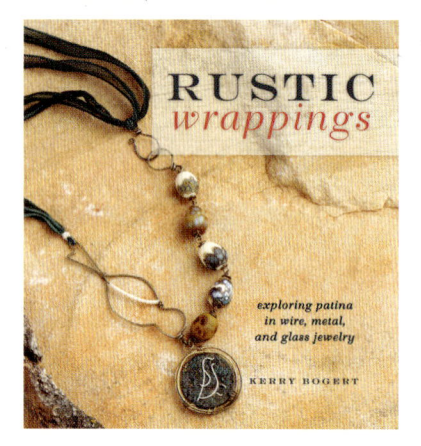

Rustic Wrappings

Exploring Patina in Wire, Metal, and Glass Jewelry

Kerry Bogert

ISBN: 978-1-59668-549-9 | $22.95

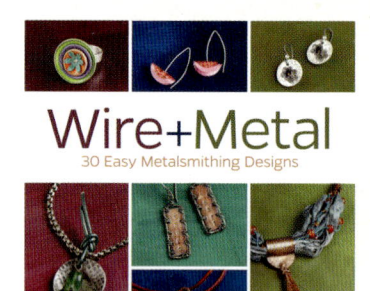

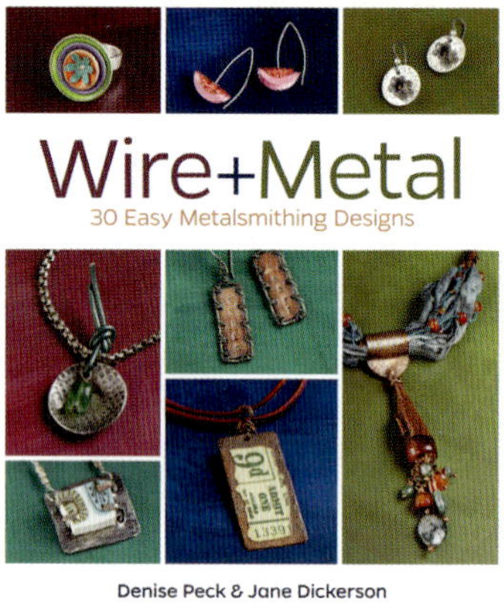

Wire + Metal

30 Easy Metalsmithing Designs

Denise Peck and Jane Dickerson

ISBN: 978-1-62033-140-8 | $22.99

Available at your favorite retailer or JewelryMakingDaily.com

Lapidary Journal Jewelry Artist

Check out *Jewelry Artist*, a trusted guide to the art of gems, jewelry making, design, beads, minerals, and more. Whether you're a beginner, an experienced artisan, or in the jewelry business, *Jewelry Artist* can take you to a whole new level. **Jewelryartistmagazine.com**

Jewelry Making Daily

Jewelry Making Daily is the ultimate online community for anyone interested in creating handmade jewelry. Get tips from industry experts, download free step-by-step projects, check out video demos, discover sources for supplies, and more! Sign up at **jewelrymakingdaily.com**.